Tell It Often— Tell It Well

To Dawnelle and David

Tell It Often- Tell It Well

MAKING THE MOST OF WITNESSING OPPORTUNITIES

Mark McCloskey

FOREWORD BY BILL BRIGHT

Here's Life Publishers

Sixth Printing, February 1989

Published by
HERE'S LIFE PUBLISHERS, INC.
P. O. Box 1576
San Bernardino, CA 92402

Library of Congress Cataloging-in-Publication Data
McCloskey, Mark, 1951-
   Tell it often—tell it well.
   Includes bibliographical references.
   1. Evangelistic work.   I. Title.
BV3790.M474   1986   269'.2   85-24923
ISBN 0-89840-124-0

Unless otherwise indicated, Scripture quotations are from *The New American Standard Bible,* © The Lockman Foundation 1960, 1962, 1963, 1968, 1971, 1972, 1975, 1977, and are used by permission.

For More Information, Write:

L.I.F.E.—P.O. Box A399, Sydney South 2000, Australia
Campus Crusade for Christ of Canada—Box 300, Vancouver, B.C., V6C 2X3, Canada
Campus Crusade for Christ—Pearl Assurance House, 4 Temple Row, Birmingham, B2 5HG, England
Lay Institute for Evangelism—P.O. Box 8786, Auckland 3, New Zealand
Campus Crusade for Christ—P.O. Box 240, Colombo Court Post Office, Singapore 9117
Great Commission Movement of Nigeria—P.O. Box 500, Jos, Plateau State Nigeria, West Africa
Campus Crusade for Christ International—Arrowhead Springs, San Bernardino, CA 92414, U.S.A.

TABLE OF CONTENTS

LIST OF FIGURES

FOREWORD

The book which you hold in your hand could well be one of the most important books you will ever read. In fact, it could change your life.

Have you had a desire in your heart to introduce your loved ones, your neighbors, friends and associates, even strangers, to the Lord Jesus Christ? But have the barriers of fear and guilt intimidated you and prevented you from being that witness you long to be? If so, this book will provide the key that can unlock the door to the greatest adventure of your life, sharing the Lord Jesus Christ with others.

It all began when God the Father demonstrated His love for us when He gave His only begotten Son that whosoever believeth in Him should not perish but have everlasting life.

God the Son so loved the world that while we were yet sinners, He died for us.

The apostle Paul was so constrained by that love that he told everyone who would listen about Christ (Colossians 1:28).

Through the centuries, God has chosen multitudes of men and women to be His ambassadors, filled them with His Holy Spirit, and anointed them to proclaim the most joyful news ever announced. There is no greater privilege.

During the last thirty years I have asked two vital, all-important questions of Christians all over the world. The first is, "What is the greatest thing that has ever happened to you in all of your life?" I have asked it of rich and poor, old and young, famous and not so famous. The answer has always been the same: "Knowing Jesus Christ as my Savior and my Lord is the greatest thing that has ever happened to me."

The second question logically follows: "If knowing Jesus Christ personally is the greatest thing that can happen to any person, what is the greatest thing the Christian can do for a nonbeliever?" Obviously, the answer is to help the nonbeliever come to know

Jesus Christ personally. Why? Because, as the Scripture clearly teaches, "What does it profit a man to gain the whole world, and forfeit his soul?" (Mark 8:36). God is holy and man is sinful, and there is a great chasm, a gulf, that separates us. No matter how hard man may try, he can never bridge that gulf thru his own self-efforts, but there is good news. Jesus Christ can bridge the gulf. In fact, He is the only one who can, for His claim is true: "I am the way, and the truth, and the life; no one comes to the Father, but through me" (John 14:6). And as we are reminded, "There is no other name under heaven that has been given among men, by which we must be saved" (Acts 4:12).

Many marvelous things happen to us when we receive Christ. We become children of God (John 1:12); our sins are forgiven (Ephesians 1:7); we become new creatures in Christ (2 Corinthians 5:17); and we have peace with God (Romans 5:1). He gives us His joy and His love. He directs our steps as we walk in faith and obedience so that our lives are filled with meaning and purpose. He gives us power to live holy, fruitful lives for His glory. And finally (though He does a thousand other things and more for us), He gives us the assurance of salvation (1 John 5:11-13).

How could anyone say no to such blessings and benefits? It is my personal conviction that no open, honest, intelligent, inquiring person will want to say no when Jesus Christ is presented as Savior and Lord if the person is approached in a loving, gracious, knowledgeable, Spirit-filled way. For many years, I have observed and experienced the truth of this invitation from the Lord Jesus: "Follow Me and I will make you to become fishers of men." It is our responsibility to follow Jesus — it is His responsibility to make us fishers of men. Since He came to "seek and to save the lost," and since He lives within every believer in all His resurrection love, power, wisdom and grace, does it not make sense that a good percentage of the nonbelievers would want to respond to Him? He is so loving, so attractive, so appealing, so convincing.

Yet, millions of surveys which we have helped to take around the world indicate that approximately 98 percent of the Christians do not regularly introduce others to the Savior. One must ask the question, "Why?" And to those who have had the privilege of training Christian workers, the answer is obvious: The average Christian does not understand the ministry of the Holy Spirit in his life nor how to share in an effective, fruitful way the love and forgiveness of God revealed in Jesus Christ. It is to meet that need that *Tell It Often, Tell It Well* was written. If you feel that need personally, this book has vast potential to revolutionize your life and your witness for our Savior.

Mark McCloskey, the author of this book, has a brilliant, logical, inquiring, creative mind. These qualities led him, as a student on the university campus, to investigate the claims of Christ. From the very beginning, he realized that there was no decision he would ever make that would compare with the decision to come to know Christ personally. Then, as he grew and matured in his faith, he began to win and disciple other students to Christ, and for years he has continued a ministry of evangelism and discipleship that has influenced the lives of many thousands. His disciples are now serving Jesus Christ around the world.

In this outstanding book, Mark presents a well-reasoned, biblically based, and philosophically unassailable rationale for sowing the seed of the gospel broadly and for initiative-taking evangelism. But it also looks beyond that to every-member mobilization for evangelistic outreach through churches. His heart, burning for the salvation of all lost men, women and children, has kept Mark motivated during the four years it took to write, rewrite, and polish the message in this book. I predict that through the influence of *Tell It Often, Tell It Well,* tens of thousands, and quite possibly millions, will become more effective, fruitful witnesses for the Savior.

Since the inception of Campus Crusade for Christ in 1951, this ministry has been committed to helping fulfill the Great Commission. Through the strategy of spiritual multiplication made possible through well-written literature and effective training, we are seeking to enable generations yet unborn to help reach their own generations for Christ, as well. This book articulates our mission, our message and our methods in attempting to proclaim the good news of our Savior and Lord to all men throughout he world. We commend it to you with the prayer that you will not only read it and be inspired and even changed because of its message, but will pass on the good news to others who will also benefit.

> Bill Bright
> Founder and President, Campus
>   Crusade for Christ
> Chancellor, International Christian
>   Graduate University

CHAPTER 1

The Shocking News

I magine that you are a skilled physician. Through a research project you isolate an up-until-now undiscovered virus. As your research continues, you find, to your amazement, that in all probability this virus has infected 100 percent of the human race. Indeed, every man, woman and child from every culture on earth has contracted the disease.

As your research continues, you come to the shocking realization that this disease is also 100 percent fatal. Your thoughts are filled with the staggering implications. "This means I have the disease," you painfully realize. Visions of your family, friends and other loved ones race through your mind. The thought of 4.5 billion people with the disease is too frightening to appreciate fully. Further research only confirms your findings. Though the symptoms may at times be almost unnoticeable and are often subtle and unalarming, though they may vary from person to person and from culture to culture, the result is the same. This virus is a killer.

After the shock of your discovery abates, your concern turns to some practical and pressing questions. Can the world bear to hear? Is there hope for a cure? You press on with your research. It would be unthinkable to break this devastating news without also announcing the good news of a cure.

Your research pays off — you find the cure. You develop a means of administering it and treat yourself as the first patient. It works! Your tests indicate the virus is destroyed. You can hardly contain your joy as you remove yourself from the terminal list. Now your thoughts turn to your family and your friends — in fact, to the entire world. There is hope! But your joy of discovery is tempered by the sober realization of the critical condition of others. Even at this moment the virus continues to take lives.

You arrange a press conference to bring the joyful news of the cure to the public. To your surprise, only a few of your colleagues and some newspeople attend. Your colleagues seem to be embarrassed for you. "What virus? A universal disease? Who, me? I feel just fine," are the only comments you hear. Even your family and friends are skeptical of the idea of a "universal, terminal disease." A few take you seriously, but mostly, you are treated with polite indifference.

Convincing the Sick

In spite of this rejection and indifference, your confidence never wavers. The more your own life is changed by the cure, the more you realize what a subtle, debilitating effect the virus had on your health.

You conclude that this virus is tricky. People don't realize they have it — until it's too late. Some will admit to the symptoms, and may even grudgingly admit that they might have the virus. But they are revolted by your contention that it is terminal and needs an immediate application of your cure. What a sad irony. The cure is so powerful and efficient, the disease so deadly, but the sick don't take the matter seriously. "Why bother with a cure to a disease that I don't have or that isn't harmful?" they reason with a deadly logic.

The Patient Healer

Now you must consider the question: How can I convince the sick of their condition? *I can't pour the cure down their throats; they have to want to take it,* you reason. The crucial necessity is to open their eyes to their need so they will embrace the cure.

Through wise reasoning and persistent efforts, you reveal and communicate the nature of the disease and the marvelous effectiveness of the cure, and some are convinced. They take the remedy. Then they join you in the cause of convincing a sick world, blind to its sickness, of the great hope found in the only cure.

The Real Situation

This story accurately describes the human situation since the fall of man recorded in Genesis 3. A disease has infected the entire human race. It has many symptoms, but God gets to the root of the matter and calls it sin. It is terminal if left untreated. It is deceitfully subtle. Many do not even know they are infected with sin, though they may recognize some symptoms, and may realize their conduct is not always what it should be. But God is not content to deal with the superficial symptoms of sin. His word confronts indifferent human beings with the enormous personal consequences and eternal ramifications of sin.

Against the dark backdrop of man's spiritual dilemma, the Bible also presents the cure. Jesus Christ and His offer of salvation, secured through the cross and His resurrection, and proclaimed in the gospel, is the good news — and only hope — for our terminally ill generation. We, of course, are the physicians, following in the footsteps of the Great Physician, who came to heal sin-sick human beings (Mark 2:17). We have experienced life on the "terminal list," but have taken the cure. We have decisively met Jesus Christ, been forgiven of our sin, received the Holy Spirit and the gift of eternal life. We are grateful recipients of the grace of His salvation and participants in His Kingdom. We now want our lives to count toward bringing others to the only Savior. As would any trained physician with a sick patient, we strive to do, skillfully, sensitively and effectively, whatever is necessary to recommend Jesus to all who will listen. Indeed, we seek to persuade them to listen. This is the work of evangelism: announcing the good news of the cure to sin-sick men and women, reasoning with them and convincing them that Jesus is indeed the Great Physician who came to heal and restore them to life.

Why Another Book

This book is dedicated to the proposition that the motivational and structural barriers to personal involvement in evangelism must be addressed if the church is to mobilize its members to their maximum effectiveness.

Just what are these barriers, why do they persist, and how can they be overcome? The answers to these questions are grounded in the conviction that only a theologically informed, zealous approach to our evangelistic task can overcome the barriers and ensure that as many as possible hear as soon as possible and can decide as clearly as possible for Jesus Christ.

I am convinced that a sensitive heart and an informed mind are a necessary combination if the church is to succeed in its evangelistic calling. James Denney, the 19th-century Scottish theologian and preacher, dedicated his career to the belief that sound theological thinking must infuse the preaching and evangelistic efforts of the church. He wrote, "If our gospel does not inspire thought, and if our theology does not inspire preaching, there is no Christianity in either."[1] Denney was convinced that if our theologians were evangelists and our evangelists were theologians, we would come nearer to having the ideal church.

But the scenario described by evangelist D. P. Thomson more accurately depicts today's evangelistic scene. He writes, "Evangelism has too long been under a cloud. It has been associated with a crudity of thought and expression, a sensationalism of method, and a largely emotional appeal to which thoughtful men and women could not consciously subscribe."[2] As a result of this "cloud," we find many well-intentioned believers on the evangelistic sidelines, immobilized by the fear of being identified with these negative features. At best, a few of the more gifted communicators among us might venture out to share Christ with friends and acquaintances. This is commendable, but is a far cry from the maximum mobilization necessary to fulfill the church's evangelistic calling. To make matters worse, the very structural supports that could serve to train, equip and mobilize believers for evangelism are ignored or criticized by those intent on avoiding the cloud. It is sad but true that motivational and structural barriers continue to hinder the great majority of the body of Christ in America from personal involvement in evangelism.

But this need not be the case. The church can share the good news with a theologically informed zeal that will protect it from ineffective or harmful evangelistic practice, will motivate the membership toward personal involvement and will undergird the structures required for translating this motivation into actual involvement. Such zeal must rest on the conviction that the person involved in evangelism is on the cutting edge of what God is doing in the world. It will appreciate the fact that the gospel is such good news that it must be announced to all who will listen. At the same time, such crucial news must be communicated accurately and sensitively so that it touches the heart and brings about a life-changing decision for Jesus Christ.

This book is addressed to the great need in American Christendom for such bold and sensitive, zealous and informed evangelism. We must tell the gospel well and we must tell it often. Our evangelism must reflect a warm heart and a trained mind so that as many as possible might listen, and that those who listen may truly hear.

I trust that this book will motivate and inform you. I hope it motivates you toward personal involvement as you grasp the crucial nature of the evangelistic task and the magnificent power of the gospel to save lost individuals and restore them to new life in Christ. I trust, also, that you will be informed as to how you might pursue this work of evangelism with boldness, sensitivity, confidence and effectiveness.

God is ready, willing and able to use you right where you are. No matter what your personality type, spiritual giftedness or circumstances are, you can play a significant role in seeing the love and forgiveness of Christ become a reality in the lives of your friends, neighbors, family, and, indeed, anyone who will listen. It's my prayer that this book will give you the tracks to run on to tell the good news often and tell it well.

CHAPTER 2

The Gospel:
A Multifaceted Message

A
t its most foundational level, evangelism is the communication of a message. This message is the good news that God has acted for the salvation of the world in the incarnation, death and resurrection of Jesus.[1] To the Jew, the good news was the God's messianic promises, given to Israel, all found their "yes" in Jesus Christ (2 Corinthians 1:20). The long promised deliverance and blessings of the Messiah were now available through the death and resurrection of Christ. To the Gentile, previously separated from God, excluded from the commonwealth of Israel, and estranged from the covenant of promise (Ephesians 2:12), the good news was that he too could share in this Messiah's deliverance and blessing. But whether Jew or Gentile, the good news to all was the same: God had graciously intervened through Jesus Christ to save men and women from their sinful plight. If a person takes his lost, terminal condition seriously and sees the offer of a cure for his situation as a live option, this message would indeed be joyful, good news.

It is not surprising then that the Greek word for gospel, *evangelion,* means "good news," and that the word for evangelism, *evangelizo,* means "bring or announce good news." We see from the close connection between these words that good news is for sharing and for being heard. The gospel and evangelism go hand in glove.

17

The gospel message is designed by God to touch men and women at the core of their beings. It is God's instrument to elicit a response of faith from men and women as they realize that Jesus Christ is the answer to the deepest longings of their hearts. The gospel specializes in awakening lost sinners to the vacuum in their hearts that can be filled only by Jesus Christ.

A Multifaceted Gospel

The gospel is a multidimensional message speaking to the height, breadth and depth of the need of the human heart. Let us take a look at the gospel from this multifaceted perspective. As we do, you will appreciate how God has designed this message perfectly to meet man at his point of greatest need.

The Gospel of Truth

Colossians 1:5 says that the gospel is the "word of truth." It is the true story of Jesus, who is the truth (John 14:6). The gospel gives us correct answers to all the crucial questions of life. Who am I, what is my problem, who can solve it and why should I take this seriously are questions answered truthfully by the gospel.

I was sharing the gospel with a student one afternoon, and he was genuinely touched by the message of God's love and forgiveness in Christ. I asked him what he was thinking, and he remarked, "I know this is true, I just know it is. This is just what I need." In a world of shallow, false answers to the wrong questions, the truth of the gospel is a welcome relief.

The Gospel of Hope

Colossians 1:23 speaks of the "hope of the gospel." The gospel says to every man, yes, there is hope for you. There is a future and you have a place in it. This life, as significant as it is, is not all there is. You can be with Jesus one day, in His Kingdom and you can live, joyfully in the here-and-now based on that future certainty and the present reality of His gifts of forgiveness and the Holy Spirit.

The Gospel of Peace

Ephesians 6:15 says that we proclaim a "gospel of peace." The gospel message tells us that a relationship of harmony with God is possible. I once counseled a young man who had had a close brush with death the previous weekend. I asked him what thoughts went through his mind during the close call. His response was, "I found out I wasn't ready to meet God. Things aren't right between us." The gospel of peace assures us that any alienation and strife between God and us can be resolved. Because of the cross of Christ, I do not need to be afraid of meeting God.

The Gospel of Immortality

We are told in 2 Timothy 1:10 that the gospel is the message of "life and immortality." You who fear death can live forever. The author of Hebrews tells us that "through death, He [Jesus] might render powerless him who had the power of death, that is the devil; and might deliver those who through fear of death were subject to slavery all their lives" (Hebrews 2:14,15). The real fountain of youth has been revealed. It is the fountain of Jesus' blood, shed at the cross on our behalf, and because of it we can live forever. We will not be "food for the worms," but a glorious future awaits us.

The Gospel of the Kingdom

Matthew 24:14 tells us that we proclaim the "gospel of the kingdom." This was Jesus' message as He began His ministry in Galilee preaching, "the kingdom of God is at hand; repent and believe in the gospel" (Mark 1:15). This kingdom of God is found wherever Jesus is present and reigns in a human heart. I am His subject along with millions of others, from every race and tribe on earth. It is a kingdom with privileges, responsibilities and a certain way of life. I am not stepping into a vacuum when I trust Christ, but into His kingly rule as a member of His royal family.

The Gospel of Salvation

Paul writes in Romans 1:16 that the gospel is "the power of God for salvation to everyone who believes." In 1 Corinthians 15:2 Paul states that it is through this gospel that we are saved.

Salvation speaks to man's three most essential needs. First, and primarily, salvation speaks to man's need for forgiveness of sins and the gift of the Spirit. Second, salvation speaks to the image of God in man longing for completion. Third, salvation speaks to man's humanly impossible pursuit of wholeness and fulfillment, due to the fragmentation in his life caused by sin.[2] The gospel of salvation speaks to man as he really is: created in God's image, deeply fallen, but greatly loved by his creator.

It is impossible to comprehend the grace and magnitude of God's offer of salvation through the gospel without first understanding man's awful condition before God as a result of the fall. The fall of man recorded in Genesis 3 has thrust all people into the kingdom of darkness (Colossians 1:13, Acts 26:18) and there they are held in bondage to sin (John 8:34, Romans 6:17), blinded by Satan to their spiritual plight (2 Corinthians 4:4) and helpless to remedy this situation (Romans 5:6).

In addition to this, men are undergoing a perishing process (1 Corinthians 1:18) and a destruction (John 10:10) due to their subjugation to sin, which deceives and kills them (Romans 7:11). This present state of rebellion and alienation from God will lead inevitably to a reckoning with God's righteous judgment (2 Thessalonians 2:8,9), where man's alienation from God will be drawn out to an eternity of separation from Him. It is from this very real present and future danger that God rescues men through Jesus Christ.

The New Testament authors used two Greek words to describe this divine rescue project. *Rhyomai* means "to rescue, deliver, preserve, save."[3] This term is often used to speak of a rescue from physical danger, as when the Lord *delivered* Paul from physical harm (2 Timothy 3:11; 4:17). Paul used the word in Colossians 1:13, however, to speak of an even more dramatic rescue: God intervening to save a person from the kingdom of darkness and the penalty of sin.

The second word family used to describe this rescue is *sozo* and *soteria,* meaning "to keep from harm; preserve, rescue; salvation and deliverance."[4] These terms also mean to be rescued, saved and kept from harm in a physical or circumstantial sense. But the New Testament writers used this word primarily to describe God's intervention to rescue individuals from the results of the fall.

Seven Word Pictures

Salvation is a multidimensional, multifaceted concept. The new kingdom citizenship of the saved carries with it a dazzling variety of implications that touch on our new identity in Christ, our behavior, our attitudes and our interpersonal relationships. Not surprisingly, salvation as a theological concept forces us to consider the many dimensions of the ultimate reality it describes. Let us look at seven word pictures the New Testament authors use to describe the richness and depth of God's gift of salvation.

Regeneration: From Death to Life

In his interview with Nicodemus (John 3:1-15), Jesus told him, "Unless one is born again, he cannot see the kingdom of God." Now Jesus was speaking to one of the most moral, religious men of His day, but He also knew the spiritual condition of man. All men are in need of a change that will penetrate to the core of the human heart and break the dominion of sin, a change that will replace the self-centered bent with a new spiritual center of gravity. Man is helpless to make these changes for himself. God must do this for him, because man is dead in his sin (Ephesians 2:1-2) and cannot remedy his condition of separation from God. In short, man needs the gift of eternal life.

Alexander Pope, the English poet, was overheard to mutter, "O Lord, make me a better man."

To which his spiritually enlightened page replied, "It would be easier to make you a new man."

Regeneration is the divine act of making the repentant believer a "new" man or woman in Christ by the imparting of new divine life through the gift of the Holy Spirit. The believer is thus "born again." He now has the life of God in him, is "born of God" (1 John 2:29, 5:4, 18), and is a "new creature in Christ" (2 Corinthians 5:17).

George Whitfield, the great English evangelist, preached on John 3:1-8 over 300 times. When asked why he chose this text so often, he said simply, "Because you must be born again." He understood what a beautiful and powerful word picture regeneration is, describing the monumental event of a lost, dead sinner graciously being given the very life of God through the gift of the Holy Spirit. Being born again is not for the emotionally predisposed few, or for those with the right denominational background. It is an absolute necessity for all those who seek to "see the kingdom of God" (John 3:8). The gospel of salvation is the offer of new life to the lost.

Reconciliation: From Enemy to Friend

Reconciled is a common word used to describe a relationship of animosity that has been changed into a relationship of friendship and harmony. Someone who was once an enemy is now a friend; two parties once separated for whatever reason have been brought together.

In Romans 5:10, Paul states that the lost are enemies of God. This is strong language. But this condition certainly follows if the unregenerated are citizens of Satan's kingdom, the general course of their lives is described as being after "the prince of power of the air that works in the sons of disobedience" (Ephesians 2:2). The sin principle which controls those who are citizens of this kingdom of darkness will necessarily bring them into sharp conflict with God's holy character.

Man's reconciliation to God is made possible by the cross of Christ. All of God's claims against us were settled through Christ's death (Colossians 2:13,14). "The certificate of debt has been cancelled," Jesus has borne all of our sins (1 Peter 2:24). Our holy God has nothing against us. He is waiting with open arms, ready to restore us to friendship with Himself. God has been reconciled to us through Jesus' death. All of the obstacles preventing our fellowship have been removed, *except one:* man's rebelliousness.

It remains for us to agree to be reconciled to Him. Therefore, Paul saw the evangelist as an ambassador of reconciliation (11 Corinthians 5:19-21), inviting men to step from the precarious ground of animosity toward God onto the safe ground of a restored friendship. The gospel of salvation is the offer to the lost of friendship with God.

Propitiation: From Wrath to Mercy

Propitiation was a common religious word in biblical times, used in relation to heathen religious rites to win the favor of the gods or to avert the impending wrath and disfavor of the gods. The first-century Christians adopted this word for their own use in picturing how Christ's work on the cross had dealt with the righteous wrath of God toward all who have sinned.

Propitiation describes that facet of our salvation which takes us out from under God's righteous judgment (Romans 1:18) and places us under the safety of the cross of Christ. The believer is no longer an object of God's wrath but a recipient of His mercy. Thus, the publican in Luke 18:13 got up from his prayer of confession having been "propitiated." He had gone from being under God's wrath to being under His mercy. This word picture suggests that what was once offensive to God and deserving of His righteous judgment has now been covered by the blood of Christ, an overflowing fountain of constant mercy and forgiveness (Hebrews 8:12, 1 John 2:2; 4:10). The gospel of salvation is the offer of mercy to the lost.

Sanctification: A Change in Ownership

Sanctification in Old Testament terminology meant to separate an object (or a person) from the world, declare it as belonging to God, and to dedicate it to God's exclusive use. This term was commonly applied to all objects associated with the nation of Israel's ceremonial worship. It was extended to speak of the assertion of God's rightful claim over the lives of those He created and sustains (Ezekial 36:25,26,30).

The New Testament uses the term sanctify to describe God's exercise of His option to rescue the lost from the kingdom of darkness and to claim them for His exclusive possession and use (Acts 20:32; 26:18; Hebrews 10:29; 1 Corinthians 1:2; 6:11).

The word *saint* literally means "sanctified one," or one who now belongs to Jesus and no longer to Satan. This word reflects the radical change in our spiritual status. Kingdom lines have been crossed over. A new Christian I knew in college wore a button that said "under new management." This expresses well the change that sanctification brings. The gospel of salvation demands that God be allowed to exert His rightful claim of ownership over the lost.

Redemption: From Slavery to Freedom

The word picture of redemption was a common one to the Hebrew mind and to the first-century world. The word *redemption* comes from the Hebrew word meaning "to tear loose, to rescue."[5] This idea originated in the Old Testament practice of a kinsman redeemer, the one who came to a relative's aid by purchasing the relative's land that had been lost to the family. This property was then returned to those who had a rightful claim to it. God is said to be the redeemer of Israel because He acts as its kinsman redeemer, the one who tears Israel loose from her oppressors and restores her to her proper owner: God Himself.

In the New Testament, men are seen as captives of an array of forces that lay an illegitimate claim to man. Sin, death, the law and Satan hold men in their deadly grip. Men need to be "torn loose" from these oppressors. In a sense they, like a piece of land in the Old Testament, must be purchased out of this situation. They must be bought back by their rightful owner.

Just as a man could be released from jail by payment of money, cancelling out the certificate of debt against him (Colossians 2:13), and could be set free from the darkness of prison into the light and freedom of day, and just as a slave in ancient times might be legally purchased by a generous man and set free, so God has paid the purchase price of the blood of Christ to release sinners held captive by spiritual oppressors (Ephesians

1:7; 1 Peter 1:18; 1 Corinthians 6:18). The gospel of salvation is the offer of release to the lost.

Justification: From Guilt to Acquittal

"Justification expresses the judicial action of God apart from human merit according to which the guilty are pardoned, acquitted and then reinstated as God's children and as fellow heirs with Jesus Christ."[6] As this definition indicates, *justification* is a legal term taken from the courtrooms of the first century. Very simply, it means to be declared not guilty by a judge, whose word is final.

To the Hebrew mind, Yahweh was the supreme judge who presided over the affairs of Israel (Jeremiah 11:20, Psalm 7:7-11). "As judge, Yahweh supremely distinguishes between those who are 'in the right' and those who are 'in the wrong.' Those who are in the right are delivered and those in the wrong are punished."[7]

Justification as a word picture presents the drama of God as judge, with a guilty sinner before Him, one whose guilt is not in doubt. As the Judge pronounces His decision, instead of soberly announcing, "Guilty as charged" and sentencing the person to eternal death, He calls out in a tender voice, "Not guilty, you are set free."

God, as judge, has declared us to be *righteous,* not guilty. To be declared righteous means to be seen as conforming to a standard of acceptance. It is "The state of him who is such as he ought to be."[8] We are now in a spiritual state of not having our sins counted against us. We have escaped condemnation, but more than that, we have been declared righteous in Jesus Christ. As long as sinful men must deal with a holy God who will judge, justification will be a beautifully relevant picture of the cure that only the gospel of salvation in Christ can bring. To the lost, the gospel of salvation is the offer of right standing before God.

Adoption: A Change in Families

Adoption refers to the fact that in Jesus Christ we have become sons and daughters of the living God. We are in His forever family. The word picture of adoption communicated a *change* of families. Consider that the New Testament describes the lost as being children of the devil (John 8:44; 1 John 3:10), and children of wrath (Ephesians 2:3). But as we step into the state of salvation by responding to the gracious offer of the gospel, we claim a new set of family relationships, and a new set of affections which reflect the character of our heavenly Father. As children of God, we are said to be children of wisdom (Matthew 11:19), children of obedience (1 Peter 1:14), and children of light (Ephesians 5:8).

Obviously, Paul was familiar with adoption in Roman and Greek culture. In extreme cases a man who had no son but needed an heir to his estate would actively seek out a young man willing to fulfill the obligations of a son. The legal requirements would be worked out, and the adopted son would be brought into the family with all the rights, privileges and obligations of any true son by birth.

This picture combines nicely with the themes of regeneration and redemption, reconciliation and sanctification. They touch, like the sides of a geometric figure. We have been born again into God's family. We are sons because we have the Father's life within us. We have a new relationship of intimacy, trust and dependence. Indeed, we can cry out, "Abba, Father" (Galations 4:6) an Aramaic term for "daddy," a term of the utmost intimacy and personal endearment. The legal arrangements of the adoption were taken care of in our justification; the fact that our former family affiliation was lived out in rebellious disobedience is taken care of through our reconciliation. All of these themes touch on the fact of our adoption.

The Relevance of Salvation

These seven word pictures begin to give us some insight into the multifaceted nature of God's gracious provision for fallen human beings. In fact, every problem that I have as a result of the fall is spoken to in God's offer of salvation. Man has died spiritually, but God offers him regeneration and new life in Christ. Man is God's enemy, but God offers him reconciliation through the cross of Christ. Man is a slave to the law, sin, death and Satan, but God intervenes to purchase him out of his prison and bring him to a place of freedom. Man finds himself in Satan's family, but God reaches down and adopts him as a son. Man finds himself an object of wrath, but God sends His Son to be the propitiation for his sins. Man finds himself standing guilty before the righteous Judge, but God mercifully declares him not guilty because of Jesus' work on the cross and resurrection. The moment the nonbeliever embraces the gospel, these seven word pictures become a reality in his life. The radical spiritual status change becomes his experience.

CHAPTER 3

The Gospel:
A Precise Message

Paul concisely and precisely states the terms of the gospel in 1 Corinthians 15:1-5: "Now I make known to you, brethren, the gospel which I preached to you, which also you received, in which also you stand, by which also you are saved, if you hold fast the word which I preached to you, unless you believed in vain. For I delivered to you as of first importance what I also received, that Christ died for our sins according to the Scriptures, and that He was buried and that He was raised on the third day according to the Scriptures, and that He appeared to Cephas, then to the twelve."

Let us take a closer look at this biblical definition of the gospel.

The Gospel Defined

The main topic of this passage is Jesus Christ and the sequence of events that make salvation possible for sinful men. The gospel is that message "by which also you are saved" (verse 2). As the message is preached it takes root in a human heart that is ready to turn from sin and to trust Jesus Christ for the forgiveness of sins. The message speaks to the person's need to be lifted out of his state of danger and lostness. Salvation can be defined as the divine act whereby a person is given a spiritual status change through his deliverance from the kingdom of darkness and his transferral into the safety and blessing of the kingdom of Jesus Christ (Acts 26:18; Colossians 1:12,13).

The gospel is a description of how God has arranged for a sinner's salvation. Paul states, "For I delivered to you as of first importance what I also received, that Christ died for our sins according to the Scriptures, and that He was buried, and that He was raised on the third day according to the Scriptures" (verses 3,4).

Christ's death, burial and resurrection are the only basis upon which a sinful person can approach a holy God. The gospel has at its heart the fact that the death and resurrection of Christ have removed the barriers between a Holy God and sinful men.

Note also the phrase "according to the Scriptures" (verse 4). This refers to the fact that Jesus' death and resurrection are the fulfillment of the Old Testament Scriptures. The law, the Psalms and the prophets all pointed to the necessity of the sacrificial death of the Messiah (see Psalm 16:8-11, Isaiah 53:5,6 and Luke 24:25-27). Thus, the death of Christ for the forgiveness of sins is the focal point of God's redemptive plan. As such, it is to be the central focus of our presentation of the gospel.

Verses 4-6 speak of the resurrection of Christ and of His subsequent appearances. The implications of the resurrection of Christ are two-fold. First, the resurrection vindicates His sacrificial work on the cross. His payment for sin was accepted by God; the barrier between man and God now is abolished. The Spirit now can be given freely (John 7:37-39). The way is open for the repentant man or woman to come to God.

Second, the resurrection means that Jesus is alive and available to us today. As the risen Lord, He now sits at the right hand of God (Acts 2:32-35) from where He offers the gifts of the Holy Spirit (Acts 2:33; John 7:37-39), the forgiveness of sins (Acts 2:38; 26:28) and a share in His eternal kingdom. (Acts 26:18).

Thus, the gospel is both information concerning Jesus and His invitation to step into His kingdom, and a demand that men and women repent and embrace Christ as Lord and Savior. It is the message of God's saving grace grounded in the event of the cross. It relays the significance of God's work of reconciling men to Himself through that cross. By its very nature, the gospel compels those who know it to share it.

The Challenge of Precision

I believe that there are three compelling reasons for taking seriously the challenge of presenting the gospel with theological precision.

The first is the purity of the primary focus of the gospel. James Denney states, "The simplest truth of the gospel and the profoundest truth of theology must be put in the same words, 'He bore our sins.'"[1] As we learned from Paul's definitive statement of the gospel in 1 Corinthians 15:1-5, the death of Christ for sin is the focal point of God's redemptive plan from ages past. Paul states in no uncertain terms, "For I delivered to you as of *first importance* what I also received, that Christ died for our sins" (1 Corinthians 15:3). The point here is not so much that this was the subject matter of which Paul first spoke, but rather that Paul saw the death of Christ as that which is central to the gospel message.[2]

Why is this so crucial to the purity of the gospel? Paul writes in Romans 3:25,26 that the cross was a demonstration of God's righteous character in dealing with sin. Paul explains that God is both judge — He punishes sin on the cross of Christ — and justifier — He forgives the one who has faith in Christ. The death of Christ for our sins shows us both God's holy character and His deep mercy. "The divine necessity is not just to forgive, but to forgive in a way which shows that God is irreconcilable to evil, and can never treat it as other or less than it is."[3]

The death of Christ for sin teaches us the reality of God's love for sinners and His repugnance for sin as that which destroys His creatures and His created order. As James Denney states, "He would not do justice to Himself if He displayed His compassion for sinners in a way which made light of sin, which ignored its tragic reality, or took it for less than it is."[4]

Therefore, the evangelist must ensure that whenever the gospel is communicated, it speaks with great precision and clarity to the issue of man's greatest need, to be forgiven of sin. God is not content to deal merely with surface symptoms of the sin problem. The cure of the gospel speaks with force, frankness and insight to the root problem of sin. The purity of the gospel must be guarded. The righteous character of God is at stake.

The Spirit's Work

The second reason for taking seriously the challenge of precision is that God promises that the Holy Spirit will impress on the non-believer the validity of the gospel message. As we have seen, the gospel speaks primarily to man's need for the radical spiritual status change brought by the gift of the Spirit and the forgiveness of sins.

It is to this primary emphasis of the gospel that the Holy Spirit is said to bear witness in John 16:8-11. "And He, when He comes, will convict the world concerning sin, and righteousness, and judgment; concerning sin, because they do not believe in Me; and concerning righteousness, because I go to the Father, and you no longer behold Me; and concerning judgment because the ruler of this world has been judged." Let us take a closer look at this passage.

The word *convict* in verse 8 "is a legal term that means to pronounce a judicial verdict by which the guilt of the culprit at the bar of justice is defined and fixed."[5] John continues, "Concerning sin because they do not believe in me" (verse 9). He is referring to the Holy Spirit at work in the hearts of men and women, creating a sense of inescapable guilt and responsibility before God. The Spirit focuses squarely on the issue of lack of belief in Christ. God wants people to realize that the source of all sin lies in an attitude of active rebellion or passive indifference toward Jesus Christ, and He sent the Holy Spirit to see to it that the unbeliever understands this issue.

Note how God's Spirit, like the knife of a skilled surgeon, cuts through the superficial symptoms and gets to the root of sin. Sinful lifestyles and specific acts of sin are not His focus.

He brings men face to face with the root cause of sin in a way that blocks off all escape through excuses or rationalizations.

The Spirit is also said to convict of "righteousness" (verses 8,9). God's holiness and character form the perfect standard by which men's actions will be judged, and this righteousness is found only in Jesus Christ. As this reality is brought to light, the sinner will realize his own deficiency before God and is led to the realization that Jesus' death for sin is the only escape route from his awful state of alienation and spiritual death.

The Spirit also comes to convict the sinner of impending judgment (verses 8,11), the inescapable destiny of all who refuse to repent and believe in Christ. They have aligned themselves with Satan's kingdom and will share in its downfall, which was secured when Satan and his spiritual forces were defeated by the death and resurrection of Jesus (John 12:31, Colossians 2:15).

It becomes obvious that the primary concern of the gospel, the good news of it, is that sin can be forgiven; righteousness, or a correct status or standing from God, can be attained; and judgment therefore can be averted. We are promised that the Holy Spirit reveals these very truths in the lives of the unsaved, to prepare their hearts to respond to the gospel.

The Example of Lydia

Paul's founding of the Philippian church is an example of how the Holy Spirit works in conjunction with the sharing of the gospel. Acts 16:13 records that Paul "began speaking to the women who had assembled." One of those women, Lydia, was obviously interested in Paul's presentation of the gospel. As she listened, Luke records, "The Lord opened her heart to respond to the things spoken by Paul." What a beautiful combination of the power of the gospel to save and the Holy Spirit's behind-the-scenes work of conviction.

The point here is that the gospel needs to speak clearly to the very concerns that the Holy Spirit creates in hearts. It is as though there were a gospel-shaped keyhole in the heart of the nonbeliever, and only the gospel fits the lock. The evangelist's verbal presentation of the gospel message must be congruous with the behind-the-scenes, powerful work of the Spirit. The Spirit will create a felt need in the hearts of those to whom we present the gospel. Of course, it has been a real need all along, but the patient must personally appreciate the need if he is to accept the remedy of the gospel gladly. He must be made painfully aware of the fact that his lostness will not just go away. But once the reality of his state without Christ is made evident, what good news the gospel will be! It will speak directly to the needs of his heart, and there will be a beautiful meshing of the promises of the gospel to deliver from the darkness of sin, and the person's growing sense of need to have this happen in his life. The gospel will then be the dynamite of salvation in his life.

The Challenge of Relevance

The third reason for taking seriously the precision of the gospel is the need for relevance. It presents the Christian with both his greatest opportunity and his greatest challenge in communicating the gospel. Relevance touches the question of how to communicate the never-changing Christ to an ever-changing world of diverse and ever-changing individuals. George Peters observes, "It is a fact that the effectiveness of evangelism depends to a great extent upon our ability to make the gospel message relevant to the religious needs and hopes, the aspirations and anticipations, the yearnings and strivings, the fears and frustrations of the people."[6] Anyone who is serious about communicating the gospel to our generation must take to heart the concern of relevance.

It is sad, but all too true, that many people reject or remain indifferent to the gospel not so much because they disagree with it, but because it is alien to their world of thought and outside of their realm of comprehension. Chapters 18 and 19 will cover the matter of relevance as it relates to our personal communication style. But I want to make clear at this point that making the gospel relevant (communicating it in terms and concepts that our generation can readily relate to and understand) touches dramatically on the precision of the gospel message.

The issue is this: How can the communicator of the gospel find "common ground," a point of contact, between the gospel message and the felt needs of the nonbeliever and at the same time stay true to the primary focus of the gospel, that Christ died for our sins?

Walking this communication tightrope is no easy matter. We live in a generation that is profoundly out of touch with the real need to enter into a personal relationship with Christ. The gospel implies that all men are lost and in need of forgiveness. Its reception into the human heart depends upon men and women being in touch with the reality of personal sin. If this is not the case, the gospel is at best an irrelevant message. As C. S. Lewis states, "Christianity tells people to repent and promises them forgiveness. It therefore has nothing as far as I know to say to people who do not know they have done anything to repent of and who do not feel that they need any forgiveness."[7] Another author notes, "In some ways, having a sense of sin has become a giant anachronism to a great number of men and women."[8] Indeed, a recent poll reveals that nearly one-half of the people in a very religious midwestern state do not believe they are sinful, and 83 percent of them rejected the biblical doctrine of the depravity of man.[9]

Karl Menninger, psychiatrist and social commentator, takes our generation to task for its refusal to admit that sin is still a personal and societal reality. In his work *Whatever Happened to Sin?*, Menninger suggests that sin, of course, has not disappeared. It has just been renamed and swept under the rug.[10] The last ten years have seen the popularizing of sin euphemisms. A euphemism is the substitution of an agreeable or inoffensive expression for one that may offend or suggest something unpleasant. Thus, we no longer fornicate; we have "pre-marital sex." We no longer commit adultery; we have an "affair." We don't tolerate pornography; we attend "adult movies." Filthy language is for "mature audiences." Homosexuality is not sin but an "alternate" or "same sex" lifestyle. Abortion is not a pro-death position, but a "pro-choice" alternative.

Sin is no longer viewed as a condition of personal wrongdoing and rebellion against a Holy God. Rather, man's state of alienation from God — if it is recognized at all — is, at best, described as a psychological problem needing *treatment,* but not *forgiveness.* "Sin" is just one of the many tolerable imperfections and weaknesses of the human condition, and who can be faulted for not being perfect? Who can be held responsible for being weak? Our culture mutters Flip Wilson's "The devil made me do it" or cries out Steve Martin's "Excuuuuse me for being imperfect," and evades its personal responsibility before God and man. What the Bible calls sin is certainly not seen by most of our culture as a condition meriting eternal judgment. Just as in the days of Jeremiah when the Jews glossed over their guilt of rejecting God and mistreating their fellow citizens by reasoning "I am innocent, I have not sinned" (Jeremiah 2:35), so the present-day American culture has all but lost touch with the implications of the ominous reality of sin. In the words of Baptist theologian A. H. Strong, society is guilty of the greatest sin, which is to be conscious of none.[11]

Good News or Nonsense?

Into this theological vacuum steps the gospel message and its offer of forgiveness of sins. It doesn't take much intelligence to realize that we might have a "relevance gap" here. People usually listen to a message only to the degree that they feel it speaks to their felt needs. People are not likely to accept a solution to a problem they don't believe they have, or listen to answers to questions they have never asked, or, in the terminology of this book, pursue a remedy for a disease they think does not exist or is not serious. When was the last time you saw a telethon for the flu? So the sensitive communicator realizes that the good news might be perceived as irrelevant nonsense or, at best, nice thoughts but not really pertinent.

The Danger in Relevance

Faced with this prospect of offering an "irrelevant" message to a disinterested or passive audience, the communicator begins to feel the tension between the common ground, — the point of relevance to the nonbeliever — and the primary focus of the gospel. In the face of this tension, the communicator may be tempted to fall into the trap of what I call accommodation. Accommodation involves (1) emphasizing certain benefits of salvation over the primary benefits of the cross — forgiveness of sins, the gift of the Spirit, and a radical kingdom status change — and (2) addressing felt needs without reference to the reality of man's lostness and the provision of salvation through the cross of Christ.

The accommodation approach usually focuses on a relevant cultural need, then suggests Jesus as the one to meet that need. "Come to Jesus, for He wants you rich, perfectly healthy, popular and fulfilled." "Come to Jesus and He will assist you in your pursuit of self-actualization, weight loss or a happy marriage." The message is made clear: "Whatever your felt need, Jesus is relevant to it." What is implied is that Jesus will meet you right where you are, and on your own terms.

Of course, some of these needs are valid desires. Who doesn't want a great marriage, vibrant health and a good self-concept? Other felt needs, however, are simply extensions of sinful patterns that need to be repented of, broken and forgiven, not complemented in a personal relationship with Christ. The subtle danger in appealing to such needs — whether good or bad — is that they easily can become ends in themselves, with Jesus seen as simply the means to that end, whatever fulfillment the person is seeking.

The gospel is compromised and stripped of its saving power when it is diluted and reconstructed to speak to the needs of the human heart without reference to the cross — and that is tragic.

I once counseled a young man who had professed faith in Christ a few weeks earlier. But his life did not seem to change at all. I asked him what was going on in his heart since he had trusted Christ, and he responded, "I was lonely and I knew that Jesus didn't want me that way, so I invited Him into my life so I wouldn't be lonely anymore. But I'm still lonely." I later learned that this young man had been encouraged to trust Christ solely on the basis of his felt need of loneliness — a felt need that never led him to consider the cross and thus did not lead to his salvation and, I might add, never cured his loneliness.

This approach is a misuse of the concept of relevance. If relevance becomes an end in itself, it degenerates into accommodation and compromise. The communicator is thus constrained to search for a point of contact between God and the sinner other than the "irrelevant" sin problem.

One might protest, "Is it not valid to package the gospel in today's terms and present it as touching on today's concerns?" One might further protest, "Is it not valid and indeed wise to focus on the individual's felt need and then present Jesus as the One able to meet those needs, even if that means ignoring or postponing discussion of the sin issue?" As one author puts it, "It is more profitable to center on the fact that Christ does more to ease the pain of a frustrated life than anybody else." This author goes on to argue that to make an issue of an individual's sin problem, unless he first brings it up, is spiritually immature and manifests a "neurotic desire to appear superior at the expense of others." To do so is called "unprofitable theological or psychological speculation."[12] This line of reasoning implies that we must communicate only those aspects of Christian truth which are perceived to be relevant to the non-Christians, for they are not likely to respond to a solution to a problem they don't know they have.

Yes, there is a sense in which this desire for cultural and personal relevance is perfectly appropriate. The Old and New Testament authors borrowed words and images from their culture to convey the basic idea of the gospel. Paul borrowed word pictures from the courtroom (justification), the marketplace (redemption), domestic life (adoption), and even from pagan religions (propitiation), to package the dynamite of the gospel. The method obviously worked. People were confronted with their need for Christ in language they understood. Indeed, Jesus approached the woman at the well with the common ground of thirst, and He approached the sick and the blind on the common ground of their felt need to get well. But note the crucial difference between the practices of Paul and Jesus and the practice of accommodation. Jesus was always careful to do one thing: ensure that the packaging of the gospel did not violate the primary intention of the gospel to announce to lost sinners the necessity and opportunity to step into God's salvation. The necessity to repent, believe the gospel and enter the Kingdom of God were always center stage. Though Jesus dealt with the woman's thirst (John 4:7), He moved quickly to bring up her sin problem (verses 16-18).

Relevance and the Integrity of the Gospel

The fact that sinners do not gravitate toward discussing their sin problem, or even believe that they have one in the biblical sense of the word, is a problem that will not go away. So how can we be relevant to these people without compromising the integrity of the gospel?

I think the key is found in the communication strategy of Paul and Jesus. Here we find one principle which, if followed, will enable the Christian communicator to walk the tightrope between preserving the fidelity of the gospel and finding a relevant point of contact between God and the sinner.

The Principle of the Primary Versus the Secondary

The tension between the cultural relevance and fidelity of the gospel can be resolved partially by recognizing the distinction between the primary, secondary and tertiary focuses of the gospel (see Figure 1).

As we have noted, the primary elements of the gospel refer to those issues centered on the gospel's offer of salvation in all if its multifaceted splendor. This is summed up in a kingdom transfer (Colossians 1:33; Acts 26:18), the forgiveness of sins, and the gift of the Holy Spirit. The Holy Spirit primarily concerns Himself with the sinner's need for these gifts (John 16:8-11). It was to secure these gifts for the believer that Christ was born, died and raised from the dead.

These three gifts are the *primary* and *initial* point of contact between the gospel and a sinner. One might say that they are *normative*. In other words, all new believers share in the same experience.

FIGURE 1
PRIMARY, SECONDARY AND TERTIARY ELEMENTS OF THE GOSPEL

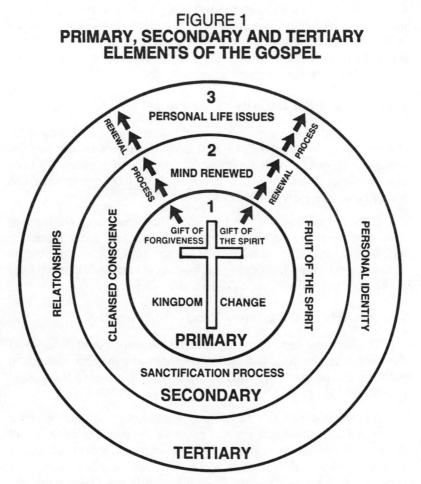

1. **Primary Elements of Gospel** —Justification/Regeneration and Kingdom Status Change. Instantaneous and normative for all.

2. **Secondary Elements of Gospel** — Renewal/Sanctification. Not immediate, but in God's timing for all believers.

3. **Tertiary Elements of Gospel** — Continued Renewal/Sanctification. A process and individually tailored.

As we move to the secondary concerns of the gospel, note that here we are dealing with *results* of the primary elements of the gospel taking root in the new believer's life. Though these lifestyle changes flow naturally and inevitably from the primary salvation gifts, they are not to be confused with the primary focus of the gospel.

The secondary elements are inevitable but not immediate, normative. All new believers do not experience these results in just the same way.

The primary gift of forgiveness of sins will naturally work itself into the life of the new believer through a conscience increasingly freed from the debilitating presence of guilt. The gift of the Spirit will naturally produce the fruit of the Spirit, resulting in a more joyful, loving person. But a distinction needs to remain between the immediate, normative and primary; and the subsequent, individualized and secondary concerns of the gospel.

The tertiary segment completes the circle. What salvation touches it changes, and salvation touches the whole person. Every thought, word, deed and relationship will come under the renewing influence of the Holy Spirit (Romans 12:2; 1 Thessalonians 5:23). In this sense, we could say that there literally is nothing in our lives to which Christ does not ultimately relate.

The Model Applied

Let us consider how this model (Figure 1) can help us in actual situations of communicating the gospel. What do we do when the nonbelieving culture in general, has no sense of sin and thus no felt need for the gospel?

First, let me suggest what *not* to do. Do not change the gospel to emphasize Jesus' relevance to a problem or felt need that is less than sin. This method only short-circuits the work of the Spirit and subverts the saving power of the gospel.

Note that nonbelievers' felt needs are most likely to fall under the secondary and tertiary concerns of the gospel.

Is the gospel of Jesus Christ relevant to a lonely person, or to one struggling with meaning and purpose in life, or, for that matter, to anyone with any of the numerous felt needs so common to the human condition? Yes, of course. Self-concept, love, joy, an integrated personality, a good marriage, purpose and direction for living are all elements of life that salvation in Christ will inevitably and profoundly touch. Jesus is concerned about all these needs and, yes, a relationship with Him will bring His healing touch to all of these areas.

But the evangelist must realize that felt needs in these areas are always a result of a real need which is addressed by the primary focus of the gospel. The root of a man's loneliness is his alienation from God. The root of man's lack of purpose, lack of direction and interpersonal problems is His rebellion toward God. The source of a man's poor self-concept is his guilt and alienation in relation to his Creator. Thus, all of a person's felt needs (at least, those that are a reflection of God's image within him yearning for completion) are symptoms of man's primary problem, which is the primary focus of the gospel: "He bore our sins."

Zero In

As an evangelist, I must indeed relate Jesus Christ to the whole person in his total predicament, but I must *initially* and *primarily* address the sin, guilt and alienation issue. Why?

First, we have discussed, the purity of the gospel is at stake. Second, I must make sure that there is congruity between the gospel I communicate and the work of the Holy Spirit in convicting men of sin, righteousness and judgment. Third, I must appreciate the power of the gospel to bear witness to its own ability to create a platform of relevance and common ground. The Word of God can and will win and hold our hearers.

Let me explain. The fact that the non-Christian has the symptoms is evidence that he also has the root problem. As an evangelist, you need to convince the nonbeliever that his symptomatic felt need is traced to his real need which is resolved only in the cross of Christ. And *how* might you convince him that his felt need is merely a symptom of this deeper issue? The answer, is simply to share the gospel with boldness, clarity and sensitivity, pointing out that the cross of Christ speaks to the core problem of the individual. Be quick to point out that Jesus is interested in bringing His healing touch to the symptom, but explain that first He desires to heal the problem which gave rise to that symptom in the first place.

As you are explaining the gospel, remember that the Holy Spirit is working behind the scenes to convince the non-Christian that every symptom can be traced to the root problem of unbelief in Christ (John 16:8-11). Wherever the gospel is proclaimed in all of its purity and simplicity, Jesus is surely at work.

God's gospel is designed to effect the response of repentance and faith in the life of a nonbeliever. God has given us the gospel to share in all of its simplicity and power because He Himself has invested the message with spiritual power to impact the human heart. Remember, it is the power (dynamite) of God for salvation (Romans 1:16) performing its work in those who believe (1 Thessalonians 2:13).

As Jonathan Edwards put it, "The warnings of God's word are more fitted to obtain the ends of awakening sinners, and bringing them to repentance, than the rising of one from the dead to warn them."[13] He further states, "He who made the faculties of our souls knows what will have the greatest tendency to move them, and to work upon them."[14] As James Denney observes, "Yet all experience shows that the gospel wins by its magnitude and the true method for the evangelist is to put the great things in the forefront,"[15] "For the preaching of the atonement has something to do with producing the very state of mind on which its reception depends."[16] Therefore, the evangelist presents the gospel that they might gain perspective on their felt needs and come to grips with their real need. We do not preach sin that they might come to Christ; we proclaim the gospel of Christ that they might come to a knowledge of their sin. Our message is Christ-centered, not sin-centered. The grace of the gospel is a magnet to the heart that is truly in tune with the convicting ministry of the Spirit. The grace of the gospel exposes the folly of the heart that is out of tune with its great need and wins the honest heart to Christ.

This truth was demonstrated to me not too long ago. I spoke to a group of men about how Jesus Christ was relevant to their future plans, especially in the area of giving them meaning and purpose in life. As I met afterward with one of the men who wanted to know more about the gospel, I asked him why he was interested in Christ. His response was that he "needed direction and purpose in life." As we talked further, it became obvious that this man had never considered the personal ramifications of Christ's death on the cross for his sins. I suggested that he give me his opinion on a short presentation of the gospel. As we came to the part that discussed Christ's death for man's sin, I asked him if he thought this was relevant to his present situation. I explained that the root cause of man's lack of direction in life was directly related to his alienation from God. I could see the proverbial wheels turning in his head as he considered for the first time the eternal ramifications of his guilt and alienation before God and their remedy in the cross of Christ. The young man was profoundly touched by the simple, gracious truth that "He bore our sins," and he later came to a saving knowledge of Christ. God got this man's attention via his lack of purpose and direction in life, but the gospel — not content to speak merely to symptoms — healed his root problem.

I would have done an injustice both to this young man and to the gospel had I been satisfied to relate Christ's relevance to his lack of purpose and to leave it at that. That would have been equivalent to treating a patient's symptoms at the expense of healing his disease. Without the cross of Christ, there is no true remedy for man's sin; there is, in other words, no true salvation, as the term is biblically understood. That is why Richard Lovelace can say, "Indeed, no conversion is complete that does not deal with the problem of sin."[17]

We do the unbeliever no favors by allowing him to make a "decision for Christ" that is motivated by a presentation of the "gospel" that fails to deal squarely with the sin issue. We are dealing with eternal matters here; men's souls are at stake. Therefore, the burden of precision weighs heavily on the evangelist. The evangelist must work to avoid what is known as a spurious conversion experience, where the potential believer believes he is entering a personal relationship with Christ when in reality he is merely using Jesus as the means to an end of meeting his felt need.

Of this burden of precision, Robert Ferm remarks, "He (the evangelist) will be particularly cautious for he knows that the stimulation of a spurious conversion may well constitute a prohibiting factor for any future, true conversion. Many persons, as it has been shown, have been very satisfied with a spurious conversion."[18]

As James Denney states, "The condemnation of our sins in Christ upon His cross is the barb on the hook. If you leave that out of your gospel, I do not deny that your bait will be taken . . . but you will not catch men. You will not create in sinful human hearts that attitude to Christ which was created in the New Testament. You will not annihilate pride and make Christ the alpha and omega in man's redemption."[19]

An Illustration

Suppose you are on an ocean liner ten miles out to sea. It is a clear day and you are walking on the deck when you see a man struggling in the water 30 yards away. He seems to be frantically swimming in the same direction as the boat. As you look more closely, you see to your great surprise that he is doing quite well. He waves at you and smiles. "Where are you going?" you ask.

"To Hawaii," he replies with great confidence.

"You will never make it," you scream. "It's over 2,000 miles from here. Why don't you come aboard?"

"No, I've made it this far," he assures you, "and I'm sure I'll see you there."

Your arguing is fruitless, but you have an idea and you return to your cabin. You come back with a map of the world, your position marked on it. You put it in a bottle and throw it to the swimmer. "Here, look at this and you'll see how far you have to go," you tell him. "You'll drown. There's no chance you'll ever make it."

"I'd like to prove I can make it myself," he retorts. "I don't need a boat ride. I can swim it. It's not that far."

Upon further encouragement, he takes the map out and while treading water notes, "Boy, it's a lot farther than I thought, but I can make it, I think."

The hours pass and, to your relief, the swimmer begins to look exhausted. His strokes are less assured. You call to him, "Are you ready to ride? Please grab on to this life preserver and I'll pull you aboard."

Now you will see if he really understands that Hawaii is beyond his range and that he would eventually drown in the insane pursuit of trying to swim the Pacific. You are delighted when he begins to swim toward the life preserver. He grabs hold, and you drag him aboard. Then you ask him why he finally changed his mind. His answer reveals that he never did really understand his predicament. "Seventy miles of swimming can make a man hungry. Besides, I was getting waterlogged and felt that I needed to dry off. And it sure was lonely out there, with only you to talk to. And it seemed like people on the boat were having such a good time, I just wanted to join in."

Application

This rather silly story illustrates the point quite, well. The swimmer's reasons were all wet. He displayed the profound gift of being able to avoid the primary issue of the matter: He would eventually drown if he kept on because the goal was beyond his reach. Why did he need to get on the boat? Because otherwise he would die. Did coming aboard alleviate his wetness, hunger and loneliness? Of course it did. But this was not the correct reason he needed a "change of heart." This was not the primary issue that the helpful man was speaking to. That was not why he threw him the map or life preserver or experienced the great joy and relief upon the swimmer's return to the ship. The swimmer had profoundly misunderstood the reason for his rescue.

On a spiritual level, this has serious ramifications. Apart from the gospel being clearly and precisely presented, it is very likely that no true conversion will take place and no salvation will be experienced by those who are superficially interested in Jesus. It is true that whosoever will, may come, but those truly prepared by the Holy Spirit to do business with Jesus will not come with their fingers crossed behind their backs. They must do business with Jesus on His terms and His terms alone. "God is there for the desperate man, for the man who needs Him; there is no point in offering faith to the man who is not ready to repent."[20]

In Summary

I am convinced that we can have both a relevant message and a cross-centered message. As George Jackson sums it up, "Questions of the hour, interesting topics, meeting felt needs may serve some useful end. They may help, like the ringing of a bell to gather a crowd, but there is nothing people tire of more or much sooner, than the sound of a bell. The bellman must have something to say."[21] Attempted shortcuts may really be the longer way around. In our eagerness to achieve relevance to get a hearing for the gospel, we must not forget the true gospel for which the hearing is to be gained. As Dr. E. V. Hill says, "Preach Christ — He's preachable."

CHAPTER 4

A Look at New Testament Evangelism

Now that we have a clear understanding of the gospel message, the definition of evangelism can be brought into focus.

It is interesting to note that the Bible does not use the term *evangelism,* but it does talk a lot about the activity of "proclaiming the good news." In fact, more than fifty times the New Testament speaks of such proclaiming (evangelism) taking place.[1] Our term *evangelism* is derived from the Greek word *evangelizo* meaning "to bring or announce good news." Acts 5:42; 8:4, 12, 25, 35, 40; 10:36 and 11:20 tell us that the first-century church was busy about the work of evangelizing. Luke 2:10 says the angels evangelized the shepherds with "good news of great joy." In 1 Corinthians 15:2 we see that Paul evangelized (preached the word to) the Corinthians. It is obvious from these references that evangelism is the activity of communicating the good news of the gospel. Evangelism, then — at least in the New Testament — is a verb, not a noun. It is always something that is done, not just studied, encouraged, or discussed.

Contemporary Definitions of Evangelism

The Lausanne Covenant offers this definition of evangelism: "To evangelize is to spread the good news that Jesus Christ died for our sins and was raised from the dead according to the

49

Scriptures, and that as reigning Lord, He now offers the forgiveness of sins and the liberating gift of the Spirit to all who repent
and believe. Evangelism itself is the proclamation of the historical,
biblical, Christ as Savior and Lord, with a view to persuading
people to come to Him personally and so be reconciled to God."

The Berlin World Congress on Evangelism offered this definition: "Evangelism is the proclamation of the gospel of the crucified
and risen Christ, the only redeemer of men, according to the
Scriptures, with the purpose of persuading condemned and lost
sinners to put their trust in God by receiving and accepting Christ
as Savior through the power of the Holy Spirit, and to serve
Christ as Lord in every calling of life and in the fellowship of
His Church, looking toward the day of His coming in glory." It
is "an affirmation concerning all that is central in the work of
Christ for men and in men; and all that is fundamental in that
transforming experience to which the exercise of personal faith
in Christ gives rise."[3] Thus, evangelism might be summed up as
the communication of all that is fundamental and primary to
entering a personal relationship with Christ.

Evangelism could also be defined as the offering of the "cure"
to a terminally ill patient. It brings lost men and women into
contact with the love and forgiveness of God. As such, it is the
believer's opportunity to be on the cutting edge of God's redemptive plan for the world. As the Christian participates in the work
of evangelism, he aligns his efforts with God's work to redeem
the lost from the tragic consequences of the fall and restore them
to a personal relationship with Himself.

Focus of Evangelism

Note that both the Lausanne and Berlin definitions of
evangelism emphasize its persuasive nature. God has given the
gospel message for the purpose of bringing a very specific result:
the conversion of sinners to Jesus Christ. The gospel message is
indeed a magnificent message, but it was not given to be admired.
It was given to *persuade* men and women to put their trust in
Christ. It demands that lost sinners change their minds and "do
business" with Christ.

So, to be involved in evangelism is to be involved in a persuasive activity. Evangelism assumes that men and women without Christ can be won and, indeed, will be won. God desires nothing less than to see the lost found and transferred from the kingdom of darkness to the kingdom of Jesus Christ (Colossians 1:12,13; Acts 26:18). "The primary purpose of the evangelist message is not general Christian instruction in an improvement of the moral life; its first concern, rather, is to awaken souls from spiritual death, to bring them rebirth by the power of the Holy Spirit."[4] Indeed, the gospel is both good news and a gracious offer. As an offer, it is the most decisive question ever put to a person and calls for nothing less than a response of radical obedience. Heaven and hell hang in the balance, so the evangelist can do nothing less than seek a verdict for Christ.

One day I approached a young man who was lounging in his college student union, and I took the opportunity to talk about the gospel. His first words to me were, "I'll talk with you as long as you don't try to talk me into accepting Jesus." I had to be honest with this student and said that, while I would not try to force him into making a decision he did not want to make, the gospel message is inherently persuasive. Jesus calls people to decide about Him; there is no getting around this.

God's RSVP

We can have great confidence that asking for a decision for Christ is not only appropriate to, but also inherent in, the work of evangelism, for our God is an inviting God. From beginning to end, the Bible is filled with God's invitations to man to repent and return to Him. The Bible ends in an invitation to all to come. Revelation 22:17 says, "And let the one who hears say, 'Come.' And let the one who is thirsty come; let the one who wishes take the water of life without cost." The gates of heaven have been thrown wide open, and all may enter on the merit of the finished work of Christ. The invitation of the gospel cuts across all human distinctions and dividing lines. Gradation of morality and religiosity are meaningless in the face of the gracious offer of the gospel.

It is also very clear from God's Word that His invitations come with an RSVP. A response is demanded. Thus, the children of Israel are told by Moses and Joshua to decide whether they will or will not follow God (Exodus 32:26; Joshua 24:15). The first words of Jesus' public ministry were an invitation for men and women to repent and believe the gospel (Mark 1:15). He did not just announce that the kingdom of God was here and leave it at that. Rather, we find Jesus calling for a radical decision. Men are asked to repent (Mark 1:15; Matthew 11:20,21; 12:41; Luke 5:42), to follow Him (Mark 1:16-20; 2:14,15; 8:34), to deny themselves (Mark 8:34), to take up their cross (Matthew 10:32) and to lose their lives (Mark 8:35; Matthew 10:39). His first words to His disciples were, "Follow Me." They were asked to decide between fishing for fish or fishing for men.

At one point Jesus told the parable of the wedding feast for the king's son. When those people who were first invited refused to RSVP, the king sent out his servants to the main highways and streets to find anyone to attend (Matthew 22:1-14). Let it be firmly stated that there will be no guests at the last great wedding feast who did not decide to attend. Jesus called, and still calls, men and women to a deliberate decision; He addresses and challenges their wills to action. He calls them to a personal decision; they alone can decide their own destinies. He calls them to an urgent decision; the kingdom of God is here and life is no longer business as usual. And He calls them to an indispensable decision; the battle lines have been drawn, and all must choose whom they will serve.

It is no surprise, then, that since God places a premium on human decision, He charges His ambassadors with the responsibility of calling for a decision from nonbelievers. We are to persuade (2 Corinthians 5:11; Acts 17:1-4), entreat and beg (2 Corinthians 5:20), to the end that men and women clearly and soberly face the question, "What will you do with Jesus Christ?" This is the most decisive question that can ever be put to a person, for his answer is the hinge on which his eternal destiny swings.

The point is that we need to see the decision phase of the evangelistic encounter as necessary and distinctly appropriate, in light of our role as ambassadors for the God who invites. We are to communicate in order to influence, to see change wrought in the attitudes of nonbelievers. We are to present the gospel for a verdict.[5]

As we look at New Testament evangelism, we see that it was carried on in a variety of styles.

Proclamation Evangelism

The New Testament authors used two words to describe the activity of announcing, proclaiming and generally making known the gospel. The Greek word *kerysso* means "to announce, preach or sound forth." It is derived from the Greek term *keryx*, meaning a herald, the one "who is commissioned by the ruler or state to call out with a clear voice some item of news and so to make it known."[6]

The Greek word *evangelizo* carries much the same sense as *kerysso*, meaning "to bring or announce good news, proclaim, preach."[7]

The very nature of the gospel demands that it be proclaimed, announced and generally made known to all who will listen. The first-century Christians were obviously gripped by the fact that the gospel is both a gracious offer that all should want to hear and a solemn call to a life of submission and obedience to Christ that no one can afford to ignore or misunderstand. As such, it is mandatory that all who are willing to listen have the opportunity to hear and understand the best and most crucial news ever told.

New Testament Examples

The New Testament church's practice of proclamation evangelism usually took the form of public group meetings. The distinguishing feature of proclamation evangelism is that the ratio of hearers to speakers is usually quite large, thus minimizing the opportunity for immediate feedback from the audience and per-sonal interaction between the speaker and audience.

Examples of proclamation evangelism are Peter's sermon in Acts 2:14-36, and Paul's sermon to the Athenians in Acts 17:21-53. In each case the gospel was presented publicly to a large audience comprised of anyone willing to listen.

Proclamation evangelism was practiced anytime and anywhere a crowd could be gathered. Synagogue preaching (Acts 13:16ff; 14:1ff; 17:3ff) was one of Paul's main strategies for communicating the gospel. The success of this strategy is obvious, as the proclamation of the gospel provided the spark for the founding of many New Testament churches. Paul also spoke in the marketplaces (Act 17:17) and in the formal lecture halls of his day (Acts 17:19, 19:9). Paul's use of this type of evangelism implies that the New Testament church sought to proclaim the gospel to any group, in any place, and at any time within the bounds of propriety.

Benefits

The benefits of proclamation evangelism are many. First, it exposes a large number to the gospel message at one time. Second, it is a screening procedure. By this I mean that the ones who return for more information are likely to have a genuine spiritual interest. Thus, in Acts 2:37, immediately following Peter's sermon, many in the crowd were "pierced to the heart," and asked, "Brethren, what must we do?" Luke records that immediately following Paul's proclamation of the gospel to the Athenians, some in the crowd said, "We shall hear you again concerning these things" (Acts 17:32).

Third, proclamation can prime the spiritual environment by planting the seeds of the gospel in the minds of the listeners. In my experience, I have found it is not unusual for one who has heard the gospel at a large group meeting to be more open to the gospel the next time he hears it. I happen to be one who heard the good news at a large meeting and could not get the message out of my mind. Six months later I received Christ as my Savior, largely due to the impact the gospel had made on me at the mass gathering.

Fourth, the proclamation of the gospel in a large group setting is usually a "no risk" venture for the nonbeliever. Those who showed up to hear Paul's public evangelistic sermons knew that they had no obligation to respond to the message. The one who was curious about spiritual things could hear the gospel while hidden in the crowd if he so chose. This is an attractive setting for many who, for whatever reason, are reluctant to talk to someone face to face about the gospel.

Finally, the proclamation of the gospel can lead easily to an opportunity for face-to-face interaction over the content of the gospel. We must not assume that the sole purpose of proclamation is merely to impart gospel information — a sort of once-for-all-take-it-or-leave-it activity. Proclamation is more than a bare offer of the gospel. From 1 Thessalonians 2:9, we learn that Paul proclaimed the gospel in the context of his own intense personal interest, persuasion, love and self-sacrifice (1 Thessalonians 2:7-12). Paul saw proclamation as the doorway to further interaction with the Thessalonians. Remember that the Lausanne definition of evangelism states that proclamation is done "with a view to persuading people to come to Him personally and so be reconciled to God."

In my own experience of sharing the gospel with large groups, an opportunity is always provided for feedback from the audience. Those who respond positively are contacted for an opportunity to discuss further how to have a personal relationship with Jesus Christ. Many desire to talk more; thus, proclamation gives way to dialogue-persuasion, a face-to-face conversation concerning the claims of Christ on one's life.

This is exactly what happened with Paul in Thessalonica. Acts 17:1-4 records that Paul proclaimed Christ to the people there. "This Jesus whom I am proclaiming to you is the Christ" (verse 3). At the same time he was "reasoning, explaining and giving evidence from the Scriptures that Jesus was indeed the Christ" (verses 2,3). So we see that while proclamation and dialogue-persuasion are distinguished from one another, at the same time they are inseparably linked in their function.

Persuasive Dialogue Evangelism

As we have seen, the proclamation and persuasive elements of evangelism are both necessary ingredients in defining the nature and focus of evangelism. While proclamation centers on the mass announcement of the good news of the gospel, persuasive dialogue focuses on the one-to-one interaction between the Christian communicator of the gospel and the non-Christian. While it is true that proclamation is persuasive in nature, it lacks the element of dialogue and the personal or small-group setting featured in persuasive dialogue evangelism. Thus, we might say that the gospel is such good news that it must be proclaimed and shouted far and wide, yet such crucial news that it must be communicated in the context of a dialogue to ensure that it be clearly understood.

The Power of Persuasion

The Greek term for *persuade* is *peitho,* meaning to prevail upon or win over, to persuade, bringing about a change of mind by the influence of reason or moral considerations. The word has the basic meaning of trust, and implies that the one persuaded is ready and willing to let himself become convinced and thus puts his trust in the information made available by the communicator. *Peitho* is also translated as "trust" (Mark 10:24), "obey" (Acts 5:36) and "being confident" (Philippians 1:6).

Persuasive dialogue evangelism takes seriously the fact that there is a compelling reasonableness to the gospel. The message makes sense. Thus, people need to engage their minds to consider the claims of Christ, asking themselves if He indeed is their only hope for eternal life. Persuasive dialogue evangelism also acknowledges that the reasonableness and personal implications of the gospel are best communicated person to person. The truth of the gospel must often be amplified, clarified and personalized if it is to take root in a human heart prone to doubts and misconceptions about spiritual truth. Often, this can take place only in a personal context where the nonbeliever feels free to raise his doubts and concerns. It is in this individualized situation that the persuasive efforts of the evangelist become a tool in the hands of the Holy Spirit to communicate to the nonbeliever that the gospel not only is true but also is meant for him. The result is that the nonbeliever is given every opportunity to make a fully informed decision for Christ.

New Testament Examples

The first-century Christians were eager to take advantage of all opportunities for personal witness. Their evangelistic spirit is typified in Colossians 4:5,6 as Paul writes, "Conduct yourselves with wisdom toward outsiders, making the most of the opportunity. Let your speech always be with grace, seasoned as it were with salt, so that you may know how you should respond to each person." The church manifested an incredible availability to be used as an instrument of God to convince the lost of His saving power.

In the New Testament we see persuasive dialogue evangelism often taking place from stranger to stranger. For example, Philip had never met the Ethiopian eunuch before he preached the gospel to him (Acts 8:26-40), and Paul had never met Lydia (Acts 16:14) before. We see persuasive dialogue evangelism also taking place from family member to family member. Lydia shared the gospel first with her family (Acts 16:15), and the Philippian jailer with his family (Acts 16:34). Andrew told his brother Peter about Jesus, and Philip told his brother Nathaniel (John 1:40-46). The network of social relationships, whether among family members, close friends, or acquaintances, was an arena for New Testament evangelistic activity.

One cannot mention person-to-person evangelism without thinking of Jesus' interview with Nicodemus (John 3:1-15) and His encounter with the Samaritan woman at the well (John 4:4-26). The Gospels record over thirty such meetings where Jesus engaged in dialogues with seekers of spiritual truth.

Paul as Persuader

Paul's ministry is a vivid demonstration of the power and priority of persuasive dialogue evangelism. Acts 18:4 states, "And he was reasoning in the synagogue every Sabbath and trying to persuade Jews and Greeks." Paul's ministry in Ephesus was no different. Acts 19:8 states, "And he entered the synagogue and continued speaking out boldly for three months, reasoning and persuading them about the kingdom of God." Here, Paul's proclamation was complemented by his persuasive efforts. Finally, Acts 28:23,24 states that Paul continued, most likely to his dying day, to persuade people of the truth of Christ: "And he was explaining to them by solemnly testifying about the kingdom of God, and trying to persuade them concerning Jesus, from both the Law of Moses and from the Prophets, from morning until evening." Indeed, Paul was so intensely committed to bringing his persuasive skills to bear on the minds of the unbelievers that a Roman attorney, Tertullus, called him "a real pest" (Acts 24:5).

Paul understood that the gospel is more than information. It is information that asks for — even demands — a decision. Paul understood that persuasive dialogue evangelism provides the evangelist with a platform to "combine teaching and decision so that a man's heart and mind combine to leave him no alternative to accepting Jesus Christ as Lord."[8] To stop short of calling for a decision would be a disservice not only to his role as an ambassador for Christ (2 Corinthians 5:21), but also to the very nature and intent of the gospel message. The gospel must be not only heard, but also understood and decided upon.

Clarity In Persuasion

The Christian communicator must leave no question in the listener's mind as to what is at stake in the call for a decision to trust Christ as Lord and Savior. The listener must know exactly what he is doing or his "decision" could do more harm than good. David Hesselgrave describes this danger in picturesque terms: "The mission fields are well populated with men and women who have been ushered into the heavenlies without knowing why they got on the elevator. Once back on earth they have no intention of being taken for another ride."[9]

This danger was felt by Paul on his first-century journeys. Paul knew that the call for a decision for Christ could be construed as just one of many other calls for decisions in a world flooded with various religions and ideas. How much more is this true today, in an age of overchoice, where we are asked to decide on various issues hundreds of times a day, thousands of times a year.

Paul faced such a problem with his audience in Athens, the Greek world's marketplace of new ideas. The audience, so used to new ideas in the religious realm, responded to Paul's presentation of the gospel with only mild curiosity. Some called him an "idle babbler" or a "proclaimer of strange deities." The gospel of Jesus Christ was just another "new teaching" which brought "some strange things to our ears" (Acts 17:16-20).

There was always the possibility of great misunderstanding when the gospel was presented. On Paul's first missionary journey visit to Lystra (Acts 14:8-28), he and Barnabas were even mistaken for the Greek gods Zeus and Hermes.

Noting the potential for confusion, it is not surprising that Paul called for a decision for Christ through a cognitive decision-making process. Paul knew that even lost men and women retain God's image, and thus require intellectually sound reasons to make heartfelt choices. Thus, in Thessalonica Paul "reasoned with them from the Scriptures, explaining and giving evidence that the Christ had to suffer and rise again from the dead" (Acts 17:2,3). As a result, some in the audience were "persuaded." The words "reasoned," "explaining," "giving evidence" and "persuaded" all point to the fact that Paul thought it very important that people decide to follow Christ with their minds fully engaged. He wanted new believers to understand who Jesus is, what their need was and how Jesus met that need. Paul was not content to let people come to Christ for motives less than those based on a clear understanding of the issues of the gospel.

Integrity in Persuasion

The watching world often sees as ethically suspect any attempt to convince others of the truth of Christ and to ask them to follow Him. Some accuse us of proselytizing. This word is usually used in a derogatory sense, implying that the evangelist, whose enthusiasm may overstep his sense of propriety, is out to convince others that their way is wrong and his way is right, or get them to leave their group and join his. In all honesty, the evangelist *must* be sensitive to the concerns raised by this accusation. Are we trying to win others to *us* or to *Christ?* Are we asking others to change outward, sociological or cultural allegiances without a corresponding inner change? Do we merely want to see our group get larger and more powerful, or do we want to see the kingdom of God grow? Do we want nonbelievers to decide for Christ for our benefit or for theirs?

Recruiting others to join an organization, often at the expense of another group, for ends other than their personal benefit will always be open to charges of proselytizing, and rightly so. But true scriptural evangelism cannot be charged justly with proselytizing. True evangelism seeks to win others first to Christ, for their own benefit. Of course, as this happens, it is only natural that these new believers may want to identify with their newfound forever family, as they did with Paul in Thessalonica. "And some of them were persuaded and joined Paul" (Acts 17:4). It is also possible that this will make the group they left very angry over their departure, as was the case with the Thessalonica Jews (verses 4-13). But charges of proselytizing in cases like this are usually the rhetoric of sour grapes. As persuaded people persuading others, we will always be susceptible to such charges, but as long as we are winning people to Christ, for the glory of God and for their own eternal gain, we need not feel that our persuasive efforts are ethically suspect.

Propaganda Versus Persuasion

Propaganda differs from persuasion on two major points. Both are an attempt to elicit a decision from others. But propaganda does this by distorting the facts and the true nature of the situation by either withholding certain information or by over- or under-emphasizing certain facets of the information. The propagandist is out to convince any way he can. If he can do this by appealing to purely emotional factors, he will. If the facts must be manipulated to gain the desired response, then so be it. The end justifies the means. But we must affirm with Ghandi that evil means, even for a good end, produce evil results. Propaganda is inherently unethical and should be avoided by the evangelist.

The second area of departure closely follows the first. Propaganda is inherently self-centered. Its goal is to elicit a decision that is favorable for the communicator or his group. The welfare of the listener is secondary at best.

A good case could be made for the contention that almost all communication is propagandistic in that most messages are sent for the benefit of the communicator. Most messages contain only that information which puts the communicator's cause in a good light so that it will be accepted or supported. The decision that stems from propagandistic communication will therefore be based on less than adequate information, often with the mind being less than fully informed and engaged.

The evangelist must avoid both proselytizing and propaganda. Affirmation VI of the International Conference for Itinerant Evangelists states: "In our proclamation of the gospel we recognize the urgency of calling all to decision to follow Jesus Christ as Lord and Savior, and to do so lovingly and without coercion or manipulation."[10] The Christian communicator must affirm in his attitudes and actions that Jesus came not to trick or coerce, but to win men.

Sensitivity in Persuasion

The need for sensitivity on the part of the communicator is of utmost importance as he calls for a decision. The evangelists must ask, "Is this person truly ready for such a decision? Does he know the issue? What barriers, if any, remain between him and inheriting eternal life?" In short, the evangelist must work to create the proper climate for an authentic decision to take place.

True, our communication is purposeful and persuasive, but we also realize that there is a point where the nonbeliever must decide for himself. Here is where we must respect the moral responsibility of each person created in God's image and the behind-the-scenes work of the Holy Spirit in the conversion process.

The communicator of the gospel must walk the fine line of using all of his godly wisdom to persuade the nonbeliever while

still respecting the nonbeliever's free choice and the work of the
Spirit in his life. On one side of this line is the mistake of not
challenging the nonbeliever to make a decision for Christ in the
very near future. As Paul wrote, "Behold, now is 'the acceptable
time' behold, now is 'the day of salvation'" (2 Corinthians 6:2).
It would be a mistake not to bring all of our persuasive power
to bear on the nonbeliever who is truly under the conviction of
the Spirit and has ample information to make a biblically informed
decision. On the other hand, it would also be a mistake to push
a nonbeliever into deciding before he is convinced that the decision
is necessary and in his best interest. If the issues of eternity
remain unclear, or if valid barriers continue to hinder his response
to Jesus Christ, these must first be dealt with.

There is an old saying, "Don't try to teach a pig to sing; it
wastes your time and annoys the pig." Another old saying is,
"A man convinced against his will is of the same decision still."
In St. Augustine's words, we as communicators are "not merely
imparting knowledge about things that ought to be done but
rather moving them to do that which they already know must
be done."[11]

The point is that the communicator must use all of his
persuasive powers and marshal all the evidence necessary to
convince the nonbeliever that to remain undecided about Jesus
is in reality to decide against Him, and this is life's greatest
possible tragedy. But to decide to accept the free offer of salvation
in Christ is life's greatest responsibility and joy. A definite, clearcut
verdict for Christ is our goal, and this is possible only when the
nonbeliever's heart is set in motion by the convicting work of
the Spirit of God, propelling him into the kingdom.

Jesus' ministry displayed His great regard for the dignity of
man's freedom of choice and the moral responsibility God has
entrusted to each man and woman. Richard Lovelace describes
this extremely well: "Jesus' whole ministry reveals a controlled
dignity which did not force persons beyond the moving of the
Holy Spirit detectable in their words and actions, so that in
bringing them to commitment, even the Son of God waited upon
the Spirit."[12]

The key is to understand our role in the evangelistic encounter and, more specifically, the limits of our role. We are to present the gospel clearly. We are to persuade, even beg, the nonbeliever to respond as he grasps the issue of the gospel. We are to convince the nonbeliever of the truth of the gospel and his awesome responsibility to decide yes or no for Jesus Christ. We are to make it quite clear that Jesus stands at the door of his life waiting for an answer. But here our persuasive efforts reach their limit. We must never entertain the thought or act as though we are able, through the power of our personality or the application of our carefully devised communication technique, to bring about the spiritual change in the listener's heart. Only Christ can do that. The decision is between the nonbeliever and Jesus, and we must grant every person his right to decide for himself. He must have the genuine freedom to disagree, or to postpone his decision. Remember, we are not out to win an argument, but a person.

The Foundation of New Testament Evangelism

Whatever the method of New Testament evangelism, the work of sharing the gospel was usually enhanced by the visibility and availability of the loving fellowship and compassionate service of the church.

We are not to confuse fellowship and the good works that comprise compassionate service with evangelism per se. Technically they are not evangelism, but at the same time they are crucial to its long-range success. The Lausanne Covenant keeps this distinction in mind: "Our Christian presence in the world is indispensable to evangelism, and so is that kind of dialogue whose purpose is to listen sensitively in order to understand. But evangelism itself is the proclamation of the historical, biblical Christ as Savior and Lord, with a view to persuading people to come to Him personally and so be reconciled to God."[13] Whatever form our good works and our personal presence takes, they are not the good news. The presence of the church or an individual is, of course, a prerequisite for most evangelism[14] and, as the first-century church demonstrates, is integral to the long-term success of the work of taking the gospel to the world.

First Century Presence

Acts 2:41-47 gives us a picture of the corporate quality of life
of the first-century church. This quality of life, I believe, was
foundational to its success in evangelism. Verse 41 records that
three thousand new members were added to this new church in
Jerusalem following Peter's first evangelistic sermon. Imagine taking three thousand additional people into your church. Think of
the incredible burden this would place on the church in terms
of meeting the total range of needs of these newborn babes in
Christ. Spiritual nurture, of course, would need to be given. But
because many of these new believers were travelers from around
the world, in Jerusalem to celebrate Pentecost, they also must
have had many material needs as their travel provisions ran out.

What kind of Christians unselfishly reached out to embrace
these needy brothers and sisters? Verses 42-47 give us their profile:
"And they were continually devoting themselves to the apostles'
teaching and to fellowship, to the breaking of bread and to prayer.
And everyone kept feeling a sense of awe; and many wonders
and signs were taking place through the apostles. And all those
who had believed were together, and had all things in common;
and they began selling their property and possessions, and were
sharing them with all, as anyone might have need. And day by
day continuing with one mind in the temple, and breaking bread
from house to house, they were taking their meals together with
gladness and sincerity of heart, praising God and having favor
with all the people. And the Lord was adding to their number
day by day those who were being saved."

What an attractive group of people. Here we have the epitome
of a loving fellowship, ready to serve as needs became apparent.
In a Roman world where the unlovely were shunned and the
poor had no alternative but to go hungry because there were no
such things as social welfare systems, this new fellowship of
believers must have been startling. Their loving fellowship was
a powerful testimony to the life-changing power of the gospel
and the living presence of the risen Jesus Christ. Their unselfish
service, intimate personal relationships and evidence of God's

supernatural presence in their midst produced the kind of social environment that was conducive to the spread of the gospel. As we note in verse 47, "the Lord was adding to their number day by day those who were being saved."

Just as the individual must live a life that bears testimony to the purity, truth and power of the gospel, so must the corporate fellowship of believers. The medium must not be incongruous with the message. But it is more than a matter of just not contradicting the gospel. The medium must also support and enhance the gospel.

This is our "salt" responsibility. As Jesus states, we are the salt of the earth (Matthew 5:13). In the ancient world, salt was considered a necessity, due to its preserving qualities. The word *salt*, therefore, acquired connotations of high esteem and honor in ancient and modern languages. Cakes of salt were used as money in Africa, and when an Arab says, "There is salt between us," he speaks of an intimate, enduring friendship.[15] A person who is the salt of the earth is a man or woman of high honor and esteem.

Thus, the Christian's presence (his character, conduct, fellowship and service) is to parallel the highly esteemed function of salt. As salt stabilizes a food product, inhibiting the perishing process, so we as Christians, by our holy living, are to inhibit the spread of sin, to the glory of God and for the good of our nonbelieving friends and enemies alike. As salt flavors and spices up otherwise bland food, so we flavor the gospel, enhancing its already self-authenticating and powerful message, by the living testimony of the grace of God in our lives. As salt causes thirst, so we too, by the visible demonstration of the power of Christ in and among us, make the world thirsty for the One who alone is the living water. We may not be able to make the world — or the stubborn horse — drink water, but we can certainly feed them salt. All three of these salt functions — preserving, flavoring and creating thirst — support the work of evangelism. They augment our proclamation and persuasion efforts, providing a "sermon in shoes," a living object lesson of the power of the gospel unleashed in human lives.

This is exactly what we find happening in the evangelistic ministry of the early church. The Athenian philosopher Aristides observed, "When they see the stranger, they take him to their dwellings and rejoice over him as over a true brother. And if anyone among them is poor and needy, and they have no spare food, they fast two or three days in order to supply him with the needed food. The precepts of their Messiah they observe with great care. They live justly and soberly as the Lord their God commanded them."[16]

Years later, Bishop Dionysius of Alexandria would write that "most of our brethren (during the Alexandrian plague) did not spare themselves and held together in the closest love of their neighbors. They were not afraid to visit the sick, to look after them well, to take care of them for Christ's sake and to die joyfully with them. . . . Many of them lost their own lives after restoring others to health, thus taking their death upon themselves. . . . In this way some of the noblest of our brethren died — some presbyters, deacons and highly esteemed lay people. But the heathen did exactly the opposite. They cast out any people who began to be too ill, and deserted those dearest."[17] Imagine the testimony of such living to the truth, power and relevance of the gospel to the watching world. The faithful proclamation of the gospel by the early Christians, by whatever method, was enhanced by their loving fellowship.

CHAPTER 5

Evangelism as an Event and a Process

A nyone who has been involved in evangelism realizes that time constraints and social factors often make it impossible to communicate the entire gospel with an interested non-believer. The social context may be inappropriate for such a dialogue, or you may simply run out of time. It may be that the nonbeliever does not understand a major element of the gospel. Perhaps he does not grasp the implications of his problem and its remedy in Jesus' atoning death, or does not believe that God loves him and is interested in his welfare. In such a situation, it is easy to reason that it would be not only foolish, but also inappropriate to ask for a decision for Christ.

These are valid concerns and raise an important question that touches on the nature and definition of biblical evangelism. When can we say that true evangelism has taken place? Is it always necessary to share the gospel in its entirety to consider our ambassadorial duties fulfilled? Will our evangelistic efforts always result in reaping (i.e., seeing others make a decision for Christ), or should we expect to do our share of sowing? And what are we to do in those situations where lack of time or lack of personal preparedness of the nonbeliever prevents a complete presentation of the gospel or makes calling for a decision unwise? I believe that a proper understanding of evangelism as both an event and a process will help to resolve this issue.

Evangelism as an Event and Process

Evangelism as an event could be defined as the communication of the gospel, both in a proclamation or persuasive dialogue context, in such a manner that an informed decision for Christ is appropriately called for. The hearer(s) may or may not be ready to believe, but nonetheless the crucial and decisive nature of the gospel has been clearly, boldly, sensitively and persuasively communicated.

Thus, we find Peter proclaiming the gospel to thousands on Pentecost and calling for a decision for Christ (Acts 2:14-42). Three thousand responded, but many others probably went away angry at Peter's message or just scratching their heads in confusion. Nevertheless, the event of evangelism had taken place.

Paul reasoned with a group of Jews and Greeks in Thessalonica (Acts 17:1-4). Some were persuaded and followed Paul and his companions as their disciples (verse 4). Others left without making a decision, and still others left having made a decision to return with an angry mob to run Paul out of town (Acts 17:5-9). Here, the good news had been proclaimed, explained, discussed and reasoned out. The audience knew that a decision was called for. Thus, the event of evangelism had taken place. The number of valid conversions is not the issue, for evangelism is not defined as converting nonbelievers, but as giving nonbelievers the opportunity to make an informed decision to trust in Christ.

Whether or not people are saved when they hear the gospel is up to God. He alone can convict the heart of sin, lack of righteousness and impending judgment. He alone is capable of confirming the grace, hope and truth of the gospel to the heart and mind of the nonbeliever. As the messenger, I cannot take great pride in many responses or feel bad about few responses. God is sovereign in the matter.

Evangelism as a Process

In Acts 18:4, Paul gives us an example of the process of evangelism. In Corinth Paul reasoned with the Jews in the synagogue every Sabbath, with mixed results. The leader of the synagogue, Crispus, believed, but many of the Jews "resisted and blasphemed," until Paul felt it necessary to leave and set up shop in a personal home next door. The point is that Paul kept coming back to explain, clarify and reason with these people. Paul followed much the same pattern in Thessalonica (Acts 17:1-9). Over a period of three Saturdays he reasoned with them, explained and gave evidence that Christ was the Messiah. Luke says that Paul did this "from the Scriptures." The idea seems to be that Paul progressively built a case for Jesus as the Messiah. Thus, his evangelism in Thessalonica could be described as a process.

I have had many experiences like this. One young man in particular, John, would invite me to sit down with him almost weekly to explain more about Christ. He asked me many times to repeat things so that they would sink in. He asked me more than once to tell him how crucial this issue was and how he really needed to trust Christ as soon as he felt he could make a sincere decision. He was always eager to hear more, but for some reason the gospel never "clicked." He later moved away, and I did not hear from him for a year. Then by divine providence, I'm sure, I ran into him. The first thing he told me was that he had finally put together all the pieces and that he had trusted Christ through the help of a friend in his new church. He thanked me for hanging in there with him. My evangelism with John was definitely a process of sowing, so that another could have the joy of harvesting.

I would have been greatly amiss had I told John that since he was not ready to decide for Christ I did not have time to talk with him. The fact that a person is not ready to make a decision to trust Christ now does not mean that he is not serious about pursuing the matter. I need to meet him where he is and be a patient 'sower' in his life. I need to answer his questions, listen to him carefully, explain and clarify so that the issue of "Christ and Him crucified" is the only stumbling block to his receiving Christ. Misconceptions need to be cleared away so that the real matter at hand — "What will you do with Christ?" — can take center stage. Understanding evangelism as a process gives me the freedom to do this.

Some Cautions

Evangelism as a process, however, must be practiced with some cautions. First, we must be true to the persuasive nature of the gospel message. Look at what Paul did in Acts 18:4. "And he was reasoning in the synagogue every Sabbath and trying to persuade Jews and Greeks." Even though he was involved in evangelism as a process, he did not allow the expanded time frame to dilute his sense of urgency. Paul stood ready to be *both* sower and harvester. The gospel was still to be believed as soon as it was possible for the listener to make an informed decision. He was "trying to persuade." In other words, the process had a specific direction to it. And don't bet that his hearers were oblivious to this fact. They knew exactly where he was headed.

Paul gave them the gospel information and demands and then backtracked to answer questions and clarify issues. We might say that the *process* of evangelism took place in the context of the *event* of evangelism; Paul spoke the gospel with every intention of leading others to Christ (reaping) but with an awareness that in the lives of some he would assume the role of sower.

Whether evangelism is a 'sowing' process or a reaping event is not so much to be determined by the intention of the evangelist, but by the response of the listeners. For some in Thessalonica, Paul's first Saturday synagogue message was an evangelistic event; an experience of reaping the fruit born by God's Spirit. They believed the first time they heard the gospel. For others it was the first step in a process that took weeks or even months and years. Paul assumed the role of sower in their lives and it would be up to others to reap where he had sown. He appreciated the truth that, at any moment, as he sowed the seeds of the gospel, someone could have his last question answered, his last issue resolved, and he would then be ready to be harvested. The persuasive nature of the gospel demands that it be shared with a sense of urgency grounded in an awareness of this truth. The time for decision is always now.

The danger is that the process can degenerate into a nonpersuasive dialogue that sacrifices the cruciality and urgency of the gospel for the sake of an expanded time frame. In such a context, it might be easy for both the evangelist and, consequently, the hearer to lose sight of the direction of their interaction. This is unfair to both the listener and the persuasive nature of the gospel.

It is unfair to the non-believer in two ways. First, the ethics of persuasion ask that we honor a person's autonomy and freedom of choice. A hidden agenda is inappropriate and unethical. The gospel and Jesus Christ need to be the up-front issue if the Christian is to engage the non-Christian in a long-term dialogue or relationship for the purpose of sharing the gospel (see Figure 2). The nonbeliever needs to know what it is he is discussing and the intention of the evangelist before he commits himself to participating in the dialogue or relationship. Second, the crucial necessity of salvation demands that we give the nonbeliever enough information to decide to trust Christ. Some people will be ready to believe the first time they hear the gospel (or the first time they hear it from us), and we dare not tiptoe through the spiritual tulips with them.

Therefore, I submit that it is appropriate and necessary to make sure that the gospel is explained, the call to decision is given, and the opportunity to decide is given, even in the context of evangelism as a process. This, of course, needs to be done in a way that appreciates that the listener may not be ready to take decisive action. I need to remember that even though no decision is made, my persuasive efforts need not cease. I pursue the work of evangelism with the awareness that, in any given situation, I may be a sower or harvester. My witness may be used by God to plant the seeds of the gospel in their heart that another may one day harvest. Or, my witness may be the last link in a chain of events started long ago through the sowing efforts of others, resulting in the non-believer's conversion. The matter is completely in the hands of God.

With these truths in mind, a proper balance will be maintained between the fact that salvation is crucial and urgent — and thus my witness should provide ample opportunity for decision — and the reality that not everyone is ready for conversion at the same time, or has the same amount of insight into the personal implications of the gospel — and thus my witness may be a seed-sowing

FIGURE 2
EVANGELISM AS A PROCESS

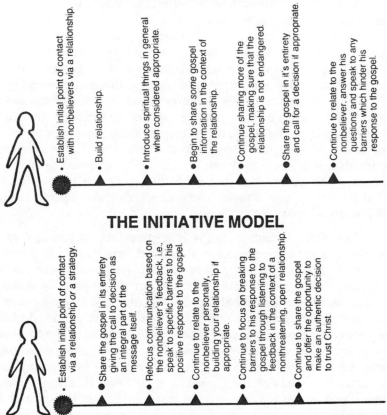

THE RELATIONAL MODEL

- Establish initial point of contact with nonbelievers via a relationship.
- Build relationship.
- Introduce spiritual things in general when considered appropriate.
- Begin to share *some* gospel information in the context of the relationship.
- Continue sharing more of the gospel, making sure that the relationship is not endangered.
- Share the gospel in it's entirety and call for a decision if appropriate.
- Continue to relate to the nonbeliever, answer his questions and speak to any barriers which hinder his response to the gospel.

THE INITIATIVE MODEL

- Establish initial point of contact via a relationship *or* a strategy.
- Share the gospel in its entirety giving the call to decision as an integral part of the message itself.
- Refocus communication based on the nonbeliever's feedback, i.e., speak to specific barriers to his positive response to the gospel.
- Continue to relate to the nonbeliever personally, building your relationship if appropriate.
- Continue to focus on breaking barriers to his response to the gospel through listening to feedback in the context of a nonthreatening, open relationship.
- Continue to share the gospel and offer the opportunity to make an authentic decision to trust Christ.

NOTE: The varied sizes of the dots illustrate the amount of the gospel that might be given at different times, ranging from almost no gospel content in an initial meeting, to a complete presentation at another time.

The initiative model, which introduces the gospel, (with call to decision given) at the first meeting or soon after, gives the communicator freedom to intelligently address the non-believer's misconceptions and spiritual problems in light of their response to the gospel.

The relational model posits a link between the intimacy of the evanglist's relationship with the non-believer and the amount of the gospel information to be shared. As a result, the communication of the entire gospel (with call to decision given) is postponed, leaving the communicator with little opportunity to sensitively deal with the non-believer's questions concerning the gospel.

experience that sees the nonbeliever moving one step closer to trusting Christ. An understanding of this truth will assist us in our pursuit of being bold yet sensitive communicators of the gospel.

So When Has True Evangelism Taken Place?

As we can see from our discussion, the element of evangelism as a process makes this a rather tricky question. The unpredictable elements of time and human response muddy the water. Maybe there is no definite answer, but using some of the criteria we have established, we might be able to say when biblical evangelism has *not* taken place.

Evangelism has not occurred if less than the essential ingredients of the gospel are presented. First, the declaration of the gospel events: Jesus' death and resurrection. Second, the promise and offer of forgiveness of sin and eternal life. And third, the imperative of repentance and faith in Christ. Thus, if the gospel events are communicated but no call to decision is given, evangelism by definition has not taken place. The good news is good news because it touches on the sinner's present situation of lostness and lifts him out of the awful state of spiritual death. Robbed of the call to decision, the gospel is not good news at all because it has stopped short of touching the sinner's helpless plight with the healing option of conversion. In the patient-cure analogy, announcing to a dying patient that a cure has been found for his illness, at first glance, would be good news. But what if it stopped there? He would continue to lie in bed and eventually die. He must be shown how to make the cure work for him. He must grasp the fact that the cure is for him and will save him. Then the cure must be *taken*. Evangelism must take the element of decision seriously. It is the door leading to rescue. Therefore, the evangelist needs to give the nonbeliever enough gospel information so that he has the opportunity to make an informed decision for Christ. Only when this is accomplished has biblical evangelism taken place.

CHAPTER 6

The Person God Uses

E vangelism is not a task that God does Himself. Rather, He sovereignly chooses to accomplish this work *through* His children. Of course, if God saw fit, He could use the stones to bear witness to the truth of the gospel (Matthew 3:9). He could use animals (Numbers 22:28) or angels (Luke 2:8-15). But He has chosen to use us, weak and sinful as we are, for this eternally significant work. Why is this?

One reason is that all the glory for the results of men and women responding to the gospel might go to God alone. Paul states in 2 Corinthians 4:7, "But we have this treasure [the knowledge of the glory of God in the fact of Christ] in earthen vessels, that the surpassing greatness of the power may be of God and not from ourselves."

Paul writes elsewhere, "But thanks be to God, who always leads us in His triumph in Christ, and manifests through us the sweet aroma of the knowledge of Him in every place. For we are a fragrance of Christ to God among those who are being saved and among those who are perishing; to the one an aroma from death to death, to the other an aroma from life to life. And who is adequate for these things?" (2 Corinthians 2:14-17). Paul adds, "Not that we are adequate in ourselves to consider anything as coming from ourselves, but our adequacy is from God, who also made us adequate as servants of the new covenant, not of the letter, but of the Spirit; for the letter kills, but the Spirit gives life" (2 Corinthians 3:5,6).

A biblical philosophy of evangelism must take note of the truth that God uses people to effect spiritual change with eternal results in the lives of others. With all our sin and weakness we still count. He can and does make flesh and blood people adequate for His service. This truth should cause us to respond with both humble gratitude and a sense of healthy responsibility. It should cause us to ask, "If God uses people toward His eternal ends, what kind of person does He use?"

A popular Bible teacher was once asked, "Why doesn't God use me any more than He does?" His answer was, "God is using you as much as He can." Indeed, the New Testament has much to say about the issue of our usability for the work of God. God uses not just anybody (though I'm sure He could if He wanted to), but the one who is usable. Thus, the issue is, are we usable for Him?

Is there a general profile of a "usable person"? I believe there is. However, I want to make clear that this is not a list of criteria to check off, and if you pass the test, you are "usable;" and if you don't, forget it. We are continually growing in all facets of our Christian experience. No one can boast that he has "arrived" in any one area of his spiritual development. Ultimately it is only God's grace that enables us to be usable.

It is clear, however, that to accomplish His redemptive purposes, God uses people who exhibit certain spiritual and character qualities. Our lives, therefore, should reflect a willingness to trust God to make us useful as "fishers of men" by producing these qualities in our lives through the power of His Holy Spirit.

Availability

Evangelism is not only for "specialists." True, the New Testament speaks of those with the gift of evangelism (Ephesians 4:11) who, as a result, are called specifically to a personal ministry that will emphasize evangelism. Philip is one example (Acts 21:8).

But we must not conclude that the work of evangelism is reserved only for these spiritually gifted few. The fact that God graces His church with certain spiritual gifts, such as serving, teaching, leading, giving and showing mercy (Romans 12:7,8) does not limit activity in these areas to the exclusive ranks of those endowed with those particular gifts.

The Bible stresses that all Christians are to be involved in each of these areas, even though some will lead the way by exercising their particular spiritual gifts. The fact that I do not have the gift of giving does not exempt me from being a wise steward of my possessions and talents. In like manner, the fact that I do not have the gift of evangelism does not exempt me from the wise stewardship of my time, talents and treasure in the work of sharing the good news.

Consider the example of Timothy. He was a relatively young man when he assumed leadership of the church at Ephesus. Although He had been through many frontline experiences with Paul on his second missionary journey (Acts 16:1ff), Timothy was still by nature a timid person. "The general picture of his [Timothy] character, seen chiefly from the Corinthian letters and the Pastorals, is of an affectionate and loyal companion of Paul who lacked forcefulness of character and was self-conscious about his youthfulness."[1] Timothy's spiritual gift was more likely that of pastor-teacher rather than evangelism. In fact, we probably would not find two men further apart on the personality scale than Paul and Timothy. Paul was aggressive, not minding a confrontation and willing to take the initiative in meeting people. Timothy, on the other hand, probably would have preferred to stick to a close circle of friends and avoid confrontation and conflict. He did not fit the stereotype picture of a person likely to be involved in evangelism. Nevertheless, Paul wrote to him, "But you, be sober in all things, endure hardship, do the work of an evangelist, fulfill your ministry" (2 Timothy 4:5). Paul reminded him, "For God has not given us a spirit of timidity, but of power and love and discipline. Therefore do not be ashamed of the testimony of our Lord, or of me His prisoner; but join with me in suffering for the gospel according to the power of God" (2 Timothy 1:7,8).

The lack of the gift of evangelism and the fact that I do not possess the outgoing personality usually associated with having this spiritual gift are no reason to remove myself from availability to "do the work of an evangelist."

The Professional Syndrome

A football game has been described as an event where 22 men greatly in need of rest are cheered on by 80,000 greatly in need of exercise. I guess it will always remain a general rule of life that 80 percent of the work will be done by 20 percent of the people. There are those who make things happen, those who watch things happen, and those who return to their seats from the concession stand to ask, "What happened?" The church's experience in taking the gospel to the world is much like a football game, for the American church is experiencing a spectator glut and a participant vacuum.

Evangelism was not meant to be a spiritual spectator sport with only a certain few experts doing the work while the rest of us cheer them on or go about other business. But there is a strong temptation to assign to the professionals the work that rightly belongs to us all.

Some "Every-Member" Reminders

Remember that Jesus' first call to discipleship was the call to become fishers of men (Mark 1:17). To be a first-century follower of Jesus meant to be involved in His mandate to take His message to the world. The twelve were commissioned to do this (Mark 3:14), the seventy were sent out to evangelize (Luke 10:1-16), and the entire church's destiny was wrapped up in being a witness of the gospel to their homes, their cities, their nations and the entire world (Acts 1:8). Acts 8:1-4 recounts the first great persecution of the church in Jerusalem: "And they were all scattered throughout the regions of Judea and Samaria, *except the apostles.* . . . Therefore, those who were scattered went about preaching the word." (Acts 8:1,4, emphasis added). Note that the professionals, if we could call them that, were left in Jerusalem, while the rest, the ordinary rank and file, "went about preaching the word." Those with the most experience, the ones trained by Jesus Himself, were not expected by the rest of the church to be the only ones doing evangelism. The average member of the First Church of Jerusalem obviously took it on himself to be available for the task of preaching the good news. Michael Green writes, "One of the most striking features in evangelism in the early days was the people who engaged in it. Communicating the faith was not regarded as the preserve of the very zealous or of the officially designated evangelist. Evangelism was the perrogative and the duty of every church member."[2]

God uses the man or woman whose life is characterized by a spirit of availability. Are you willing to let God use you to have an eternal impact on another by the sharing of the gospel? No matter what your spiritual giftedness or personality type or level of spiritual maturity is, God wants to use you as His "ambassador for Christ" (2 Corinthians 5:21).

In the Spirit's Power

If evangelism is a task that the New Testament assigns to all believers, then it would make sense that the personal equipping necessary to fulfill the task is also made available by God to all believers. Remember Paul says, "Our adequacy from God, who also made us adequate as servants of a new covenant, not of the letter but of the Spirit; for the letter kills, but the Spirit gives life" (2 Corinthians 3:5,6).

Affirmation VII of the International Conference for Itinerant Evangelists in Amsterdam reads: "We need and desire to be filled and controlled by the Holy Spirit as we bear witness to the Gospel of Jesus Christ, because God alone can turn sinners from their sin and bring them to everlasting life."[3] We must appreciate the fact that the work of evangelism; is an exercise in spiritual warfare. Men and women are in the grip of the enemy's kingdom, and a great spiritual battle is even at this moment raging over the souls of men. Paul says, "For though we walk in the flesh, we do not war according to the flesh, for the weapons of our warfare are not of the flesh, but divinely powerful for the destruction of fortresses" (2 Corinthians 10:3,4). The spiritual weapons of our warfare are prayer (Ephesians 6:18) and "the sword of the

Spirit, which is the word of God" (Ephesians 6:17), described by the author of Hebrews as "living and active and sharper than any two-edged sword" (Hebrews 4:12).

It follows, then, that if evangelism is an exercise in spiritual warfare, requiring spiritual weapons, the messenger must also be spiritually equipped by God.

Thus, it is not surprising to find that Stephen, the first recorded Christian martyr, was "a man full of faith and of the Holy Spirit" (Acts 6:5). He was a man full of grace and power and was performing great wonders and signs among the people (Acts 6:8). His eloquent witness to the Jewish leaders was grounded in the fact of his spiritual vitality.

New Testament evangelism was accomplished by men and women who were spiritually in tune with their Lord and, therefore, ready at any moment to be used by God in the work of being witnesses to the gospel. We may not all be used in the radical way that Stephen was but witnessing opportunities are there for the one who is spiritually prepared to make the most of them (Colossians 4:5,6). Ephesians 5:18 commands us to be "filled with the Spirit." We are to walk in the light as He is in the light (1 John 1:7). Our attitude of availability needs to be in the context of our being filled with the Spirit, for we must be equipped with God's power through the Holy Spirit in order to engage in spiritual battle.

Understanding and applying the ministry of the Holy Spirit to our lives is the crucial ingredient for successful personal and corporate evangelism. It is impossible to understand the vitality and tenacity of the first-century church's witness without understanding its power source.

It is an amazing fact that after three years of walking with Jesus, seeing Him perform miracles, being trained by Him in evangelism and actually doing the work of evangelism (Matthew 10, Luke 10), the disciples still did not have what was required to be effective witnesses for Jesus. Indeed, we find the disciples a scattered band of defeated followers of Jesus after His crucifixion.

What was it that took Peter from denying His Lord before a slave girl to speaking boldly of Jesus to a large and potentially hostile crowd only two months later? The Holy Spirit — Peter's supernatural power source.

Luke 24:44-49 recounts Jesus' resurrection appearance to His disciples. As He commanded them to take the message of "repentance for forgiveness of sins to all nations," He also told them, "And behold, I am sending forth the promise of My Father upon you; but you are to stay in that city until you are clothed with power from on high."

The disciples were entrusted with no ordinary message, and their task was of no ordinary dimension. They, therefore, required a superordinary power. "The promise of My Father" that Jesus spoke of is His Holy Spirit. He alone could equip them individually and corporately to take the gospel to the ends of the earth. As He promised, "You shall receive power when the Holy Spirit has come upon you; and you shall be My witnesses both in Jerusalem, and in all Judea and Samaria, and even to the remotest part of the earth" (Acts 1:8). The Holy Spirit is the witnessing Spirit. To be filled with the Spirit is to be prepared for witness and thrust into the work of bearing witness to Christ. The Day of Pentecost marked the endowment of the church with this new power for witness. This is the reason that Peter was able to take a bold stand and present the first evangelistic sermon, bringing a great harvest of souls (Acts 2:14-41).

The Book of Acts is not so much the acts of the apostles but the acts of the Holy Spirit through the apostles. As J. B. Phillips has noted. "No one can read this book without being convinced that there is someone here at work besides mere human beings. Perhaps because of their very simplicity, perhaps because of their readiness to believe, to obey, to give, to suffer, and if need be to die, the Spirit of God found what He must always be seeking — a fellowship of men and women so united in love and faith, that He can work in them and through them with the minimum effort or hindrance."[4]

The progress of the gospel is linked inseparably to the lips of men and women whose hearts were filled with the Spirit and in communion with Him who promised His presence to ensure the success of the Great Commission (Matthew 28:20). As J. B. Phillips states in his introduction to *Letters to Young Churches,* "The great difference between present day Christianity and that of which we read in these letters is that to us it is primarily a performance, to them it was a real experience. We are apt to reduce the Christian religion to a code, or at best, a rule of heart and life. To these men it is quite plainly the invasion of their lives by a new quality of life altogether. They do not hesitate to describe this as Christ living in them."[5] The usable messenger is not only available, but is also filled with the Holy Spirit.

A Wartime Mentality

The person who is available and filled with the Spirit finds himself thrust into the midst of a spiritual battle. The first-century Christians had a keen sense of the need to maintain a wartime mentality.

Paul wrote, "For our struggle is not against flesh and blood, but against the rulers, against the powers, against the world forces of this darkness, against the spiritual forces of wickedness in heavenly places" (Ephesians 6:12). It is not surprising that the gospel met obstacles at every turn. It was not carried along smoothly paved roads with supernatural ease, but on the backs of flesh-and-blood men and women who persevered and sacrificed under the most difficult of circumstances.

J. B. Phillips comments, "Many Christians today talk about the 'difficulties of our times' as though we should have to wait for better ones before the Christian religion can take root. It is heartening to remember that this faith took root and flourished amazingly in conditions that would have killed anything less vital in a matter of weeks."[6]

Consider the fact that a crucified Messiah was a scandal to the first-century mind. Paul, recognizing this, wrote, "but we preach Christ crucified, to the Jews a *stumbling block* and to the Gentiles *foolishness*" (1 Corinthians 1:23, emphasis added). The very mention of the cross and resurrection of Christ as "good news of salvation" was, by the prevailing cultural standards, the stuff of "idle babblers" (Acts 17:18). It was equivalent to a 20th-century proclamation that "we gladly worship our leader who, by the way, was put to death as a common criminal in the gas chamber, but still lives today." This was absurd to the "thinking" first-century person. Thus, the Christian of that day faced the serious prospect of having the gospel relegated to a position of cultural and intellectual inferiority.

The Christian recipients of Peter's first letter, who resided in Pontus, Galatia, Cappadocia, Asia and Bithynia, had to deal with incredible misunderstanding on the part of their pagan neighbors as they claimed the name Christian and proclaimed the gospel. They were accused of practicing incest probably because they called one another "brothers and sisters in Christ." They were accused of being cannibals because they practiced communion, which was "eating the body and blood of Christ." They were accused of treason because they followed one who claimed to be a king, in the face of Caesar's claim to exclusive political authority. Ironically, they were also rejected by the immoral pagan for being too moral, having an ethical standard impossible to live up to.[7]

Michael Green sums up the context in which first-century evangelism was practiced: "Evangelism was a task involving social odium, political danger, the charge of treachery to the gods and state, the insinuation of horrible crimes and calculated opposition from a combination of sources more powerful, perhaps, than at any time since."[8]

In contrast to the experience of the first-century church, we live in an age where commitment, sacrifice and perseverance are considered outdated, quaint, or irrelevant character traits. Jim Elliot observed, "We are so utterly ordinary, so commonplace, while we profess to know a Power the 20th century does not reckon with. But we are 'harmless' and therefore unharmed. We are spiritual pacifists, non-militants, conscientious objectors in this battle to the death with principalities and powers in high places."[9]

A friend of mine shared that in cleaning out his grandmother's attic, he came across 40 pounds of packaged white sugar. It had been there since World War II, when sugar was rationed. Instead of putting up with the inconvenience and sacrificing for the cause of war, this woman hoarded sugar. She obviously lacked the spirit of self-sacrifice that reflects a wartime mentality.

Noting this dearth of wartime mentality in American Evangelicalism, Jim Elliot wrote, "I do not understand why I have never seen in America what missionaries write of — that sense of swords being drawn, the smell of war with demon powers." He added that our warfare is merely a "sham fight with shadows, a cold war of weary words."[10]

I often find myself lacking a wartime mentality, dominated by the concerns of comfort, convenience and social convention. I have to admit that I am prone to sacrifice as little as I must and to live as indifferently as I dare. So as not to put myself out on the limb where I have to trust God, or expose myself to potential discomfort, I find myself trying to predict who might or might not be interested in the gospel. Instead of initiating conversations with anyone who will listen, I try to make sure that any evangelism I do will be immune from criticism and the possibility of discomfort.

We have much to learn from the wartime mentality of the first-century church. As J. B. Phillips states, "These early Christians were on fire with the conviction that they had become, through Christ, literally sons of God; they were pioneers of a new humanity, founder of a new Kingdom. They still speak to us across the centuries. Perhaps if we believed what they believed, we might achieve what they achieved."[11] Let us pray with Jim Elliot, "O that God would make us dangerous!"[12] As 19th-century American preacher Phillips Brooks states, "O, do not pray for easy lives; pray to be stronger men! Do not pray for tasks equal to your powers; pray for powers equal to your tasks. Then the doing of your work shall be no miracle, but you shall be a miracle."[13] The usable evangelist must be available, he must be Spirit-filled and he must possess a wartime mentality.

Commitment to Integrity

The New Testament posits an intimate link between the messenger and message in the success of evangelism. It is assumed that the life and character of the one bearing witness to the truth and life-changing power of the gospel will always be a crucial factor in the success of the evangelistic enterprise.

There must be congruence between the high ethical and spiritual quality of the gospel message and the life of the ones delivering it. The gospel message is the "gospel of God" (Romans 1:1). Its source and author is the Holy One, the Lord of heaven and earth. As such, it is a message of ultimate truth and purity. The messenger's character and conduct must never contradict, but rather must harmonize with, the character of the one who gave us that message and who sends us to speak it as His personal ambassador (2 Corinthians 5:20). God's gospel must travel along paths that substantiate, not violate the purity and truth of, the gospel. Anything less would bring the confusion of a mixed message to the onlooking, unbelieving world and great dishonor to the name of God.

Integrity in Action

Peter and Paul recognized that it was impossible to do the work of an evangelist without living a life that was consistent and honoring to both the message and the Lord who gave it. There is one overwhelming reason for this.

All humans have an innate sense of the truth being congruent with the practice of high moral and ethical standards. Even sinful, fallen men insist on this. At first glance it seems incredible that a moral-ethical issue could have been a serious stumbling block to the immoral, pagan population of Peter's day. But we find Peter's reading audience "slandered as evil doers" and, therefore, needing to counteract this charge by "keeping their behavior excellent" (1 Peter 2:12). In Peter's mind, nothing less than the progress of the gospel was at stake. Even the morally deficient pagan population could demand, "If you have the truth and expect us to believe it, your lives had better not be open to moral criticism." As immoral as they already were, they still insisted on a link between truth and the purity of life of those committed to this truth.

A friend of mine learned this lesson the hard way. He was scheduled to give an evangelistic talk to a group of college students one evening. That afternoon he played a game of "pick up" basketball at the college gym. Unfortunately, in the heat of the game he became involved in a shoving match with one of the players. Nothing came of it, but that evening as he was addressing the college group, his eyes fell on this same student in the crowd. As the student saw who was to speak, he got up and left the room. This student obviously presumed that a witness to the truth should be above a shoving match on the basketball court.

Paul's ministry came under almost constant criticism from his opponents on moral and ethical grounds. Because of this, he was willing to go the extra mile in exhibiting the qualities of integrity and honesty in his evangelistic ministry.

Paul wrote in 2 Corinthians 4:2, "Rather, we have renounced secret and shameful ways; we do not use deception, nor do we distort the word of God. On the contrary, by setting forth the truth plainly we commend ourselves to every man's conscience in the sight of God" (New International Version). Some say that integrity means doing the right thing when no one is watching. But Paul knew that he always had God as his audience. God was his witness (2 Thessalonians 2:5).

One must understand the first-century context in which Paul preached. "So many wandering charlatans made their way about the Roman world, peddling their religious or philosophical nostrums, that it was necessary for the apostles to emphasize the purity of their motives and procedure by contrast with these."[14] Those men made their living as touring speakers. They were self-proclaimed authorities on various topics, usually areas of current religious or philosophical interest. These professional philosophers were masters at "tickling the ears" of their audiences. Their goal was to gather a following and earn public recognition, not to mention economic profits. The first-century churches that Paul visited and later wrote to were all too familiar with these men. Vanity, opportunism and self-seeking motives typified their persuasive efforts as they toured the ancient world looking to peddle their verbal wares.

Paul had to deal with the fact that at first glance the traveling evangelist looked like a run-of-the-mill traveling philosopher. Paul went out of his way to make sure that he would be set apart from them in both character and ethical conduct.

Paul understood the truth that even though God had vested in him the authority of an apostle and the rank of ambassador, a crucial commodity of the evangelist was his personal integrity. Indeed, the New Testament concept of spiritual authority is never divorced from integrity of character. "Bible scholars point out that the New Testament concept of authority as expressed in the Greek word *exousia* does not have the connotation of jurisdiction over the lives of others. Rather, it is the authority of truth, the authority of wisdom and experience which can be evidenced in a leader who is held up as a special example, who can commend himself to 'every man's conscience in the sight of God.'"[15]

Paul addressed this issue head-on in 2 Corinthians 3:1-3: "Are we beginning to commend ourselves again? Or do we need, as some, letters of commendation to you or from you? You are our letter, written in your hearts, known and read by all men being manifested that you are a letter of Christ, cared for by us, written not with ink, but with the Spirit of the living God, not on tablets of stone, but on tablets of human hearts."

As Paul explains to the church at Thessalonica, "You are witnesses and so is God, how devoutly and uprightly and blamelessly we behaved toward you believers; just as you know how we were exhorting and encouraging and imploring each one of you as a father would his own children, so that you may walk in a manner worthy of the God who calls you into His own kingdom and glory" (1 Thessalonians 2:10-12). Paul recognized that the power of persuasion, not the power of position, was the legitimate avenue by which his spiritual authority was to be expressed. This distinction is grounded in the recognition of our humble state as sinners saved by grace. D. T. Niles put it well: "Evangelism is witness. It is one beggar telling another beggar where to get food. The Christian does not offer out of his bounty. He has no bounty. He is simply a guest at his master's table and, as evangelist, he calls others, too."[16]

Paul's clearest defense of his motives comes in 1 Thessalonians 2:3-6: "For the appeal we make does not spring from error or impure motives, nor are we trying to trick you. On the contrary, we speak as men approved by God to be entrusted with the gospel. We are not trying to please men but God who tests our hearts. You know that we never used flattery, nor did we put on a mask to cover up greed — God is our witness. We were not looking for praise from men, not from you or anyone else" (New International Version).

Paul states here that he is not guilty of four shortcomings. The first shortcoming is error: The messenger's motives may be correct, but his message is dead wrong and thus inherently misleading to the audience.

The second shortcoming is impure motives: Even though a message may be correct, the messenger's motives may not necessarily be above-board. They may be tainted by greed, selfishness or, as alluded to here, sexual impurity.

The third shortcoming is deceit or trickery: Here both the message and motives are wrong. Whereas the person in error may not realize his error, the one practicing deceit knows full well the error of his message, but still presents it to the audience. He is out to deceive them into accepting the message as true, even though he knows it is not, and into accepting the messenger as having pure motives, even though they are impure. The word for deceit also can be translated "guile," "pointing us to cunning craft: It properly signified catching fish with a bait, and hence came to mean any crafty design for deceiving or catching."[17]

The last shortcoming is pleasing men by flattery. Paul argued that his ministry was devoid of both impure motives and message error. In fact, God Himself had searched his heart and found it worthy of the stewardship of the gospel.

Because of this transparency before God, he had nothing to hide from men, and nothing to gain by tricking them. Paul was not out to build a personal following, or to make money, or to fulfill any selfish motive whatsoever. His goal was simply to please God and pursue the eternal benefit of his audience.

Thus, Paul did not have to resort to flattery — to say nice things for selfish motives. Paul was not out to win his audience for his own benefit and thus careful to hide the presence of a greedy heart. Paul could be himself because there was nothing to hide. He knew the gospel had the power to attract a hearing, hold an audience and bring the assurance of full conviction (1 Thessalonians 1:5) of its saving power. Thus, the Christian communicator never need resort to flattery to gain a hearing.

Summary

The Christian message spread by the first-century church was distinct in large part because the messengers were distinct. The first-century evangelists were men and women who stood apart in their availability, spiritual power, commitment to a wartime mentality, and in their lives of integrity. Of these evangelists, Michael Green writes, "The simple directness of this wandering preacher, accepting no fees and content to get temporary accommodation where he could, a man utterly convinced of the truth of his message, must have been unusual among the open air preachers."[18] I might add, such men and women are just as unusual today.

CHAPTER 7

The Secular Person

Leo Tolstoy, the Russian novelist and reformer, observed, "To believe is as essential as air and water." Men and women down through the ages have never managed to escape their built-in need to express faith. As Ralph Waldo Emerson states, "We are born believing. A man bears beliefs, as a tree bears apples." Whether they have faith in self, in an ideology, in another person or in a cause, men are drawn to seek an object for their trust as a moth is drawn to a light on a dark night.

The 20th-century secular person is no exception. Because we are designed in the image of our Creator, we come equipped with a God-given design that draws us, often imperceptibly, to find an object, person or cause to serve and to worship. Indeed, faith, defined as the act of placing one's trust in an object considered worthy of one's allegiance and service, is a psychological necessity. We must fill this God-shaped vacuum in our hearts if we are to avoid life's most dreadful prospect: a meaningless existence. Man is designed to serve and to trust. Therefore, "he must choose, . . . not whether he will serve, but which God he will serve, the God who made him or the gods he has made."[1]

Sadly, the 20th-century secular man has chosen to serve the gods he has made. Pascal observes that "it is natural for the mind to believe, and for the will to love; so that, for want of true objects, they must attach themselves to false."[2] These false gods are many: materialism, technology, hedonism, the pursuit of power and prestige, self-actualization, and on and on. I will not attempt to catalog the endless expressions of the spirit of secularism. Rather, I hope to accomplish two things in this chapter.

First, I hope to give the Christian communicator insight into the thought patterns of the secular person. If we are to communicate the gospel with boldness, sensitivity and relevance to our generation, we must appreciate how the spirit and assumptions of secularism affect that person's response to the gospel message. What are the most common points of disagreement between the secular person and the gospel message? Is that person even asking the right questions, the kind answered only in Jesus Christ? And if not, how can we get him to start? The answers to these questions will help us to fulfill our role as ambassadors for Christ more effectively.

Second, I hope to equip the Christian communicator to challenge the assumptions of secularism boldly and confidently, especially as they touch on the perceived relevance of the gospel. The gospel must shine the light of eternity into the heart of the secular person, exposing his assumptions as dangerous misreadings of the human condition. We must be ready to challenge these men and women with an accurate biblical analysis of their predicament before their creator. If evangelism is the offering of the cure to a terminally ill patient, we must help the patient to realize the true nature of his disease.

Seeds of Secularism

The Oxford English Dictionary defines *secular* as "belonging to the world and its affairs, as distinguished from the church and religion," and "not concerned with or devoted to religion, caring for the present world only." *Secularism* is defined as "the doctrine that morality should be based solely in regard to the well being of mankind in the present life, to the exclusion of all considerations drawn from belief in God or in a future state."[3] This tendency to care for the present world only, to exclude all considerations drawn from belief in God or in a future state, are the thought seeds of secularism.

These seeds were germinating in the soil of Adam's heart as he renounced his creature status and rebelled against his Creator. These seeds broke ground and bore the bitter fruit of Cain's decision to be the judge of his own values as he murdered his brother Abel. Generations later we find the family of Cain, "by the erection of a city, and the invention and development of worldly arts and business . . . laying the foundation for the kingdom of the world"[4] (Genesis 4:16-26). By the time we reach Genesis 11, we find the human race permeated with the spirit of secularism, reasoning, "Come, let us build for ourselves a city, and a tower whose top will reach into heaven, and let us make for ourselves a name; lest we be scattered abroad over the face of the whole earth" (Genesis 11:4). This tower of Babel was to serve as the first monument to man's independence from God. The Lord intervened and dispersed these ancient secularists, graciously confusing their language to prevent further hardening of their sin of rebellion through their ungodly association.[5]

But the seeds of secularism live on, for at the heart of this philosophy is the rejection of the Creator by the creature:. Paul speaks of this rejection in Romans 1:25: "For they exchanged the truth of God for a lie, and worshiped and served the creature rather than the Creator. . . ."

This is idolatry, man's attempt to order his life around that which is less than God. While God has designed man to serve and worship Him alone, secular man, often unknowingly, serves and worships various aspects of the created order. While God has designed man to be finite, dependent and insufficient apart from Him, secular man lives instead in a world of illusion, inaccurately perceiving himself to be infinite, independent and self-sufficient. The secular person supposes that his autonomy is real, making himself the author of his own existence, judge of his own values and, of course, master of his own destiny. Sadly, however, this independence is a figment of his fallen imagination. As Paul states, "But they become futile in their speculations, and their foolish heart was darkened. Professing to be wise, they became fools" (Romans 1:21,22). The independence and self-sufficiency of the secular person is comparable to the "freedom" of a man falling off a cliff. On the way down he is free to wave his arms, kick his feet or recite the Gettysburg Address if he wishes. But the illusion of his "independence" will inevitably be exposed, as the reality of gravity turns this supposed freedom into a tragic one-way trip.

Thus, the spirit of secularism is nothing less than a theological problem of misplaced worship. As Karl Menninger states, "Secularism is idolatry, the worship of the means as if it were the end."[6] It is one expression of man's attempt to fill the God-given void in his heart, a void which will refuse to be filled except through a personal relationship with Jesus Christ.

Mastery and Self-Sufficiency

The most crucial consequence of man's fall into sin was that he began to relate all matters of truth and morality to himself, instead of to God. But his enthronement of self demands an exaltation of human beings far beyond the limits set by God. Man was never designed to be the center of his own universe. He is not capable of assuming the role of final reference point, interpreting for himself right and wrong, truth and error, by the compass of his five senses and his fallen conscience.

The secular philosophy is nothing less than a glorification of the self-deification introduced into the human race through Adam's rebellion. Rather than recognizing that the creature will surely be crushed under the weight of assuming the role of "self-sufficient master of the universe," the secular man has applauded this perspective and seeks to further these illusions. To this end, He has admirably succeeded. The spirit and assumptions of secularism have so penetrated and permeated our western culture that Carl Henry has commented, "We live in a generation captivated by the temporal and seduced by the sensate, a generation whose hallmarks are the loss of the transcendant and the surrender of the supernatural."[7]

The Illusions Exposed

At the heart of this assumption of secularism is man's mortal fear of finiteness. The secular person cannot deal rationally with his own mortality and human limitations. The reason for this fear is that men and women are created in the image of God with a built-in sense of eternity. Man has a gnawing suspicion that there must be more than this life, but his secularized world view will not allow him, at least logically, to pursue this suspicion much further. As a result, the secularist lives with a non-verbalized, subconscious fear of his own finiteness.

Instead of confronting this anxiety, the secular person marshals a vain attempt to convince himself that he is not finite. Harry Blamires, in his book *The Secularist Heresy,* gives us an insightful analysis of this outworking of man's fear of finiteness. He says, "It is man's special tragedy that the God-given impulse to transcend and transfigure the finite should be perverted into a demonic zeal for disguising the finite as absolute."[8]

Blamires notes that the secular man ingeniously manages to treat the finite cause-and-effect world, including his own life and mortal condition, as though they were indeed infinite and, therefore, the source of ultimate satisfaction for the "eternity in his heart."

Describing the mental gymnastics necessary for such an accomplishment, Blamires states, "He adjusts his mind and his will, not to the finite as it in fact is, but to the finite as he would wish it to be."[9] The secular man glorifies the temporal as an end in and of itself as an exercise in wishful thinking. Secular man has learned to make the best of this fallen world. He has devoted all of his ingenuity and resources to the task of filling his God-shaped vacuum with counterfeit gods that, to be sure, supply a measure of counterfeit relief, but are just as sure to disappoint eventually. Ralph Barton, a successful satiric writer, committed suicide in 1931. He left this note: "I have had few difficulties, many friends, great successes. I have gone from wife to wife, house to house, visited great countries of the world; but I am fed up with inventing devices to fill up 24 hours of the day."

Secular man has mastered the art of creating an intellectual and cultural climate that ignores the issue of what Blamires calls "the finitude of the finite." As a culture and as individuals, most of the 20th-century western world has failed to recognize and deal with the finiteness built into the human condition. "Man behaves as though he were not a dependent creature with a limited and temporary existence in a limited and temporary universe."[10]

Of the questions of death, suffering and guilt, Deitrich Bonhoffer comments in *Letters and Papers from Prison*, "It is now possible to find, even for these questions, human answers that take no account whatever of God."[11] Such an attitude of self-sufficiency is grounded in pride. As Blamires puts it, "Pride in all its forms is the rejection of finititude."[12] C. S. Lewis observed, "Pride leads to every other vice. It is the complete anti-God state of mind."

This attitude of self-sufficiency approaches outright arrogance in some, but in most it reveals itself as a subtle, yet efficient insulator of the individual from the harsh realities of the "finititude of the finite." The secularist is a master of what social psychologists call "selective perception." As Simon and Garfunkle sang in "The Boxer," "A man hears what he wants to hear, and disregards the rest." This principle guarantees that one sees only what he wants to see so that his life-operating assumptions are safely insulated from the challenges of life's uncertainties. Pascal observed over two hundred years ago, "Between us and heaven or hell there is only life, which is the frailest thing in the world."[13] He added, "Nothing is so important to man as his own state, nothing is so formidable to him as eternity; and thus it is not natural that there should be men indifferent to the loss of their existence, and the perils of everlasting suffering."[14] The secular person has been so ingenious and inventive at ordering reality to avoid the implications of this truth that life's uncertainties no longer prod him to consider the issues of one's eternal destiny and need for God.

How can men and women consistently practice such an unnatural, short-sighted analysis of their human condition? How can many continue to ignore or treat as irrelevant the message of good news that resolves the problem of alienation from their Creator and determines eternal destinies? Although it is impossible to probe fully the deception of the sin-sick human heart, Blamires offers at least a partially satisfying answer to this question. He suggests three ways in which the cultural climate of the 20th century West insulates people from the reality of their finiteness and thus inhibits an accurate assessment of their real problem and its only resolution in the gospel. Let us examine these three components.

Remoteness of Man From Nature

The secular person imagines himself as dependent only on other human beings for his survival. By and large, 20th-century western man has failed to recognize God's gracious design in nature that provides for man's every need. The relative success of man's technological feats to control the natural order has given many the idea that we humans are doing just fine fending for ourselves. There is no disease or problem that will not one day eventually fall to the superior might of science and technology. Occasionally a drought or an earthquake will impress some with the inherent uncertainty, finiteness and dependency of the human condition. But instead of taking this revelation to heart, secular man reaffirms his faith in the ability of science and technology to shield him from life's uncertainty.

Of course, we *should* move ahead with a greater technological capacity to fight disease and to harness the natural order for the human good. The point I am making is that man's distance from the awesome power of nature and his technological progress in harnessing it for man's temporal benefit insulate from appreciating the true dependent and finite nature of his human existence.

Disassociation From Disease and Death

At a conference I attended, a speaker discussed how the gospel's offer of eternal life and victory over death found listening ears and prepared hearts in the first century. He explained how these men and women appreciated their finite status only too well. The average life expectancy was well below fifty years. Life was full of uncertainty. Death was out in the open. Nearly everyone in the Middle East in the first century had seen a member of his family die or had at least seen a dead body, the speaker noted. Then he asked us to raise our hands if we had actually seen someone die. Only a handful of the eight hundred people acknowledged that they had.

The Census Bureau reports that one out of every one person will eventually die. Your insurance agent and local funeral director are counting on that fact. But because society increasingly insulates us from death's harsh reality, few consider the need to prepare for life beyond the grave.

Jonathan Edwards, the great 18th-century Puritan author and preacher, wrote more than two hundred years ago that men and women are "greatly deceived about the things of another world." He also stated, "Some flatter themselves with a secret hope that there is no such thing as another world."[15]

One day as I was eating lunch with a young medical doctor, we began to discuss the gospel. He admitted that he was not a believer, and he did not seem to be open to the gospel. I asked him if he witnessed death much. He commented that he saw someone die almost every week. I then asked him if he ever wondered where he was going when he died. He laughed and said, "Of course not. What good would that do?" I responded that it might be good to know where we were going, especially if there really were a heaven and a hell. He shrugged his shoulders as if these were irrelevant considerations. He then smiled and said, "I guess I'll worry about it when I get there."

In an interview with *People* magazine, psychologist B. F. Skinner was asked, "What advice do you have for those who are afraid of dying?" He responded, "What arouses fear is not death itself, but the act of talking and thinking about it, and that can be stopped. We brood about death most when we have nothing else to do. The more reason we have to pay attention to life, the less time we have for attention to death. A properly executed will can give you the satisfaction of knowing your possessions will go to the right people, and you can extend the life of part of yourself by donating any organs that might still be useful. When those things have been done, it is probably better not to think about death."[16] Skinner's attitude is typical of those adhering to secularist assumptions. Just ignore death and it might go away; besides, what can we do about it?

The secular person is devoid of a realization of his own finiteness and the finality of eternity. Thus, it is no surprise that the gospel, offering hope beyond the grave and answers to questions of one's eternal destiny, is perceived as irrelevant by many secularists.

Diversions, Diversions, Diversions

Few of us are content to sit down and contemplate the mysteries of life. Our hurry-up, get-it-done-yesterday culture is not designed to give people time to reflect on life's unanswered questions. As I have shared the gospel in the university community, I have been amazed at the many students who remark that they never have an opportunity to discuss matters of eternal significance. They claim that they just do not have time.

Video games, movies, sports events, every possible diversion under the sun is pursued with gusto. It is not surprising that even in difficult economic times, the entertainment industry does well. Pascal accurately assessed this curious tendency: "Nothing is so insufferable to man as to be completely at rest, without passions, without business, without diversion, without study. He then feels his nothingness, his forlornness, his insufficiency, his independence, his weakness, his emptiness. There will immediately arise from the depth of his heart weariness, gloom, sadness, fretfulness, vexation, despair."[17]

The diverted person, intuitively aware of this truth, has taken a raincheck on dealing with his real needs and as a result does not have a sense of the inherent relevancy of the gospel as the answer to those needs. This is why we find few people preoccupied with their concern over their alienation from their Creator, the certainty of their death and the uncertainty of what lies beyond the grave. Sure, a thought here and there may pop into one's mind as he sees a tragedy reported on the news, walks by a cemetery or feels the tug of an unfulfilled need of the heart, but these thoughts fall short of recognizing his real need, which finds its resolution in Jesus Christ.

At best, the secularist may feel a nagging uneasiness in the face of his desire for security and meaning. But the fallen human heart is a master at keeping the truth of the human condition under wraps. The secular person, laboring under the illusion of his own mastery and self-sufficiency, is intent on modifying reality in order to avoid its challenge to his finiteness and his corresponding need for God. A guilty conscience, restless heart or tragedy should point him to his need for God. But instead he finds his resolution to these concerns in an affirmation of faith in man's ability to take care of himself, or in a commitment to shallow diversions.

CHAPTER 8

The Gospel and the Secular Mind

T he illusions and assumptions of secularism are held with varying degrees of emotional intensity and self-awareness by the secularists. It would be a mistake to assume that if you have seen one secularist, you have seen them all. Although all secularists, by definition, share a common set of operating assumptions grounded in the illusions of mastery and self-sufficiency, these assumptions are manifested in a variety of patterns. To help give an understanding of some of this variety, especially as it touches on varying patterns of response to the gospel message, I have divided the secular world into three categories: the intellectual secularist, the self-fulfillment secularist, and the despairing secularist.

A Profile of the Intellectual Secularist

Of the three categories, the intellectual secularist is the one most likely to possess a well-reasoned, internally consistent world view. His distinguishing presuppositions include:

(1) God is non-existent or irrelevant to matters of this life. Instead, the scientific method and our five senses are the only reliable standards for determining matters of truth and judging the reliability of information. As my former sociology professor used to say, "If I cannot measure it, I'm not interested."

(2) Belief in God, Christ and the Bible are inconsistent with a "scientific" world view; therefore, "intelligent" people are not concerned with spiritual matters. The gospel and Christianity are consigned to the scrapheap of history. Edmond P. Leach, professor of anthropology at Cambridge University, is an articulate spokesman for this position. He says, "Our idea of God is a product of history. What I now believe about the supernatural derived from what I was taught by my parents, and what they taught me was derived from what they were taught, and so on. But such beliefs are justified by faith alone, never by reason and the true believer is expected to go on reaffirming his faith in the same verbal formula even if the passage of history and the growth of the scientific knowledge should have turned the words into plain non-sense."[1]

Stanford University professor Michael Novak writes, "It is taken for granted in most intellectual circles that an intelligent person does not believe in God, and certainly not in any institutional religion." Novak goes on to state, "Indifference to religion is the ordinary mark of the serious intellectual."[2] He later concludes, "Indeed, the thesis of the intellectual life in America is that there is no God.[3] The intellectual secularist has reversed the biblical formula. To him, it is the wise man, not the fool, who says in his heart there is no God (Psalm 53:1).

(3) Man is the apex of an impersonal evolutionary process and is therefore ultimately accountable to no one in matters of personal values, morality and behavior. Man is seen as a highly sophisticated, technological animal. He is, in the words of French theologian Tiellhard de Chardin, "the evolutionary process becoming aware of itself." As such, he is answerable to no one, especially God.

The secular person is at home in such a universe, free to pursue the illusions of mastery and self-sufficiency. As Albert Camus states, "The universe, from now on without a master, seems to him neither sterile nor futile. The struggle toward the summit itself is enough to free the heart of man."[4] As Timothy Leary reasons, "Trust the evolutionary process. It's all going to work out all right."[5]

The Intellectual Secularist and the Gospel

This type of secularist poses a unique set of challenges to the evangelist. His position will be defended rigorously from a materialistic, naturalistic, pseudo-intellectual framework that is internally consistent and at least partially satisfying to him. We need to realize that as communicators of the supernatural message of the gospel, we are, in a sense, coming as a visitor from another world. Here are some helpful points that will enable you to communicate confidently to this type of secularist.

(1) The Christian communicator must be prepared to deal with the contention that the gospel is irrelevent to the human condition. This response is a logical extension of the secular presuppositions about God and man. Any thoughts of God as creator, redeemer, judge and lawgiver are nonsense to the intellectual secularist given his view of man as a mere product of the evolutionary process. The problem of sin and its effect on his eternal destiny is irrelevant, since he acknowledges no eternity to deal with and no objective standard from which to determine sin. Here we see that one's view of human nature is inseparable from his view of the relevance of the gospel.

We must acknowledge that man's likeness to God points to his capacity and need for redemption. Jesus' call to repent and enter the kingdom of God presupposes that He viewed all men as sinners, helpless to remedy their own situation, responsible before God and in need of conversion. It also implies that He saw men as valuable and worth redeeming for the purpose of spending an eternity with Him.

(2) The Christian communicator must guard against the fear of intimidation. It would be easy to labor under an intellectual inferiority complex as he contemplates talking to the intellectual secularist.

In my experience, I have found that the intellectual secularist's antagonism toward the gospel is not grounded in a well-thought-through response to the biblical data. I first realized this as I attempted to share the gospel with my college history professor who had been openly hostile toward Christianity in his classroom lectures. In fear and trembling I made an appointment to discuss the gospel with him. To my surprise, and relief, I found that the last time he had read the Bible was in the eighth grade. His knowledge of Christianity had been picked up in barroom discussions and fraternity bull sessions. His views on the gospel were not grounded in a vigorous intellectual analysis of the content and implications of the gospel. They were simply the result of his ignorance of the spiritual realm.

The point is that the Christian communicator need not back away from the intellectual secularist for fear of being "eaten alive" in a scholarly argument. Even though an intellectual secularist may be brilliant by the world's standards, he may be surprisingly uninformed on matters of the gospel's relevance and power. Expertise in an area of intellectual pursuit does not ensure even a modest amount of insight into spiritual truth.

It is also important to consider that the antagonism of the intellectual secularist toward the gospel may be grounded in his desire to maintain his autonomy in matters of personal behavior. The concerns of the intellect may be nothing more than a smoke screen for issues of the will and morality. This is not to say that all intellectual questions are a smoke screen for moral issues, but one must consider this possibility as he seeks to communicate the gospel confidently to these men and women.

The famous British novelist and critic of Christianity Aldous Huxley was candid about his use of intellectualism as a smoke screen to cover the morality issue raised by a biblical perspective on man and God. "I had motives for not wanting the world to have a meaning; consequently assumed that it had none and was able without any difficulty to find satisfying reasons for this assumption. . . . For myself as, no doubt, for most of my contemporaries, the philosophy of meaninglessness was essentially an instrument of liberation from . . . a certain system of morality because it interfered with our sexual freedom."[6]

This issue of the "will not to believe" was made apparent to me after having a debate with two college professors on the relevance of religion to the 20th-century world. One man was an atheist political science professor. As we talked, both during and after the debate, it became apparent to me that he had never dealt seriously with the claims of Christ. He told me that he could not intellectually justify pursuing something that he could not prove. I then asked him if he would be interested even if someone could convince him beyond a reasonable doubt that Jesus was raised from the dead and that He was the Son of God.

The professor quickly responded, "No, even if I could be shown that Jesus was raised from the dead and that He was the Son of God, I wouldn't be interested." I asked him why this was so, and he said, "I guess I just don't care to know." Even for this obviously brilliant man, the issue came down to a matter of his will. It was not that he *could not* believe, but that he *would not* believe.

I had a similar experience with a sociology professor after I spoke in his classroom on the Christian perspective of love, sex and marriage. As we ate lunch together the next day, I asked him if he had ever considered the claims of Jesus Christ. He said, "Yes, partially, but I don't think I want to know any more for moral reasons. You see, I've been recently divorced and now am living with another woman. I'm just not open to talking about those things now."

By these examples, I do not mean to assert that every intellectual secularist has moral problems, but rather that we should not assume that their hostility to the gospel is due to a well-reasoned intellectual response. It may come down to a matter of the person's moral disposition to pursue spiritual truth.

The Self-fulfillment Secularist

The self-fulfillment secularist is less likely than the intellectual secularist to have an intellectually grounded, internally consistent philosophy of life. This person is more or less the "beneficiary" of the intellectual secularist's success at imposing his world view and its operating assumptions on 20th-century western culture. He is a child of a culture that has systematically laid a foundation for, and catered to, those who desired to interpret their lives from a purely materialistic perspective which holds that any meaning, purpose or ultimate fulfillment is to be found in the worship and service of the finite.

Although man is not seen in the stark evolutionary terms of the intellectual secularist, he is seen as a one-dimensional consumer, a "need machine" that exists for the opportunity to have needs met. The self-fulfillment seeker is the person who made *Pulling Your Own Strings, Winning Through Intimidation* and *Looking Out for Number One* best sellers. He is the market for the flood of self-help books lining the supermarket checkout counters.

Definitions of what it means to be self-fulfilled vary greatly. Francis Schaeffer has suggested that two of the operating principles of the self-fulfillment secularist are the pursuit of personal peace and affluence. Personal peace is defined as "just to be left alone, not to be troubled by the trouble of other people, whether across the world or across the city — to live one's life with minimal possibilities of being personally disturbed. Personal peace means wanting to have my personal life pattern undisturbed in my lifetime, regardless of what the result will be in the lifetime of my children and grandchildren." Affluence is defined as "an overwhelming and ever-increasing prosperity — life made up of things, things and more things — a success judged by an ever higher level of material abundance."[7]

Daniel Yankelovich, in his book *New Rules,* estimates that over 80 percent of the American public has bought into this idea of "need fulfillment being the stuff of life" philosophy.[8] Seventeen percent are what he terms "hard core" self-fulfillment seekers. To them, needs are seen as sacred objects that one has a "moral obligation to fulfill." Yankelovich goes on to say, "The majority of Americans gladly echo the classic retort of Samual Gompers, founder of American organized labor, who, when asked the objective of the labor movement, replied with a single word, 'more.' For the overwhelming majority of All Americans, an important part of living the good life simply means 'more.'"[9]

The self-fulfillment seeker wants to control and dominate, as does the intellectual secularist, but his sphere of control is directed primarily at his immediate surroundings and personal life. Questions of eternal destiny and life's true meaning are bothersome sidetracks to his goal of "getting ahead." Pleasure, position, power and possessions are some of his objective criteria for determining the meaning of life.

We may find this person quite indifferent to spiritual issues because of his preoccupation with the needs of the here and now. Some may be very happy with their lives as they see a certain degree of success in meeting their goals. This spurs them on to an even greater commitment to their philosophy of life.

The Hopeless Secularist

Belonging to the same family, but on the other side of the spectrum, is the hopeless secularist. This person is in a tragic situation. He has inherited the assumptions and ramifications of secularism without laboring under the illusion of any of its false hopes.

To him, science and technology hold no hope of making life better. The aggressive pursuit of self-fulfillment holds no promise of personal satisfaction. This person is usually painfully aware of his finiteness and lack of answers to his most basic needs and questions. He may even wonder what the questions are at times. Life has overwhelmed him. Difficult circumstances or his own despair make it impossible for him to see beyond his own next unfulfilled need: an empty dinner table, loneliness, alienation, fear of death, lack of personal worth, etc.

Thus, the hopeless secularist is unable to find meaning or fulfillment in the pursuit of things, relationships or a vague hope for the future. He faces the stark realities of the human condition, and in that sense his is the most intellectually honest of the secular family. But his honest appraisal of life has left him in a state of personal despair.

Woody Allen has accurately described the plight of the hopeless secularist. In an article in *Esquire,* Allen comments on the life of those who are intellectually honest about the human condition but who, as he, had abandoned the "religious answers." Allen divided their existence into two categories: the "horrible" and the "miserable." "Life is a concentration camp" and "people don't know why they are here, where they are going or when they are going to die." The hopeless secularist has run out of diversions, so there is nothing left to divert his attention from the fact that life in a "universe without a master" is indeed meaningless. In Allen's words, death "is absolutely stupefying in its terror and it renders anyone's accomplishments meaningless."[10] The secularist has been victimized by his own assumptions and tragically fails to trace the despair of this world view to the fact that God has been left out. As atheist Bertrand Russell stated, "Only on the firm foundation of unyielding despair can the soul's habitation henceforth be safely built."[11] He learned the "secret of secularism", that "there is no end to hiding from the ultimate end of life, which is death," and that on "humanistic [secular] assumptions life leads to nothing, and every pretense that it does is a deceit."[12]

The Christian's Response to the Secularist

We have already looked at some things to consider in the unique case of the intellectual secularist. Now let us pursue some issues certain to be raised as we confront the rest of the secularist family with the gospel.

(1) *Don't generalize.* Even though all secularists share in the assumption of the irrelevancy of God, are blind to the finiteness of the finite and see morality as relative, do not be too quick to generalize. While all secularists share in the same root problem, their lostness and separation from God are manifested in a myriad of symptoms. These symptoms range from a blatant denial of God and an arrogant confidence in man's self-sufficiency, to a selfish preoccupation with temporal pursuits, to outright despair. The secular person runs the gamut from pessimism to presumption. One may consider himself a slave of the grim task of just getting by in a hostile world, a fleeting whimper in an impersonal cosmic drama; another may be a total optimist, bullish on his own personal future. He may be a hedonist, or pragmatist, fully devoted to humanity's future, or selfishly in pursuit of "actualizing" his own potential. He may have bold hope in the wrong object or may have abandoned any hope at all.

(2) *Recognize secularism's weaknesses.* It makes sense that if the secularist philosophy posits an unreal world in all of its

dimensions, there will be glaring inconsistencies and weaknesses in the secularist's attempt to assess life's meaning and purpose accurately. Wayne McDill observes, "God has so constructed His creation that any concept of reality contrary to the biblical view will ultimately find itself moving farther and farther away from practical truth, from the way things really are."[13]

Secular man has, in a very real sense, profaned reality by his pretensions of mastery and self-sufficiency. It is a sad irony that secularism, desiring to exalt man by pronouncing him free from the "bonds" of his creature status, actually denigrates him. On the other hand, Christianity, which asserts that true freedom is found only in man's affirmation of his creature status — and is thus rejected by the secularist as denigrating — actually exalts man. As C. S. Lewis commented, "In modern, that is, in evolutionary thought, man stands at the top of a stair whose foot is lost in obscurity; in this [medievel thought] he stands at the bottom of a stair whose top is invisible with light."[14]

The simple truth is that if man is a mere product of an impersonal evolutionary process, and if "all characteristics of human nature and behavior are capable of explanation simply in terms of the normal operation of the laws of physics in inanimate chemical matter,"[15] then man is nothing more than a highly sophisticated, technological animal. He might be at the top of the heap, but a heap of what? "When man bears the price tag of matter only, human life is dirt cheap. Why not regard man as worthless if he is simply a soulless organism brought into existence by the same forces that produce rust on a tin roof and fungus on a rock?"[16]

As Christians, we must recognize that secularism offers no legitimate basis for human dignity and is consequently bankrupt in terms of bringing lasting, satisfying answers to man's quest for significance, meaning and fulfillment. Man's search for these precious commodities east of Eden can end only in a denial of his own humanity. Apart from Jesus Christ, secular man loses now and in eternity. He is doomed to live in a world of illusion in this life and faces the horrifying prospect of eternal judgment in the life to come.

(3) *Be sensitive.* We must approach the secularist with empathy and insight into his attitudes and operating assumptions. We must have the wisdom to understand his reasons for believing as he does, without falling prey to any of the erroneous assumptions that he holds. This is a balancing act that will be developed in our lives only through study and practical experience. The challenge is to empathize so as to understand, but to be equipped with the proper biblical data so that we might expose wrong thinking.

How can we do this? First, we must approach the secular person not as an enemy, but as a fellow human being, created in God's image, whose deepest need in life is to realize that he is meant to be a redeemed child of God.

Second, we must ask probing questions. Historian Arnold Toynbee posed the ultimate question to the secularist: "Are we accidents that have no meaning in terms of this reality from which, as persons, we are temporarily differentiated? Or are we truants, who have alienated ourselves from the source of our being by a perverse tour de force that we cannot sustain beyond the brief span of a human life's trajectory?"[17]

We must ask the secularist to consider whether the vague uneasiness of his heart could be the image of God in him crying for completion. Might not his guilt, or loneliness, or frustration, be a symptom of the deeper problem of his alienation from and rebellion against his Creator? Might his desire for joy, peace, love, hope and life beyond the grave be authentically met only through the forgiveness and restoration found in Jesus Christ? These are the types of questions that will challenge the secular person's assumptions and cause him to ask questions that find their answers only in Jesus Christ.

We must work to engage the secular person at his point of greatest felt need and trace these symptomatic problems to his real need, which is resolved only in the cross of Christ. We must present the gospel in such a way that the secularist realizes that true fulfillment will never be realized apart from renouncing his independence from his Creator and bowing before Him, recognizing Him as Lord. The secular person must realize that his pursuit of the gods of materialism, power, pleasure and success brings a fulfillment that is temporary. Only Jesus Christ can bring lasting satisfaction to the eternity in his heart.

(4) *Be confident.* The Christian communicator must be confident in recommending the gospel to the secularist, who needs to understand its clear statement that he is a creature, responsible to his Creator. The gospel must be understood as a clarion call to turn from a life of self-deification and to submit humbly to one's appropriate status as a creature in his Creator's kingdom. The gospel assures the secularist that apart from such a response there is no escape, for one day these self-destructive illusions will be brought to light and judged by God Himself. In short, the Christian communicator must bring the truth of the gospel to bear on the mind and heart of the secularist, convincing him that a life lived by his operating assumptions will result only in self-destruction.

Although the secularist often will give the impression of being truly self-sufficient, under this thin veneer lies a human being with a God-shaped vacuum in his heart. As Christian communicators, we realize that "the real situation is that man who is made in the image of God is unable, precisely because of those qualities in him which are designated as 'image of God,' to be satisfied with a god who is made in man's image."[18] God has left Himself a witness in the heart of every person that bears testimony to the fact that finite things — whether material possessions, relationships, fame or power — can never satisfy an eternal need.

This unsatisfied longing of the heart, common to all men and women because they *are* designed in God's image, assures us that the message of the gospel will always be relevant to those who are willing to appraise the human condition honestly. As Reinhold Neibuhr observed, "Faith in Christ could find no lodging place in the human soul, were it not uneasy about the contrast between its true and its present state."[19] Or, as Pascal put it, "For who finds himself unhappy at not being a king, except a deposed king?"[20]

Walter Lippman, the columnist and avowed humanist, reconsidered his secularist assumptions in his later years. Once a believer in the ability of science and education to solve all of man's problems, he came to the point of expressing disappointment in their failure to bring about an improvement in the human condition. He wrote, "If ever there was a generation who could have done it, we could have. We meant so well, we tried so hard, we failed so miserably. What the world needs is a different kind of man." Atheist Bertrand Russell conceded, "It is in our hearts that the evil lies, and it is from our hearts that it must be pulled out."[21] As Christians we must boldly suggest to the secularist that this different kind of man is made possible only by the heart-changing power of Jesus Christ.

The Christian communicator must never lose sight of the fact that the gospel is fallen man's only hope for true meaning and fulfillment. Daniel Bell, professor of social sciences at Harvard, states, "We've gained enormous power over nature via technology, and yet the 20th century is probably the most dreadful period in human history." The writer of this article, reporter Fran Schumer, observed, "A century that has seen the Gulag, the Holocaust, Hiroshima and the spread of nuclear arms has caused some who used to champion rationalism and science to humble themselves. Since their secular gods have failed, they are beginning to view more traditional gods with a new curiosity."[22] Yes, even the avowed secularist must admit that the secular "gods" have failed miserably. The Christian communicator can therefore boldly, confidently and unapologetically recommend Jesus to all who will listen, the secular person included.

CHAPTER 9

The Misdirected Religious Person

S trange posters filled downtown Cincinnati in the fall of 1973. They pictured a Korean man named Moon, and it seemed that he was starting a new religion. I commented to a friend that the cult market was already glutted with the likes of the Children of God, transcendental meditation, Indian gurus and twelve-year-old "perfect masters." There was no room for another group.

I was wrong, however, for the human race's capacity to create and embrace religions will never be depleted. Why is this? And what does this mean to the Christian communicator? Gaining insight into the attitudes, motivations, and spiritual predicament of the misdirected religious person will enable us to be better communicators of the gospel to this segment of the population.

Part of the Design

Man's being indelibly stamped with the image of God is responsible for his incurably religious nature. He has a built-in need to know truth; to be able to explain his world; to be free from guilt, the fear of death, loneliness and alienation; and, most of all, to be secure in a relationship with his Creator.

The fall has tarnished and perverted, but not obliterated, these healthy desires. These longings find their inevitable expression in religion: man's attempt to meet his God-given needs through his own man-made system, designed to explain a perplexing world and make himself acceptable to God.

The Great Exchange

All expressions of religion are grounded in an "exchange" of the glory of the true God for what Paul calls the "speculations of foolish hearts" (Romans 1:21-23). But man does a poor job in putting back together the pieces broken in the fall. Because of his tendency to see himself as the center of this fallen world and to live in revolt against God, man will always have religions that will run roughshod over God's remedy for repairing the damage caused by the fall.

While the secular person seeks to lift an unregenerate humanity to a position of exaltation through a denial of God and an affirmation of his own independence, the misdirected religious person seeks religious systems which ignore the cross of Christ. Both equally and miserably fail. Both overlook the cross of Christ as the solution to man's sin problem. Both lead man to an eternally tragic dead end.

The Misdirected Religious Person

As with the secularist, there are many categories of misdirected religious people. Neither time nor the limited expertise of this writer will allow for an exhaustive study of these. Suffice it to say that a misdirected religious person is anyone who professes allegiance to a religion but who fails to possess the inward reality of a personal relationship with Christ, due either to the false teachings of his religion or to his personal failure to apply the truth of the gospel to his life.

This diverse group includes followers of American-based cults, such as the Jehovah's Witnesses, Mormons and Christian Scientists. It includes adherents of the major world religions such as Buddhism, Islam, Judaism and Hinduism. It also includes many, though not all, adherents of religious traditions that more or less conform to orthodox biblical standards but ignore the necessity of a vital personal relationship with Christ. Here we find the nominalist, a Christian in name, but lacking the inward reality of a personal commitment to Christ. (We will discuss the nominalist further in the next chapter.)

A close analysis of these groups and many others like them would yield a dazzling array of overlapping and contradictory truth claims, as well as a variety of responsibilities that the "faithful" must fulfill to qualify for their eternal reward.[1]

The Least Common Denominator

In light of this variety, I will list a few assumptions held by most misdirected religious people. On the positive side, more or less agreeing with the biblical perspective, they acknowledge:

(1) Man was created by God (or their concept of ultimate reality), is designed for some sort of relationship with Him, and is in some ways responsible to Him.

(2) Man has a problem that to some degree inhibits his relationship with God.

(3) The degree to which this problem is resolved in this life affects one's eternal state.

(4) The religious system adhered to by the misdirected religious person will in some way help him to overcome this problem, thus giving him meaning and purpose in this life and hope for the life to come.

In spite of these premises — similar to our own — we must realize also that the misdirected religious person is guilty of profound errors in theological judgment, which betray the person's spiritual bankruptcy and a heart that is out of touch with the grace of God.

(1) While he acknowledges God, his view of Him is either anti-biblical (contradicting what the Bible teaches) or sub-biblical (not saying enough about what the Bible teaches). The crucial question, "What is God like?" is answered by an endless array of futile and foolish speculations because the only source of

knowledge as to His character and purpose — the Bible — has been either rejected and replaced with another source of authority, or compromised and diluted by combining it with another "authoritative" sourcebook. Thus, the Mormons have their *Book of Mormon* to "inform" the Bible. The Jehovah's Witnesses have their writings of Charles Taze Russell. The followers of Islam have their Koran. And the followers of a multitude of other groups look to the authoritative teaching of an individual leader.

As a result, the nature of God is grossly misrepresented. The usual result is that a distorted quality of holiness is ascribed to God instead of the true holiness He claims for Himself. The next logical step is to propose a man-made system for earning God's favor, which places right standing with God fully within the reach of the devoted. In essence, the grace of the cross of Christ is substituted by the rigorous devotion of the religious adherent. Man is seen to be less in need of the grace of the gospel than he really is.

(2) A second and related error of the misdirected religious person is his lack of precision in dealing with man's basic problem. Unlike the secularist, he will readily admit that a problem exists, but what is it and how serious is it?

We have already mentioned the secularist's incredible ability to ignore or rationalize the existence of sin. The misdirected religious man, while operating from a different set of assumptions, ends up in the same place as the secularist. While he admits that a problem exists, he wrongly defines sin and minimizes its effects. There are three classic patterns reflective of this thinking:

(1) Man's problem is that he does not act correctly. His behavior falls short of what God (or ultimate reality) requires of him. Since sin is said to be grounded in our actions, man's problem is focused on his behavior. Immorality, violence and selfishness are the root of man's problem. If he only acted better, if his propensity to misbehave could in some way be repressed, then things would be right between him and God. Of course, cleaning up one's behavior is one's moral duty and fully within the realm of man's capability. God smiles His approval on man's attempts to do so.

(2) Man's problem is rooted in his ignorance of God. He merely lacks all the facts. This person reasons, "If only I had sufficient knowledge of God (or the nature of spiritual reality), then my problem would be resolved." Of course, overcoming this ignorance and attaining understanding is said to be well within the capacity of the religiously devoted. Making an attempt to gain such knowledge is one's "religious duty."

(3) Man's root problem is that he is weighted down by the cares of this world and, as a result, fails to appreciate the spiritual dimension of life. If he were given a "spark" or experience to lift him off the treadmill of daily living and put him in contact with God or spiritual reality, then his problem would be substantially resolved. Of course, the attainment of such an experience is said to be the believer's responsibility and is well within his capacity to initiate.[2]

All three views take the existence of a problem seriously. This problem might even be called "sin," and might be defined as "a shortcoming in one's relationship with God." But all religious men agree that "as bad as things are, self-effort can repair any damage to the relationship between me and God."

The Gospel and the Religious Person

At first glance, it would appear that the misdirected religious person would present less of a challenge to the Christian communicator than the secularist. After all, he has affirmed, not denied, the creature-Creator relationship. He has embraced, not rejected, the finiteness of this life and the awesome prospect of eternity.

Nevertheless, we dare not allow this surface agreement with a biblical world view to cause us to mistakenly assume that the misdirected religious person is less in need of the gospel than the secularist, or that he will present less of a challenge to the Christian communicator.

We must be aware of three major areas of concern as we seek to communicate the gospel to the misdirected religious person.

First, we must recognize that religion, regardless of the noble-ness of its intentions and the greatness of many of its adherents, is at cross purposes with God's plan to restore a lost humanity to fellowship with Himself. Religious systems invariably negate the cross of Christ as the solution to man's sin problem.

The religious man's assessment of his "root problem" (grounded in his lack of appreciation of the holiness of God) is but a vague reflection of the biblical perspective on sin and its violation of God's character. While it is true that sin will manifest itself in wrong behavior, spiritual ignorance, and slavery to the treadmill of daily, materialistic concerns, we dare not label these symptoms the root cause of man's spiritual dilemma. They are but surface manifestations of the true problem of man's rebellion, spiritual death, and alienation from a holy God.

This insufficient diagnosis of man's spiritual predicament will always lead to a wrong cure, a cure that will one day prove to be a tragic failure in removing the sting of sin, which is death. The religious man assumes that a fallen humanity can be discip-lined, educated, sparked or otherwise directed into attaining a right relationship with God. Man, he assumes, needs only edu-cation and modifications, not a radical change of heart brought about by regeneration.

Thus, the Christian communicator must not fall prey to the assumption that the religious are in tune with the truth of man's predicament before God and are therefore in touch with their real need for the grace of the gospel. We must address the sin problem of the religious person with the same precision, boldness and sensitivity as we do with the secularist. Only through confront-ing the religious with their true spiritual predicament by emphasiz-ing the radical solution of the grace of the cross will we be able to drive them to the realization of their need for Christ.

Second, the Christian communicator must be aware of the subtle, satanic deceptiveness of religion. It would be a mistake to assume that all religions are utterly false, ugly and blatantly evil. No, the devil is too smart to allow that to happen. As C. S. Lewis observes through Jill in The Last Battle, "And then she understood the devilish cunning of the enemies' plan. By mixing a little truth with it, they had made their lie far stronger."[3]

The devil, who disguises himself as an angel of light (2 Corinthians 11:14), is an expert at ensuring that most, if not all, religious systems include some measure of truth, beauty and morality. The devil is quite aware of the accuracy of Tolstoy's observations: "It is amazing how complete is the delusion that beauty is goodness.

Satan knows that to keep those designed in God's image in his grasp, he must appeal to their innate desire to know truth and to experience security and acceptance with God and with others. Not coincidentally, this appeal is the bread and butter of religion.

Thus, it is not surprising that the misdirected religious person embraces behavior and assents to certain aspects of spiritual truth that all men find praiseworthy. The humanitarian concerns of Albert Schweitzer, the commitment to peace of Ghandi, and the cohesive family units of the Mormons all find their just commendation, even among believers in Christ.

But the Christian communicator must remember that religion is spiritually lethal. At the heart of all religious systems is the poison of spiritual death and blindness to the glory of God's grace in Jesus Christ. Religion, grounded in the foolish speculations of fallen human nature, insulates its adherents from their need for the cross. For millions, religion is the ultimate barrier between them and the grace of the living God. Thus, the misdirected religious person, regardless of his level of personal morality, or his surface agreement with certain aspects of biblical truth, is in desperate need of a personal relationship with Christ.

The False Security of Spiritual Blindness

Religion, while putting its adherents on the road to destruction, offers them a first-class ride all the way there. C. S. Lewis observed, "Indeed, the safest road to hell is the gradual one — the gentle slope, soft underfoot, without sudden turnings, without milestones, without signposts."[4] Religion offers a false security that might indeed alleviate its adherents' fears and even instill in them a confidence and hope for eternity. But this is a cruel illusion. The only thing worse than being on a road to destruction is to be on the road to destruction and think that it is safe, secure and destined for eternal life.

Satan is a master at blinding the lost to the spiritual reality of their lostness and its resolution in the cross of Christ. The minds of misdirected religious men and women are filled with spiritual delusions, giving them a false sense of spiritual security.

Jonathan Edwards suggested that these delusions are expressed in four patterns: (1) "They are deceived about their own hearts; they think them much better than they really are." (2) "Men are very prone to be deceived about their own state . . . they suppose themselves to have need of nothing; when they are wretched, and miserable, and poor, and blind and naked." (3) "They are vastly deceived about their own righteousness . . . they think their tears, reformation, and prayers sufficient to make atonement for their sins." (4) "They are greatly deceived about their own strength . . . they think they are able to mend their own hearts."[5]

Blaise Pascal observed, "It is vain, O men, that you seek within yourselves the remedy for your ills. All your light can only reach the knowledge that not in yourselves will you find truth or good."[6] Religion specializes in shielding the lost from realizing that such reasoning is indeed vanity.

As we have discussed, the Christian communicator must appreciate the fact that to do the work of evangelism is to engage in spiritual warfare. The weapons of our warfare are prayer, the Holy Spirit and the gospel message. Only by these means can the lost be released from the delusion of false religious commitment and appreciate the solution of the grace of the gospel.

The misdirected religious person is no better off than the secularist. Both are on the road to destruction. Both are equally lost. Both are guilty of a profound misreading of the nature of God and of man's problems, and therefore they ignore the cure of the gospel. Such reasoning is a tragic, eternally consequential mistake.

In Summary

There is always a tendency to struggle with such a pessimistic appraisal of the condition of the misdirected religious person, especially in light of those who sincerely practice their faith, sometimes with more commitment than followers of Christ. But sincerity is never an issue in matters of truth. Sincerely believing one can fly does not change the size of the grease spot one makes at the foot of the sky scraper. If the evangelist is to be true to the one who said, "I am the way, the truth and the life, no man comes to the Father except by Me," he must not err in granting sincerity any worth beyond its human attractiveness. Sincerity does not wash clean our sins; only Jesus can do that. Sincerity can never take away the sting of death; only the cross of Christ is powerful enough to fill that order.

The preceding pages have been written to make one point alone. The misdirected religious person, no matter his sincerity, no matter his degree of adherence to Christian terminology, no matter his attractive lifestyle, is as much in need of the gospel as his secularist counterpart. To underscore this point, I have emphasized the shortcomings of misdirected religious systems and the danger these bring to their adherents.

The challenge is to convince the misdirected religious person of his need and the relevance of the gospel to his situation, without treating him in a harsh judgmental manner. We must heed Paul's warning to Timothy, "And the Lord's bond-servant must not be quarrelsome, but be kind to all, able to teach and patient when wronged, with gentleness correcting those who are in opposition, if perhaps God may grant them repentance leading to the knowledge of the truth" (2 Timothy 2:24,25). The wise communicator of the gospel who wishes to be used of God with this segment of the population must work to cultivate a winsome, gentle spirit in his evangelistic efforts.

A proper appreciation of our own humble state as ambassadors for Christ — sinners saved by grace and incredibly blessed with the privilege of sharing Christ with others — will keep us from any judgmental attitudes toward those aligned with falsehood. The phrase "there but for the grace of God go I" must typify the spirit of our approach to these men and women. We need to expose the error and dangerous position of the misdirected religious person, but must do so in the context of a sensitive appeal to repent and believe the gospel.

CHAPTER 10

Nominalism

"**C**hristian" nominalists make up one of the largest mission fields in the world and quite possibly the largest in the United States.[1] Any treatment of evangelism in the American culture would be deficient without a discussion of the peculiar challenges presented by the nominalist mindset.

Definition

The term *nominal* is derived from the Latin term *nominales,* meaning "belonging to a name." Thus, a Christian nominalist is one who claims the name Christian, but who has no authentic, personal, sin-forgiving and life-changing relationship with Jesus Christ. His allegiance to Jesus is in name, not heart.

The Lausanne Committee for World Evangelization has identified five types of nominalists in terms of their relationship to a church congregation:

(1) One who attends church regularly and worships devoutly, but who has no vital personal relationship with Jesus as Savior and Lord.

(2) One who attends church regularly but for cultural reasons only.

(3) One who attends church only for major church festivals (Christmas, Easter, etc.) and ceremonies (weddings, baptisms, funerals).

(4) One who hardly ever attends church but maintains a church relationship for reasons of security, emotional or family ties, or tradition.

(5) One who has no relationship to any specific church and who never attends, yet considers himself a believer in God (in a Protestant traditional sense).[2]

These five categories are helpful in that they show us both the broad range of differences among nominalists and the common thread that ties them all together. While one nominalist may be a regular and devout churchgoer, another may have no relationship with a church. One nominalist may hold a sincere religious commitment to spiritual truth as they see it, while another may be indifferent to spiritual matters altogether.

Regardless of the wide range of diversity, however, all nominalists could be described as *professors*, not *possessors*, of Jesus Christ. While claiming the title of Christian they have all failed to comprehend the cruciality of a personal commitment to Jesus Christ for the forgiveness of sins. As one of my friends described his nominalist roommate, "He had all the right words, but none of the music in his heart."

The nominalist has been spiritually inoculated. He has been so exposed to what he believes is true Christianity that he reasons there is nothing more to it beyond his present experience. Some nominalists think this condition is just fine, glad that Christianity asks nothing more of them than church attendance or intellectual agreement with certain doctrines. There is no sense of need here. Such intellectual assent is thought to be sufficient personal involvement in spiritual matters. Anything more would be approaching fanaticism.

Others, however, feel let down. "If this is all that being a Christian is, it's sure not life-changing or personally relevant," they reason. Many of these nominalists are ready to respond to the gospel.

At the Heart of the Matter

The nominalist, for whatever reason, has failed to come to terms with his sin problem and its resolution in Christ. While he may correctly analyze the problem and the solution, he will fall short of dealing with sin on God's terms but will insist on approaching God on his own terms.

The nominalist's attitude toward forgiveness betrays his unbiblical thinking on the seriousness of sin and the holiness of God. We can divide this thinking into three categories:

(1) Forgiveness is not required. This nominalist has reasoned either that sin is not serious enough to fall under God's judgment or that God is not serious enough about sin to judge it. This person is the one who made *I'm OK, You're OK* a best seller. He worships the easy-going God of whom Omar Khayyam wrote, "He's a good fellow and 'twill all be well." God sits on a rocking chair, not a throne of judgment, and forgiveness is not even an issue worth discussing. Pascal said of such people, "Truly it is an evil to be full of faults; but it is a still greater evil to be full of them and to be willing to recognize them, since that is to add to the further fault of a voluntary illusion."[3]

(2) Forgiveness is required, but earned. This person reasons, "Yes, we need God to forgive, but this forgiveness is secured on the basis of good deeds." He operates on a vague notion that if his good deeds outweigh his bad, forgiveness has been earned. The means of earning this right standing with God usually includes "being good" and following the rules of one's religious group.

Of these people, Campbell Moody wrote, "Everywhere men seek, as of old, to satisfy their conscience by the performance of duty, or by telling themselves that they have done their duty, that they have never harmed anyone, or that, at least they are as good as those who make a profession of religion, and better, perhaps, for they are not hypocrites. . . . nothing so shuts men from God's Kingdom as self-justification does."[4]

(3) Forgiveness is required, but automatic. God is concerned about sin, but thanks to His great mercy and love, all will be

forgiven eventually. Thus, while sin is indeed an issue, it is swallowed up in God's overwhelming love. This theological error is called universalism and fails to take seriously the holiness of God and Jesus' warnings about the grim possibility of an eternity of separation from Him.

The nominalist has traveled a different route from the secularist, but he has arrived at the same destination. Both have refused to come to God on His terms. As a result, they pursue an inadequate solution for their inadequately defined problem, which will leave them inadequately prepared to meet God.

An Ancient Nominalist

In Luke 18:9-14, Jesus gives us a classic picture of the nominalist mentality in action. Luke records in verse 9, "And He also told this parable to certain ones who trusted in themselves that they were righteous, and viewed others with contempt." Jesus told this parable to expose the folly of those who attempted to relate to God on the basis of their own character, religious efforts, or religious affiliation, as if they had the ability to secure God's righteousness on their own merit.

Jesus continued, "Two men went up to the temple to pray, one a Pharisee and the other a tax gatherer" (verse 10). The Pharisees were the leaders of the Jewish religious establishment. They knew all the right things to do and say and were enthusiastically committed to their expression of the Jewish faith. They knew the Old Testament Scriptures and claimed to be the spiritual guides of the nation of Israel. At first glance, someone from this category might be your pick for the one "most likely to relate properly to the living God."

On the other hand, the publican (the tax collector) was hated by his countrymen for his complicity with the Roman oppressor. On the spectrum of the Jewish religious scene the publican fell on the opposite end from the Pharisee. The Temple is the last place we would expect to find this man.

With the stage set, Jesus recounted the words of the Pharisee, "God, I thank Thee that I am not like the other people: swindlers, unjust, adulterers, or even like this tax gatherer. I fast twice a week; I pay tithes of all that I get" (verses 11 and 12).

This man reasoned, "I belong to the people of God, the nation of Israel, and even more than that, I have achieved a high position of religious leadership. I do all the right things. I deserve God's approval; what more could He want? Right standing before God is certainly a must, but thankfully I'm up to the task of earning it. It wasn't easy, but I'm glad I am who I am instead of being like this publican over here."

What a complete contrast to the publican. "But the tax-gatherer, standing some distance away, was even unwilling to lift up his eyes to heaven, but was beating his breast, saying, 'God be merciful to me, the sinner!' " (verse 13). The publican saw matters clearly. He was helpless, a sinner, totally dependent on the grace of God to remedy his hopeless situation. All he could do was appeal to God for mercy. The verb *be merciful* means "be propitiated." As we have noted, propitiation is that theme of salvation that refers to averting God's anger and wrath by dealing with God on the basis of His mercy. The publican knew this was his only hope.

Two diametrically opposed heart attitudes are contrasted here, one prideful, the other repentant. Jesus closed the parable by telling His listeners which one was approved by God. "I tell you, this man [the publican] went down to his house justified rather than the other; for everyone who exalts himself shall be humbled, but he who humbles himself shall be exalted" (verse 14). Only the publican found God's mercy that day. By inference, the Pharisee continued in an unjustified state, out of touch with God's grace, still under His condemnation, an object of His wrath.

This parable gives us two insights into the importance of the heart attitude, as opposed to the external concerns of religious sincerity and religious affiliation.

(1) Mere religious affiliation is not enough to secure God's approval. If it were, the Pharisee would have been approved by God. He was one of his generation's most religiously committed people, but this was not good enough.

(2) The issue in anyone's relationship to God is one of heart attitude. Paul states in Romans 2:28,29, "For he is not a Jew who is one outwardly; neither is circumcision that which is outward in the flesh. But he is a Jew who is one inwardly; and circumcision is that which is of the heart, by the Spirit, not by the letter; and his praise is not from men, but from God."

This was the failure of the Pharisee. The externals were all in order. But his religious affiliation, commitment to religious observances and the degree of intensity with which he held his religious convictions were all for naught. The external label, "Pharisee," and the thin veneer of religious practice served only to hide a heart that was radically out of tune with God's perspective on his spiritual need.

The Pharisee, like many nominalists, was deceived by his pride and sense of self-justification into making some serious miscalculations. As C. S. Lewis observed, "As long as you are proud, you cannot know God. A proud man is always looking down on things and people: and of course, as long as you are looking down, you cannot see something that is above you."[5] The nominalist's heart, blinded to the reality of God's holiness, will invariably overestimate its own righteousness and, therefore, its ability to please God. In his own eyes, the nominalist is not helpless, nor is his situation hopeless. He assumes that his own opinion of himself is true and that God must therefore concur. Pascal observed, "There are only two kinds of men: the righteous who believe themselves sinners; the rest sinners who believe themselves righteous."[6] As the Pharisee elevated himself, he simultaneously lowered God's standard of holiness and nullified the grave of God.

Nominalist reasoning is grounded in the ignorance of pride and is oblivious to the theological realities of man's sin, God's holiness and grace's necessity. The nominalist suffers from the same spiritual blindness as does the secularist.

The Nominalist Alive and Well

According to a 1979 Gallup Poll, the vast majority of Americans still identify to some degree with biblical terminology, if not a biblical framework for interpreting life.

Consider that 80 percent of those polled believe that Jesus Christ is divine. Ninety-four percent believe in God or in a universal spirit. Eighty-seven percent of those who said they believe in God find comfort in their belief; about half said this belief gives them great comfort.[7] Fifty-seven percent of American adults said that their religious beliefs are "very important"; only 15 percent said they were "not too important" and 4 percent "not at all important."[8] Ninety-eight percent of American homes have at least one Bible.

This weekend 54 percent of the adult population of Americans will go to church or synagogue. Only 33 percent will watch a football game on TV. Thirty-one million adults claim to be evangelicals. It is not surprising that in this cultural context "almost half (45 percent) of the American adults are clear on how to go to heaven and are quite willing to say they believe it to be true."[9]

This segment of the population is what Gallup calls "the company of the orthodox."[10] They believe that "the only hope for heaven is through personal faith in Jesus Christ," that Jesus Christ is God or the Son of God, that He was raised from the dead, and that the Bible is the Word of God.

Even a majority of the "unchurched" (those who are not members, or do not identify themselves with the institution of the church) believe that Jesus is the Son of God and was raised from the dead. Forty percent of the unchurched claim to have made a "personal commitment to Jesus Christ." Nine in ten have some sort of traditional religious background.[11]

These statistics led *Christianity Today* to conclude that basic Christian doctrine is "pervasive" in American society. But what does all of this mean, especially as it relates to communicating the gospel to a culture such as ours?

Before we answer this, we must consider the negative side of these statistics. While 84 percent believe that the Ten Commandments are for today, only half of the population can name five of them.[12] While 94 percent said that they "believe in God," only 39.5 million out of 155 million adults claim a conversion experience that fits even a minimum biblical norm. That leaves more than

100 million American adults who say they believe in God but do
not claim to have had a genuine personal encounter with Christ.
Eighty percent believe that Jesus Christ is divine, but only around
50 percent — or 69 million adults — say they are hoping to go
to heaven because of their faith in Jesus Christ. While these same
69 million American adults are "hoping to go to heaven only
because of their personal faith in Jesus Christ," only 29.5 million
claim a conversion "that included asking Christ to be personal
Savior."[13]

Ann Landers for Theologian of the Year

No one better typifies mainstream American thinking on
various topics than our own Ann Landers. In a recent column
she, albeit unknowingly, clearly articulated the nominalist perspective on the gospel.

The couple who wrote her were nominal "Christians," and
they were aghast that two of their children would suggest to
them that they should be "born again." Indeed, these children
had the gall to tell their parents that they would not go to heaven
otherwise.

Ann came to this couple's rescue by assuring them that
although the phrase, "born again," is in the Bible, it certainly
need not apply to them if they are uncomfortable with it. Ann
wrote, "I have no quarrel with those who are sincere in their
beliefs, but I feel it is unfair of your children to try to proselytize
you. A kind and generous God has room in heaven for a wide
variety of believers, including those who were only born once.
. . . your credentials for passing through the pearly gates are as
good as theirs."[14]

The lesson is obvious. "It is religious affiliation that ensures
heaven, not one's heart response to the gospel."

The Gospel and the Nominalist

What are we to conclude from this brief analysis? Gallup
interprets these statistics as indicating a huge gap between belief
and commitment. For instance, while 68 percent of the teenagers

say they feel they have been in the presence of God, only 22 percent say their religious beliefs are the "most important influence in their lives." This is not to pick out teenagers as the only ones with this commitment gap. Gallup observes that while the solid majority of Americans regard religion as important, relatively few say it is one of the most important influences in their lives.[15]

The implication is that we are a nation of spiritual illiterates. Gallup observes that "a significant proportion (in the case of Christians) can articulate only in the most vague fashion the significance of the resurrection of Jesus Christ for mankind."[16]

This spiritual illiteracy, or what Gallup calls "a glaring lack of knowledge about the basic facts of our religious heritage and a fuzziness about the central tenets of our religions,"[17] is evidence that a populace that seems to be spiritually in tune with Christian truth is, in reality, sadly ignorant of it.

These findings touch on the work of evangelism in two areas. First, we should expect a vast reservoir of good will and initial interest in the gospel from our audience. From these statistics, it is obvious that the vestiges of Christian truth remain in the consciousness of a majority of Americans. The grand biblical themes of the incarnation, redemption in Jesus Christ and God's revelation to man in the Bible are at least somewhat familiar ideas to most Americans. Thus, we are dealing with an audience who, in large part, consider themselves to be "Christian." We are more likely to run into a person who went to church last Sunday than one who watched a professional football game, and this fact should encourage us.

Many nominalists are dissatisfied with the barrenness of mere "belief." They are ready for the life-changing power that comes only from a personal commitment to Christ. They need only a clear, concise presentation of the gospel, with an emphasis on how Jesus wants to make that twelve-inch journey from their head to their heart.

Nice, But Not Necessary

Second, we can expect to encounter a curious cultural climate in which nominalists are relatively open to the gospel, but are ignorant of the personal implications of Jesus' crucial call to repentance and faith. They are content to live with the gap between belief and commitment. They treat Christian truth much like chewing gum. They taste it, chew it a bit, but never swallow it. When is loses its taste, they spit it out. Such nominalists find the gospel interesting, even somewhat relevant, but hardly the best news ever told.

I picked up one such nominalist who was hitchhiking in Iowa. During our hundred miles together we had a good chance to discuss the gospel. "I like talking with people like you," he said. "Jesus is great because He makes people happy and harmless." When I asked if he didn't think that trusting Jesus Christ was life's most crucial decision, he replied, "Of course not. It's nice to be into Christ, but not necessary."

The challenge to the Christian communicator lies not in convincing these nominalists of the general relevance of Christianity. They are already convinced. Rather, the challenge lies in personalizing the gospel — communicating Christ with precision, clarity, urgency and sensitivity so the nominalist can understand that making a decision to trust in Christ really is life's most crucial necessity.

CHAPTER 11

Erosion of Urgency

The first-century Christians were well aware of the radical change Jesus had made in their lives and could make in the lives of others. Many had been saved from lives of demon-possession, blatant immorality, even sickness and certain death. Others had been saved from the dead end of idolatry or religious pride.

Regardless of their lifestyles before they came to know Christ, all had a vivid sense of having been rescued from a spiritual condition that would have eventually led to their eternal destruction. They were so convinced of the difference Jesus made that they came to see their former existence outside of Christ as a sort of living death (Ephesians 2:1; 4:17-19; Colossians 2:13).

Sadly, however, this perspective is lacking in today's evangelical circles. To make matters worse, the generation with which we seek to share the gospel is generally not the least bit interested in seeking us out. The result is a sort of spiritual truce: They don't bother us, and we don't bother them.

Given this state of affairs, one must ask, "Have the assumptions of the secularist person or nominalist gained a foothold in the average Christian's attitude toward evangelism?" I believe the answer is a resounding, "Yes!" To a large degree, the Christian community has been sucked into the ethos of our culture, shaped by the operating assumptions of those we are attempting to reach. It is not that followers of Christ have agreed with the secularist that God is irrelevant. Nor have we taken sides with the nominalist, affirming religious affiliation as more important than a personal relationship with Christ. No, the process is a little more subtle than this.

Behind the Schemes

The story is told of an apprentice demon, soon to be sent to earth on his first mission, who is preparing for a last-minute strategy session with his master. The young demon is a fast learner. He has realized that the unbelieving world is already in his master's power and that it would be a poor use of his time and resources to focus his schemes on the lost. Rather, his strategy is to focus on neutralizing the Christians in their evangelistic work. "They could do the most harm" he reasons, "so I must keep them from the destructive work, modeled so well by Paul 2,000 years ago, of 'opening the eyes of the unbelieving that they might turn to God from Satan'" (Acts 26:18). He shudders at the thought of Paul's success.

The demon then shares his strategy with his master. "I'll try to convince Christians that there is no such thing as sin," he says. "Then they will stop sharing the good news. The answer will soon become irrelevant if I eliminate the question."

"This is only a part of my plan," says Satan, "but it cannot be the focus, for most of our enemies realize the reality of sin. Even those in our power sometimes, in rare moments of clear thinking, realize sin's destructiveness. You'll confuse some of the enemy, but not all of them on this."

"Well then, I'll convince the church that there is no hell, that even if there is sin, there are no eternal consequences."

"Good thinking," replies Satan. "You will confuse some with this, but still, the prospect of judgment is so ingrained in men, even those in our power, that this will not neutralize the enemy. Most will see through the deception."

The young demon thinks for a moment, and then a look of triumph floods his face. "I've got it! I'll convince them that there is no hurry. They can have their doctrines of sin, heaven and hell. I'll just help them rationalize away their lack of conviction on these matters by whispering in their ears, 'There is no hurry; don't inconvenience yourself. Save it for later.' They are all so prone to be concerned with their own cares and problems anyway, that they will buy right into it."

"You have done well," says Satan. "You will see great success in neutralizing the enemy with this strategy."

This story illustrates the root cause of lack of motivation for evangelism in the Christian community. It is not that we have affirmed secular or nominalist assumptions. Rather, we have unconsciously succumbed to the spirit of "non-cruciality" fueled by those assumptions having permeated our culture. This spirit whispers to us in many voices, some loud, some soft, all appearing quite harmless. But the message is always the same: "Jesus is nice, but not necessary. There is no hurry. Don't inconvenience yourself." Our evangelistic strength is sapped when we take our marching orders from the culture rather than from the Bible.

The Blind Leading the Sighted

Jesus described the Pharisees as "blind guides of the blind" (Matthew 15:14). This terminology generates a ridiculous mental picture of two men stumbling along, one thinking he is secure in the other's leadership, oblivious to the danger and pitiful reality of their situation.

But the present cultural situation conjures up an even more ridiculous image, that of the blind leading the sighted. It is understandable how a blind man led by another blind man would fail to discern the danger of their situation. But the blind leading the sighted can only cause one to question the judgment and sanity of the sighted.

This is exactly where we find multitudes of Christians today. Why are we not taking every step possible to provide for the sharing of the gospel with every person possible as soon as possible? Because, in large part, those we are trying to reach are

oblivious to the eternal cruciality of the gospel. They, generally
show no overt signs of interest in Jesus Christ. And instead of
exposing their spirit of indifference for the spiritual blindness it
is, we join in their indifference.

The Convenience Undertow

We live in a culture that worships convenience. The word
convenience means "absence of trouble; attuned to one's personal
comfort; ease of action." It means to have the external circumstances of my life in harmony with my inner desires so I
can avoid difficulty of any sort. The voice of convenience whispers,
"If it's hard, count me out. Let's find the easy way and build a
monument of golden arches to it."

Of course, there is nothing wrong with convenience per se.
I am a regular customer at our neighborhood convenience store,
and I am glad that it stays open until 11 P.M. I use the drive-
through window at our bank, and I am thankful for pop-top
cans and for being able to let my fingers walk through the yellow
pages. There is nothing inherently wrong with the *items* of
convenience. It is the *ethos* of convenience that endangers our
evangelistic motivation. By ethos I mean a prevailing cultural
pattern that permeates one's thinking to the degree that he
unwittingly conforms his behavior to that pattern. It is a short
step from reasoning that my banking should be easy, to reasoning
that all other areas of my life should be easy, including my
responsibilities to God and to others.

Water And Oil

How does the convenience factor relate to evangelism? Very
poorly. The ethos of convenience and the process of developing
biblical convictions on the practice of evangelism go together like
oil and water. I am convinced that the convenience factor is more
likely to rob the Christian of his motivation in evangelism than
any other aspect of our culture. Why? No biblically oriented
Christian will consciously buy into the secular and nominalist
assumptions that render the gospel meaningless. This is too
blatant. But we are seduced by the soothing voices that urge,

"Don't go against the grain." The would-be evangelists who have been subtly molded by these voices will find themselves overwhelmed by the rigor of evangelism. They will then settle for a practice of evangelism that falls far short of the biblical specifications. The result is the same as if he had embraced the secular or nominalist perspective: Little, if any, evangelism is done.

Paul writes, "Therefore, my beloved brethren, be steadfast, immovable, always abounding in the work of the Lord, knowing that your toil is not in vain in the Lord." Paul states that his ministry is one of "labor" and "striving" (Colossians 1;20); a "struggle" (Colossians 2:1); and one that caused him great hardship (2 Corinthians 6:4,5).

Avoiding the Undertow

The one committed to developing personal convictions that will carry him toward a *lifetime* of involvement in the work of evangelism must come to grips with the fact that it is just that, the *work* of evangelism (2 Timothy 2:4). But how can we develop the kind of motivation that will neutralize the cultural undertow and equip us for the lifetime task of sharing the gospel in any and all circumstances? There is a saying: "He who sees only half the problem will be buried by the other half." Recognizing the cultural undertow that could discourage us from doing the work of an evangelist is indeed seeing half the problem. But the other half remains, and that is to develop biblical convictions on evangelism that will motivate us to do the work "in and out of season"; to join with Paul in an evangelistic ministry sure to require labor and striving (Colossians 1:29), and possibly even hardship (2 Corinthians 6:4,5).

CHAPTER 12

The Content of a Conviction

I am convinced that only those who have made the effort to develop firmly rooted biblical convictions about evangelism will be able to overcome the cultural undertow of convenience. As Flannery O'Conner wrote, "And more than ever now it seems that the kingdom of heaven has to be taken by violence, or not at all. You have to push as hard as the age that pushes against you."[1]

Our evangelistic motivation dare not hang on the thin thread of emotional or circumstantial factors. Our passion for souls is not an emotion, but rather a conviction based on a well-thought-through theology of evangelism. In 2 Corinthians 5:11-21 Paul tells us how four theological convictions fueled his motivation to pursue the work of evangelism even against great odds and in spite of personal suffering. These four building blocks are (1) the fear of the Lord (verse 11), (2) the love of Christ (verses 14-15), (3) the reality of man's predicament and possibilities (verses 16-17), and (4) the role and responsibility of an ambassador (verses 18-21).

The Fear of the Lord

Paul writes, "Therefore knowing the fear of the Lord, we persuade men" (2 Corinthians 5:11). Paul is speaking of his total evangelistic ministry of persuading men of the truth of the gospel.[2] But what does a fear of the Lord have to do with persuading men?

Note that this fear is not to be understood as discomfort or fright. We are told that perfect love casts out this fear (1 John 4:18). Rather, this fear is a deep reverence for God out of respect for His awesome character and purposes. It is the response of humbly bowing before Him as Creator and Lord of history. It is recognizing that He is King of our lives, King of the universe, and therefore the one who alone deserves glory and our obedience. Above all, it is a recognition of Jesus as our judge. Note that verse 11 follows Paul's mention of the judgment seat of Christ. Verses 9 and 10 read: "Therefore also we have as our ambition, whether at home or absent, to be pleasing to Him. For we must all appear before the judgment seat of Christ, that each one may be recompensed for his deeds in the body, according to what he has done, whether good or bad." Our fear of the Lord is based on the reality of having to answer to Jesus for the way we have invested our lives.

Paul agreed with the psalmist, "The fear of the Lord is the beginning of wisdom; a good understanding have all those who do His commandments" (Psalm 111:10). It was this healthy reverence for the character and purposes of God that led Paul to conclude that the work of persuading men to enter His Kingdom is indeed a wise and understanding investment of one's time and treasure. To choose the work of persuading men is to choose the wise path of bringing glory to God through our obedience. This was the compelling intention that undergirded Paul's commitment to evangelism.

Evangelism as Reverential Obedience

As I have studied the Book of Acts from a motivational perspective, I am convinced that we need look no deeper than the issue of reverential obedience to find what fueled the fires of commitment to the first-century church's evangelistic enterprise.

These men and women regarded evangelism as a commanded and authorized work. Jesus said, "All authority has been given to Me in heaven and on earth. Go therefore and make disciples of all the nations, baptizing them in the name of the Father and the Son and the Holy Spirit, teaching them to observe all that I commanded you; and lo, I am with you always, even to the end of the age" (Matthew 28:18-20).

Jesus told His disciples in Luke 24:46-48, "Thus it is written, that the Christ should suffer and rise again from the dead the third day; and that repentance for forgiveness of sins should be proclaimed in His name to all nations beginning from Jerusalem. You are witnesses of these things." Jesus' command to go to all the nations was preceded by His statement, "All authority has been given to Me in heaven and on earth." The one whose name is above every other name and to whom every knee will one day bow (Philippians 2:10) has made His will plainly known. The King speaks, and His subjects carry out His order in the power of His authority. Therefore, to "go" is to obey; to stay is to disobey. To proclaim forgiveness of sins in His name is to align ourselves with the wise, instructed path of life. To keep this information to ourselves is to be foolish and out of step with the Master's design for our lives and His purpose for history.

This commitment to evangelism, grounded in obedience to the command of Christ, made the expansion of the church inevitable. The first-century Christians were found by their opponents to be an irresistible force, the overwhelming minority.

The book of Acts records the willingness of Jesus' early followers to take seriously His command to proclaim the gospel to the world. Acts 1:8 states: "But you shall receive power when the Holy Spirit has come upon you; and you shall be My witnesses both in Jerusalem, and in all Judea and Samaria, and even to the remotest part of the earth." This verse is not so much a command as a prediction of what the Christians would naturally find themselves doing as they walked in the fear of the Lord, appreciating God's intent for their personal lives and for human history. Indeed, Acts 1:8 is an outline of the progress of the church as it marched through Jerusalem (Acts 1:12-8:3) to the remotest part of the earth (Acts 11:19-28:31). Jesus commanded it. That fact was quite enough for Paul and the first-century church and should, in like manner, place anyone who fears the Lord on the wise path of persuading men.

Evangelism and God's Glory

It is clear that Jesus commanded and authorized the work of evangelism. But why did He do so? The answer is grounded in an understanding of God's sovereign plan from eternity past to redeem the world and so bring glory to Himself. The redemption of a fallen creation is the central focus of God's plan for the world. Since the fall, God has been unfolding His plan for the restoration of all things in Christ (Ephesians 1:10). John Calvin wrote, "God has created the entire world that it should be the theatre of His glory by the spread of the gospel."

The gospel, God's plan of redemption, reveals His character to a fallen world and to the fallen spiritual realm. Matthew 24:14 states, "And this gospel of the kingdom shall be preached in the whole world for a *witness* to all the nations, and then the end shall come" (emphasis added).

Ephesians 3:10,11 states that the gospel of Jesus Christ is preached "in order that the manifold wisdom of God might now be made known through the church to the rulers and the authorities in the heavenly places. This was in accordance with the eternal purpose which He carried out in Christ Jesus our Lord. . . ." God is glorified as His love, grace, mercy, justice, sovereignty and power displayed on the cross of Christ are further displayed to the fallen world as the gospel is proclaimed and lives are changed.

The spread of the gospel, then, is the focal point of God's redemptive plan to be worked out in the lives of flesh-and-blood people. As I am obedient to Jesus' command to "Go," I am wisely aligning myself with God's plan for the world. This is for my good, and for the good of those who will hear the gospel. But ultimately it is for the glory of God. The motive for obedience in evangelism is not only that the lost must be saved, but also — and even more important — that through the saving of these lost, great glory is brought to God.

Paul realized that the work of evangelism finds its *source* in God's plan for the world, *works* toward summing up all things in Christ and will *result* in great glory to God. Paul knew that evangelism is crucial and primary to the mission of God's people because it is the initial point of contact between a loving God who seeks to save and rebellious men who are bent on self-destruction. Thus, evangelism, the proclamation of the good news, is God's appeal to men to align themselves with His ongoing and irresistible plan to redeem this lost world.

This is why the fear of the Lord leads to a life of persuading men. The question is not, "Is God's plan for redeeming the world, the Great Commission, relevant to me?" but "Am I in tune with His well-defined purpose?" The fear of the Lord leads one to decide wisely to make such a personal alignment, to live a life that will bring maximum glory to God.

The Love of Christ

Paul writes, "For the love of Christ controls us, having concluded this, that one died for all, therefore all died; and He died for all, that they who live should no longer live for themselves, but for Him who died and rose again on their behalf" (2 Corinthians 5:14,15). Paul speaks here of the "love of Christ" having control of his life. Paul had grasped the fact that he was a recipient of God's love through Christ. His conviction was based on a specific body of information. Paul had "concluded," he had mentally processed the facts. The facts in this case are Jesus' great act of self-sacrifice — "He died for all" — and the corresponding implication for those redeemed by His death "that they who live should no longer live for themselves, but for Him who died and rose again on their behalf." Paul was thus a "love-mastered man."

This truth had so gripped Paul that its implications were irresistible. "If Christ did this for me," he reasoned, "then I must submit all facets of my human experience, my desires, personality, habits, time and resources to His grand design for the world." To live for himself in light of Jesus' sacrifice on the cross to qualify him for His kingdom would be unthinkable.

Paul could say, then, that the love of Christ "controlled," "compelled" (NIV), or "constraineth" (KJV) us. The Greek word *sunechei* means to be "held together," "confined" — to be held tightly or pressed from all sides. The picture generated by this word is of the love of Christ pressing in on and surrounding Paul, removing from him all pursuit except unselfish, radical commitment to the person and purposes of Jesus. The same word is used in Acts 18:5 and is translated "devoted himself exclusively," to the work of preaching the gospel. In other words, Paul reasoned, he had no other choice, given what Jesus had done for him, than to "offer his body a living and holy sacrifice, acceptable to God" (Romans 12:1). Paul understood this to be a "spiritual service of worship." He realized that "he was not his own," but had been bought with the precious blood of Christ. His main pursuit in life was to bring glory to God (1 Corinthians 6:19,20).

The story is told of a local church man who suggested that the community ask D.L. Moody to do a series of meetings. Moody had recently been to that community, so another man asked, "Why get Moody again? Does he have a monopoly on God?"

"No", replied the other man, "but God has a monopoly on him."

To have the love of Christ "control" us means to allow God to have a monopoly on our lives by bringing our will into conformity with His purposes for the world.

Michael Green sums up this attitude well: "If you believe that outside of Christ there is no hope, it is impossible to possess an atom of human love and kindness without being gripped with the great desire to bring men to this one way of salvation.[3]

We could say of Paul that "all the waters of his soul had gathered themselves into one mighty flood to be poured through the narrows of this single purpose — to preach unto the Gentiles the unsearchable riches of Christ."[4] An understanding of Jesus' love for him personally and His love plan for the world motivated Paul to subordinate every facet of his life to the end of proclaiming Christ to the world.

Thus, evangelism is grounded in love. It is the supreme act of love. Too often we equate love with emotional affection or intimacy of relationship. We say, "I am incapable of really loving this person until I feel a warm emotion in my heart. Then I can do something for him." Or we might say, "To share the gospel with him before I demonstrate love to him in a relational sense would border on hypocrisy." As one author puts it, "I don't relate to unbelievers in order to get them to be believers. I just relate to people and love them."[5]

But this is a confusing line of reasoning. Love does not precede action. Love *is* action. Love is acting on another's behalf to meet his need. I cannot meet anyone's spiritual need, although I can at times, meet physical and emotional needs. But I can introduce a person to the one who is the great need-meeter. Jesus is living water for the thirsty, sight for the blind, release for the captive, bread for the hungry soul, truth for the confused, and life for the spiritually dead. Introducing someone to the Savior, I am convinced, is the most loving thing I am capable of doing for another.

The Lausanne Covenant declares that "in the church's mission of sacrificial service, evangelism is primary."[6] As the Thailand Statement says concerning the primacy of evangelism, "Of all the tragic needs of human beings, none is greater than their alienation from their Creator and the terrible reality of eternal death for those who refuse to repent and believe. If, therefore, we do not commit ourselves with urgency to the task of evangelization, we are guilty of an inexcusable lack of human compassion."[7] Such is the reasonable conviction of that person who refuses to narrow God's purposes to the confines of his own soul and personal interests. As the love of Christ controls us, others' spiritual needs become our priority.

Man's Predicament and His Possibilities

Paul states in 2 Corinthians 5:16,17, "Therefore from now on we recognize no man according to the flesh; even though we have known Christ according to the flesh, yet we know Him thus no longer. Therefore if any man is in Christ, he is a new creature; the old things passed away; behold, new things have come."

Paul tells us that since his conversion to Christ, his personal perspective has changed in two areas: his view of men in general, and his view of Jesus Christ. Before his conversion Paul had seen both as "according to the flesh." His perspective had been dictated by the flesh principle, or his being in tune with the world's system. John tells us in 1 John 2:16, "For all that is in the world, the lust of the flesh and the lust of the eyes and the boastful pride of life, is not from the Father, but is from the world." To evaluate men "according to the flesh" means to see them through these lenses. But such an evaluation will lead one to see only the surface of their true selves. We might say, "There goes a man who knows how to dress; he is so successful and powerful, and doesn't he have a beautiful wife!" Or, "There is a woman who looks like she stepped out of *Vogue*. She's so socially poised and up with the latest in fashions." Certainly there is nothing wrong with such thoughts; these things may be quite true. But if our perspective on men and women goes no deeper than this we have settled for a totally inadequate assessment of the human condition. We have completely ignored the theological reality of fallen man created in God's image.

20/20 Spiritual Vision

The same temptations to dehumanize mankind were as present in the first century as they are today. But Jesus did not conform to the world system's view of personhood. He knew that the crowds who heard Him had a tendency to evaluate their lives solely in terms of "mammon," a totally materialistic perspective. Their identities were wrapped up in things — food and clothing and all the cares of life. In Matthew 6:24-34, Jesus deals with their inadequate view of their identity by asking them, "Is not life more than food, and the body than clothing? Look at the birds. . . . Are you not worth much more than they?" and by telling them, "Seek first His kingdom and His righteousness; and all these things shall be added to you."

Jesus modeled 20/20 spiritual vision. In Matthew 9:36-38, as the multitudes pressed in on Him to be healed and to hear His gracious words, He saw beyond their overwhelming physical and emotional needs and pinpointed their real need. "He felt compassion for them, because they were distressed and downcast like sheep without a shepherd." They needed Him, the Good

Shepherd, above all else. The human condition is a much more serious and potentially glorious prospect than any materialistic appraisal could represent. Theology is so practical to everyday life. Without crisp theological analysis, we cannot even view our next-door neighbor correctly.

Paul, too, had abandoned the "flesh perspective." He had realigned his thinking on man and Christ and conformed it to the serious biblical perspective of the true need of man in light of the realities of heaven, hell and salvation in Christ. Paul saw all men as eternal creatures. When we begin to appreciate the eternal ramifications of our "new creature" status, we cannot help but see others in light of their eternal possibilities. Paul could no longer look at men as mere men. In his mind, the focus was on the grand possibility of their coming to know Christ and "shining forth as the sun in their Father's kingdom" (Matthew 13:43), or the awful prospect of their eternal judgment.

C. S. Lewis wrote in *The Weight of Glory*, "The load, or weight, or burden of my neighbor's glory should be laid daily on my back, a load so heavy that only humility can carry it, and the backs of the proud will be broken. It is a serious thing to live in a society of possible gods and goddesses, to remember that the dullest and most uninteresting person you talk to may one day be a creature which, if you saw it now, you would be strongly tempted to worship, or else a horror and a corruption such as you now meet, if at all, only in a nightmare." Lewis concluded that in light of these overwhelming possibilities, there is no such thing as "ordinary people."[8]

These are sobering thoughts. But they are the truths that convictions are made of. A friend of mine tells of watching a Michigan-Michigan State football game many years ago. The highly intense rivalry brought over 100,000 screaming fans to the stadium. As the game and the crowd heated up, this man's friend asked him, "How many of the people in this stadium do you think are going to heaven?" My friend got the point. The real issue was not whom you are rooting for, or whether you had a seat on the 50-yard line. The real issue was, "Are you a new creature in Christ?"

Like Paul, we need to see all men in light of the eternal options. The fact that all men are created in God's image ensures that every person born into this world will live forever. The question is, "Where?" 1 John 2:17 tells us that the "world will pass away." There will come a day when the present world's system, which ignores God and dehumanizes man, will come to a screeching halt. The god of this world, already judged on the cross, finally will be put out of business. All those who are in his kingdom will be judged along with him.

We might say that evangelism has an "eschatological" dimension to it. This means simply that the good news is a message of "kingdom realignment" in preparation for that great day when the kingdom of the world finally passes away into judgment and the Kingdom of God is revealed in all of its fullness. On that great day, all eternal destinies will be sealed, all hearts exposed and all hope lost for those outside of Christ. But that day is, in a sense, every day. In each 24-hour period, over 175,000 people die, many without Christ; the matter is settled for them.

As C. S. Lewis observed, "There is no neutral ground in the universe: every square inch, every split second, is claimed by God and counterclaimed by Satan."[9]

This poem by Joseph Addison Alexander makes the point well.

> There is a time, we know not when
> A point we know not where
> That marks the destiny of man,
> For glory or despair.
> There is a line by us unseen
> That crosses every path
> The hidden boundary between
> God's patience and His wrath.
>
> (Source unknown)

The Responsibility of Ambassadorship

Paul writes, "Now all these things are from God, who reconciled us to Himself through Christ, and gave us the ministry of reconciliation, namely that God was in Christ reconciling the world to Himself, not counting their trespasses against them, and He has committed to us the word of reconciliation. Therefore, we are ambassadors for Christ as though God were entreating through us; we beg you on behalf of Christ, be reconciled to God. He made Him who knew no sin to be sin on our behalf, that we might become the righteousness of God in Him" (2 Corinthians 5:18-21). Paul's use of the Greek word *presbenomen* in 2 Corinthians 5:20 carries with it the idea of the solemn, official responsibility associated with his calling.[10]

Paul sees himself as having been entrusted with the ministry of reconciliation. The word *committed* could be translated "placing in us" and refers to "God's authoritative and effective ordination"[11] of men and women that they might be His ambassadors, officially entrusted with the communication of His saving message.

The Ambassador Mentality

Being an ambassador is both a high and a humble calling. It carries with it the joy of privilege and the compelling weight of responsibility. The ambassador is the highest diplomatic officer sent from one sovereign power to another, invested with power to speak and act on behalf of the one who sends him, and entrusted with messages of great importance. However, he has no authority or message of his own. Rather, the ambassador is sent to communicate his sovereign's message faithfully and clearly to the other party.

Commissioned to Communicate

The ambassador, as any other communicator, should model a congruity between the importance of his message and the clarity and force of his communication. Imagine seeing a fire start backstage in a crowded theatre. It grows larger and larger, but you are the only one who notices. You walk up to the usher and whisper very softly, "Fire." He moves his ear closer to you, and you feebly whisper again, "Fire . . . I think there is a fire." By this time the usher would be doubting your sanity. The lack of congruity between the reality of the situation and the intensity and clarity with which you delivered the message would imply one of two things: Either you were mentally imbalanced, or you were not convinced of the fact that there really was a fire.

Paul understood that God was making an appeal through him as His ambassador, literally "beseeching" lost sinners to return to Him through the reconciliation offered in the gospel. "The urgency of his message burned like a fire in his bones; his passion to win men was the divine constraint which gave him no rest."[12] Therefore, Paul "begged" men and women to come to Christ (vs. 20). This is intense language, but given the crucial nature of the gospel, this should not surprise us. The gospel is hardly a take-it-or-leave-it proposition. Our role as ambassadors is to move, persuade and convince; yes, to beg and beseech. The great evangelist George Whitfield once said, "If God did not give me souls, I believe I would die."

But here I must pause to ask myself, "When was the last time I exhibited such intense concern over the soul of a non-believer?" Might it be that we fail to move men because we are not greatly moved ourselves? Might it be that men do not listen because they see no intense concern on our part? Might they continue to grope in their spiritual darkness because we fail to provide spiritual light by speaking the gospel with clarity and boldness befitting the message we are commissioned to communicate? If we don't entreat men and women to be reconciled to God, who will? The church has no competitors in the business of bearing witness to the saving power of the gospel.

Summary

As the late Episcopalian minister Samuel Shoemaker wrote, "The test of a man's conversion is whether he has enough Christianity to get it over to other people. If he hasn't, there is something wrong."[13] More often than we would like to admit, what we do with our time is a valid reflection of our heart convictions. A man who has convictions on evangelism is one whose mind is convinced, whose heart has been gripped by the crucial realities of the eternal issues and whose will has been incited to action.

I am convinced that our passion for souls is not an emotion, but rather a conviction, based on a well-thought-through theology of evangelism. Paul had a four-dimensional conviction that motivated him to keep going in the work of evangelism:

(1) He was convinced that to be involved in evangelism is to obey Jesus' command and is, therefore, a wise investment of one's life.

(2) He was convinced that the love of Christ shown for him on the cross left him no other alternative but to show the same love to others by sharing the good news with them.

(3) He was convinced of the awesome theological reality of heaven, hell and the human responsibility to decide one's fate.

(4) He was convinced that the responsibilities of his ambassadorial calling compelled him to share the gospel clearly and intensely.

Steps to Building Convictions in Evangelism

(1) Do not expect your culture to encourage you to take evangelism seriously. The nature of man's sin problem blinds him to his real needs. Unless the Holy Spirit convicts him, the unregenerate man will at best be indifferent to your attempts to evangelize. You can expect to encounter the built-in opposition to the gospel found in any culture. Recognize this cultural lethargy and unwillingness to pursue spiritual truth, and realize that it is part of the devil's scheme to desensitize the world to its spiritual disease. Do not allow the world to dictate your commitment to proclaiming the gospel.

(2) Purpose in your heart to develop biblical convictions in the area of evangelism. Recognize that this may take time. Allow your mind to dwell on scriptural truths that point toward evangelism's crucial role in God's plans for the world and His plans for you.

CHAPTER 13

Two Philosophies of Evangelism

My wife, Dawnelle, had been pursuing an evangelistic ministry in a dormitory on a midwestern campus. She had been contacting women through a letter of introduction inviting them to meet with her to discuss the gospel. She then visited the ones who expressed an interest.

One afternoon she encountered criticism of her efforts from an unexpected source. A woman who had agreed to meet with her turned out to be a Christian, and she pleasantly but firmly expressed her disapproval of Dawnelle's approach to evangelism. She was concerned that Dawnelle, not having a personal relationship with most of the women she was meeting, was doing more harm than good for the cause of the gospel. She felt that my wife was not the "right person" to be sharing Christ with these women.

Although convinced she was not doing more harm than good, Dawnelle did agree there was a better person for the job. She asked, "Would *you* see that every woman on your floor has a chance to hear the gospel?" The student replied, "No, I don't know how to go about it; besides, I'm not sure I'm even willing." My wife then replied, "Although I'm not the most likely person to reach your friends for Christ, it's because of thinking like yours that people like me have to go about it the way we do."

This conversation typifies the philosophical differences among Christians as to how the work of evangelism should be pursued, whether in a dormitory, in a community or around the world. These differences can be traced to the evangelist's alignment with one of two philosophical approaches to evangelism. My wife, operating in the context of the comprehensive-incarnational school, believed that as many as possible should hear as soon as possible, as clearly as possible. She was thus compelled to initiate meetings with all who would listen, using any legitimate means toward this end. The other woman, operating in the context of the relational-incarnational approach, believed in the superiority of sharing Christ in the context of interpersonal relationships. She believed that to do otherwise, as my wife had done, was improper. (As is so often the case, however, this woman was inexperienced and untrained in evangelism and unwilling to back up her criticism with an alternative that would give her friends a chance to hear the gospel.)

In this chapter we will discuss these two approaches in terms of their theological presuppositions and the practical ramifications of those presuppositions in evangelism, and we will evaluate each from a biblical perspective.

The Relational-Incarnational Approach

The relational-incarnational approach claims this name because it is said to conform its evangelistic practice to the model of the incarnation of Jesus Christ. Those who advocate this approach reason, "When God wanted to communicate with human beings, He didn't hire a skywriter to fill the air with messages. He didn't send us a tract from heaven. Rather, God communicated to us by becoming a man and dwelling among us" (John 1:17).

Indeed, Jesus shared in the human condition. He got tired and thirsty, felt grief and experienced death. The writer of Hebrews states, "Since then the children share in flesh and blood, He Himself likewise also partook of the same" (Hebrews 2:14). The writer continues, "For assuredly He does not give help to angels, but He gives help to the descendant of Abraham. Therefore, He had to be made like His brethren in all things, that He might become a merciful and faithful high priest in things pertaining to God, to make propitiation for the sins of the people. For since He Himself was tempted in that which He has suffered, He is able to come to the aid of those who are tempted" (Hebrews 2:16-18).

Theological Foundation

The point of this passage, at least concerning relational-incarnational evangelism, is that the effective communication of spiritual truth is by necessity personal and relational, since the truth is an actual person, Jesus Himself. The incarnation of Christ was the context in which God chose to communicate and demonstrate spiritual truth to men.

We find Jesus beginning His earthly ministry by "preaching the gospel of God" and saying, "The time is fulfilled, and the kingdom of God is at hand; repent and believe in the gospel" (Mark 1:13,14). But Jesus did more than *say* the truth, He *demonstrated* the truth. His miracles and loving, compassionate service backed up His message.

For example, as Jesus taught in the synagogue at Capernaum, He cast out a demon. As His audience witnessed this miracle, they said to themselves, "What is this? A new teaching with authority! He commands even the unclean spirits and they obey Him" (Mark 1:21-27). The implication is that Jesus' verbal, propositional message was validated by the demonstration of the power of His miracles. What He *did* validated what He *said* to this audience.

Relational-incarnation evangelism is an attempt to integrate Christ's communication model, His incarnation and His ministry, into the work of sharing the gospel. Let us look at the practical application of this approach.

Practical Ramifications

The relational-incarnational school reasons that since the Truth is a person; it is designed to be communicated in the context of the relational and personal. The propositional truth of the gospel message should not be artificially separated from the context of a real person, who bears witness to this truth by manifesting in his own character and relationships Christlike qualities and conduct. An emphasis on propositional content without such demonstration, it is reasoned, is a truncated approach to communication and therefore an ineffective and generally inappropriate approach to communicating the gospel.

The communication principle, "Truth is a person," leads to a very logical result in philosophy and practice of evangelism. Here are some commonly taught principles of evangelism that find their source in this model.

(1) Since effective communication requires *both* content and demonstration (context), then to communicate the gospel effectively, one should do so in the context of a warm, ongoing personal relationship where the messenger's life, demonstrating the power of the gospel, has been witnessed. This makes the gospel more meaningful and believable.

(2) If such a relationship is absent, then the communicator should work to build one so that he can communicate the gospel effectively, i.e., in such a way that makes the gospel meaningful and believable.

(3) To validate the truth and relevence of its content, the gospel must demonstrate its life-changing power in human lives. Therefore, an evangelist must work at "earning the right to be heard" by his audience. He does this by living out the Christian life in their presence, letting his light shine before men in such a way that they may see his good works and glorify his Father who is in heaven (Matthew 5:16).

(4) Since effective communication demands *both* demonstration *and* content, both word *and* deed, then each is considered a legitimate expression of evangelism in its own right. Presence both individual and corporate, it is reasoned, is an aspect of true evangelism, as are proclamation and persuasion. Thus, to evangelize is to be present and *do,* as well as to proclaim, persuade and *speak.*

Given the need of the situation (i.e., the listener is a stranger or has not had the opportunity to see the good news modeled in the life of the messenger or church), it is sometimes necessary just to be silently present to reflect the truth of the gospel. To speak at such times would be a violation of the nonbeliever's spiritual sensitivities, and integrity constituting an inappropriate, ineffective and possibly unethical evangelistic practice. Thus, the development of a presence witness is given sequential priority over proclamation and persuasion as a general rule.

Strengths

I see three major areas of strength in using the relational-in-carnational model of communication in evangelism:

(1) The first strength might be called the friendship factor. Since relational-incarnational evangelism places great emphasis on the cultivation of warm relationships as a platform for evangelism, this opens the way for the development of enduring friendships between Christians and non-Christians. One builds a natural bridge for the gospel. The chances that the nonbeliever will come to a true understanding of the gospel are higher than when a person shares Christ with a stranger. Thus, we are more likely to see a higher percentage of informed decisions for Christ in this context.

The quality context developed in the relational approach also increases the chances for the new Christian to grow in his faith after conversion. He already has at least one friend in God's kingdom, and now he has a readily available and comfortable bridge into the fellowship of the local body of Christ.

(2) The second strength of the incarnational approach is the time factor. There is no rush here. Rome wasn't built in a day and neither are relationships that become fertile soil for the spread of the gospel. Trust must be cultivated. It is not automatic, especially in this day and age. The audience must be given the room to reflect on the quality of life of the evangelist and to begin to make the link between this quality and the truth of the gospel. In an age of hype and empty words, this demonstration of consistency is a welcome relief. The gospel is not just one more message in the already glutted marketplace of ideas. It is

backed up by changed lives, spiritual power, and the love of the evangelist.

(3) Time and friendship combined create an environment factor where the evangelist can be sensitive to the felt needs of the potential believer, to walk in his shoes for a while. We cannot attain a deep discernment of the hopes, fears and spiritual sight of a person without taking time to be a student of his life. This environment breeds trust on the part of the nonbeliever and sensitivity on the part of the evangelist.

The Comprehensive-Incarnational Approach

As the title suggests, this approach to evangelism takes seriously the communication principles and the theological concerns of the relational-incarnational model of evangelism.

Theological Foundations

At the same time, however, this approach seeks to incorporate other theological factors and communication principles, broadening the approach and giving it its comprehensive nature. This approach is based on several theological presuppositions:

(1) The truth of God's saving grace has been incarnated in the person of Jesus Christ, the living Word who became flesh and dwelt among us. Thus, the comprehensive-incarnational approach embraces the spirit and concerns of the relational school, implementing this approach whenever appropriate.

(2) The gospel message, the "word of the cross" (1 Corinthians 1:18), is God's Word of testimony to the saving work of the person of Christ. In this message, God Himself is "powerfully present," for it is the living message of the living, incarnate Christ. It is the light of the gospel of the glory of Christ (2 Corinthians 4:4), and in this gospel, the sinner encounters Christ in all of His saving power. The gospel is the "power of God for salvation" (Romans 1:16). As such, it has the inherent ability to win its own hearing, create its own platform of relevance and engage the hearts of the lost toward the end that sinners, convinced of its truth, can be saved. Thus, theological priority is

placed on the presentation of this Word (proclamation and persuasion).

(3) The Holy Spirit is God's seeking agent in salvation. He works ceaselessly to convict the world of sin, righteousness and judgment (John 16:8-11), and to bear witness in unbelievers' hearts to the grace, truth and saving power of Jesus as the gospel is communicated (1 Thessalonians 1:5). Thus there are always men and women ready to respond to the gospel if they could only hear it proclaimed.

(4) Every Christian is designated an ambassador for Christ and, as part of the local body of believers, he is God's chosen agent to manifest His saving concern for the world by bringing the gospel to the lost. God sovereignly has chosen to equip and use those yielded to His power and purposes in the work of drawing the lost to a saving knowledge of Christ. All believers are called to a maximum mobilization toward this end.

(5) The hope of heaven, the awesome reality of hell, the brevity of life and the responsibility of human decision highlight the urgent nature of the task of evangelism. It is imperative that all appropriate means possible be pursued so that as many as possible will hear as soon as possible and will understand the gospel as clearly as possible.

Practical Ramifications

The following principles of evangelism are grounded in the theological presuppositions of the comprehensive-incarnational approach:

(1) Since the gospel message, in conjunction with the convicting work of the Spirit, is sufficient to produce authentic conversions, legitimate and effective communication of the gospel can and often does take place in a context lacking demonstration, deed, presence and, generally, the relational element. Thus, priority is given to the persuasive-proclamation of the gospel.

(2) Whenever possible, the messenger should make every effort to highlight the harmony that exists between the gospel and the reality of his changed life, pointing to the supernatural

presence of Christ in His messengers and church, and thus enhancing the attractiveness of the gospel to the watching world.

(3) The evangelist is called to commit himself to an evangelistic ministry in which he (a) boldly takes the initiative with *all* who will listen, (b) shares the gospel in a spirit of sensitivity, (c) shares the gospel with a spiritual perception grounded in an understanding of the communication process, and (d) maximizes his impact for Christ by using *every* manner of ethically appropriate, biblically effective strategy and methodology that he can.

(4) It is imperative to mobilize the church for the work of evangelism. To do this, evangelistic training, tools and strategies are employed to ensure that the barriers of fear, inertia, lack of experience and lack of contact with the nonbelieving world are overcome. All believers should be given the opportunity for training in how to engage in evangelistic contact with friends, acquaintances and anyone else who will listen.

Strengths of the Comprehensive Approach

(1) The primary strength of the comprehensive-incarnational approach is its theologically comprehensive nature lending to its effectiveness.

For example, this approach provides a flexible and comprehensive framework for evangelistic ministry. It emphasizes the theological urgency of evangelism. At the same time it emphasizes sensitivity in communication, recognizing man's spiritual blindness and the necessity that he not only hear the gospel but also understand its personal implications.

The comprehensive-incarnational school places an emphasis on both God's role and the Christian's role in evangelism. God's role is (a) to motivate the Christian to go into the harvest fields and (b) to convict and regenerate the lost. The Christian's role is to communicate the gospel boldly and sensitively to all who will listen, giving them an opportunity to make a Spirit-led, intelligent decision for Christ.

(2) The second strength of the comprehensive-incarnational approach is that, while taking to heart the strengths of the

relational-incarnational school, it goes beyond the scope of this approach and seeks to reach those who are beyond the influence of a loving relationship with a Christian or the visible expression of the body of Christ.

As we have noted, the comprehensive approach assumes the sufficiency of the power of the gospel and convicting ministry of the Spirit to elicit a saving response from the lost. Thus, the evangelist knows that, while the "relationally contextualized," gospel may be *ideal,* the joyful truth is that the supernatural power of God's Word and Spirit do not make this a theological or practical necessity. I do not mean to downplay the relational context, but rather to emphasize the will and the awesome power of God to save sinners. He is able to use any human yielded to His purposes and power, no matter how "relationally unlikely" that person may be.

The comprehensive approach acknowledges that the scope of one's ministry is not defined by relational concerns, but by the necessity that God be glorified in the preaching of the gospel to "all nations" (Matthew 28:18-20).

(3) The comprehensive-incarnational approach embraces all means to reach all men. It acknowledges that many methods of doing evangelism are biblically sound and effective in practice. Hence strategy, training, tools and evangelistic techniques are readily utilized to enhance the effectiveness of the church. Because of this multifaceted approach, many who would not be mobilized by the relational approach are exposed to actual "frontline" evangelistic experience.

The comprehensive-incarnational approach is grounded in the New Testament data on evangelism and those theological concerns touching on the evangelistic enterprise. Within this context every effort is made to ensure that as many as possible will hear as soon as possible and understand the good news clearly.

Covering Some Tracks

It is not this author's intention in this or the next chapter to erect a "straw man," a relational evangelist, and then proceed to set fire to him. Therefore, let me make a few things clear.

I do not want to give the impression that everyone in each of these two schools is equally committed to all aspects of this philosophy and approach. There is ample room for variety and even disagreement among those in each school. Therefore, when I state that the relational or comprehensive schools adhere to a certain position, I mean that this a generally held position — not a hard and fast rule adhered to by 100% of those aligned with that approach.

Nor am I saying that each school is mutually exclusive and inherently at odds with the other. It's quite possible that some who are more aligned with the relational approach, in its presuppositions and application to evangelism, would be flexible enough to agree philosophically with, if not practice, some of the principles of comprehensive evangelism.

By definition, those who align themselves with the comprehensive approach embrace the spirit of the relational approach, seeing it as an effective, and at times, even the most appropriate, means of sharing the gospel. But they are compelled by the great need for all men to hear the gospel to go beyond this approach to embrace a more comprehensive scope of ministry and methodology.

But, with all this in mind, the fact remains that there are significant differences in evangelistic practice between these two schools. Let's take a look at this in the next chapter.

CHAPTER 14

Philosophy in Conflict

T he story of my wife and the student is not an isolated incident. My personal evangelistic efforts have been challenged time and time again by those who felt that taking the initiative to share Christ with a stranger and using a tool to communicate the gospel were at best ineffective and at worst damaging to the work of evangelism. This is perfectly understandable. For, given their relational-incarnational presuppositions, much of the boldness, strategy and methodology of the comprehensive-incarnational approach, is suspect.

Specific Points of Tension

Most of the tension in evangelistic philosophy and practice revolves around the issues of effectiveness and ethics. Let us take a look at these two issues in relationship to the two schools of approach.

Effectiveness in Communication

The relational-incarnational school suggests that evangelism done outside of a relational context is suspect as biblically deficient and an ineffective form of communication. David Wells, though not writing for the purpose of defending this perspective, nonetheless expresses the concern well. He writes, "The preaching of the gospel is not, then, a matter simply of blitzing the air waves or of impersonally distributing tracts. Christian salvation cannot legitimately be offered when it is severed from the life view in which it finds its context and meaning. And this framework cannot be reduced to brief slogans, isolated biblical texts or snappy bumper stickers."[1]

The relational school is concerned that evangelism attempted outside the framework of a relational element is "severed" from the authenticating power, relevence and meaning of the life of Christ, as manifested in the life of the evangelist. This is not a "legitimate" offer of the gospel and, therefore, would fall short of the standard of effective communication as modeled by Christ.

The relational approach reasons that such evangelism fails to place the gospel in the meaningful "life context" of the values and transformed character of the messenger. Such an approach fails to earn the trust of the nonbeliever and never gives the evangelist the chance to deal sensitively with the real concerns and issues in the non-Christian's life. Such evangelism is more than likely to fail. One auther labels non-relational, initiative evangelism as "confrontational/intrusional" evangelism. While he affirms that this is a legitimate biblical practice, he observes, "Many are being kept from making an effective decision because of bad experiences with a zealous, but insensitive witness."[2] Art McPhee asks, "Would it not, therefore, be much more . . . effective to share the Good News out of a relationship of trust, based on friendship?"[3]

Thus, evangelistic practices that emphasize taking the initiative to share Christ with strangers or acquaintances, where no relationship of trust has been established, are considered to be outside the framework of a biblically effective pattern of communication.

Ethics in Communication

The second point of contention concerns the ethical dimension of evangelistic practice. Those favoring the relational-incarnation approach believe that evangelistic practice which relies on strategy, methodology and tools to provide the point of contact with nonbelievers is subject to ethical criticism. The Christian using a tool, or relying on a systematic, strategic, initiative-taking approach to communicate the gospel, is said to be violating the listener's integrity.

James Jauncey writes, "Just buttonholing a stranger, witnessing to him and pressing for a decision will likely do more harm than good. Most responsible people react negatively and often quite violently to this kind of assault. It shows a fundamental lack of respect for human dignity and personality."[4]

Aldrich believes that "confrontational-intrusional" evangelism will often lead to a decision for Christ that is motivated by "manipulation, fear or the need to get rid of the evangelist."[5]

Church visitation evangelism, which relies on strategy and initiative in contacting nonbelievers, rather than on building relationships, is said to have its roots closer to Madison Avenue than to the New Testament. The manipulative spirit of the advertising world, which uses trickery, entrapment and deceit, is said to typify such approaches. Evangelism that dares to confront strangers using a strategy, method or tool is a "clever, quick-sell scheme,"[6] a hard-sell approach that attempts to force the gospel on presumably unwilling, unwitting listeners.

How should those who are involved in the strategies and methodologies grounded in comprehensive evangelisim respond to such thinking? Are not many of these concerns valid?

I greatly respect the concerns raised by these authors. Nevertheless, I feel some inherent shortcomings of the relational-incarnation approach and their criticism of evangelistic practice grounded in the comprehensive school must be pointed out. Those who are involved in comprehensive-incarnational evangelism need not grow discouraged in their efforts or think that they are involved in second-class, ethically suspect or ineffective evangelistic practice.

The Use of Rhetoric

Rhetoric is "the art of using language so as to persuade or influence others . . . language characterized by artificial or ostentatious expression." Rhetorical speech is contrasted to "sober statement or argument."[7]

It is obvious that some in the relational-incarnation school resort to the use of rhetoric in taking issue with the methodologies grounded in the comprehensive approach. Evangelists are said to "blitz," not "program" the airwaves with Christian messages. Tracts are "impersonally distributed," not "handed out with a smile and a prayer." Taking the initiative to share Christ outside of a relational context is pejoratively labelled "confrontation" or "intrusion."

Using methods and tools is "artificial and contrived," implying that their users are participating in a shallow, premeditated attempt to manipulate the nonbeliever. Methods, tools and simple strategies for proclaiming the good news are described as "slick," coated with a Madison Avenue veneer. Words such as "stilted," "rigid," and "rote" are also used to describe such methods, implying that the one who would stoop to use them is either misinformed or a non-thinking, uncreative person.

What ethically sensitive Christian under the lordship of Christ would want to touch such evangelism? If this were the reality of the situation, we would be ethically *obligated* to drop nonrelational, initiative-oriented evangelistism like a hot potato. But these rhetorical criticisms are, in most cases, exaggerations. The descriptions are meant to persuade, not inform; to move one to action-based emotions, not to stimulate thought and sober analysis of presuppositions, theology and practice. They are meant to make a point: If you want to refrain from committing ethical atrocities, if you want to be effective in evangelistic communication, stay with the relational approach or start using it right away.

Rhetoric persuades with power because it is grounded in a kernel of truth. It is not an outright fabrication, but rather, an exaggeration of the facts. Have there been instances of nonbelievers feeling offended, deceived, manipulated, or talked at instead of to because of well-meaning but poorly practiced nonrelational methodology? Of course there have. But it is one thing to say that such situations have occurred and quite another to maintain that they are exclusively inherent to and inevitable in the nonrelational approach. Neither approach is free from criticism on these points.

The False Dichotomy

Closely related to rhetoric is the use of false dichotomy. This is a classic form of persuasive communication. While rhetoric relies on exaggeration, the false dichotomy resorts to oversimplification.

The false dichotomy is thinking that insists on viewing situations as either/or issues instead of both/and issues. Two categories are set in opposition to each other with little or no possibility of combination or integration. You must be on one track or the other, black or white, the high road or the low road, but you cannot be on both. Such dualism betrays a lack of perception of the complexity of certain issues and the ability of humans to appreciate the ambiguities and multidimensional nature of such issues. The relational-incarnational approach has typically displayed such binary thinking by erecting a false dichotomy in two areas of evangelistic practice.

People Versus Programs

Evangelistic practices that widely use strategy and tools to contact nonbelievers and to enhance the communication process cut at the very heart of the relational approach. "Techniques aren't the most effective, especially for friends," says Becky Pippert. She adds that "techniques can be helpful to some people in limited ways, but they will not make us natural."[8] And of course, we all want to communicate our faith naturally instead of seeming artificial or contrived.

It is people or programs. Becoming programmatic (using strategies, tools and methods as bridges to initiate contact and communication) would make one so slavishly dependent on the tools and a rigid methodology, that he would be unlikely to relate naturally or sensitively to the listener as a real human being. Methods unnecessarily inhibit the communication process and serve only to "put off" the hearer. So we are left with two choices: (1) Use an "artificial" or "contrived" technique; or (2) choose the high road of "naturalness" and shun witnessing technique and tools.

This is false dichotomy at its best. It completely ignores a third option, to be committed *both* to people *and* to a method as a *means* of communicating more naturally with a person. There is no inherent contradiction between methodology and a natural, way-of-life approach. In fact, they are a powerful combination which contributes to our personal and corporate evangelistic effectiveness. (We will consider this further in Chapter 20, "A Strategy for Every-Member Mobilization.")

Like rhetoric, false dichotomy is usually based on a kernel of truth. Can a method be used to trample on the sensitivities of otherwise spiritually open nonbelievers? Of course it can. Can a gospel tract degenerate into a mere formula, to be impersonally imposed upon the hearer with no thought given to dialogue? Of course it can. Such practices probably happen every day, and those of the relational mindset are to be commended for wanting to avoid such problems. Implying that methods are likely to be ineffective, however, is not the answer. The real solution is the *proper use* of methods and tools.

Boldness Versus Sensitivity

The second area of false dichotomy is the supposition that boldness and sensitivity are mutually exclusive. As we have noted, sensitivity, trust and the testimony of a changed life all find ample room for expression in a relational framework.

But the reasoning is taken one step further this say that these qualities are likely to find normative expression *only* in the relational framework. How can the evangelist be sensitive toward a stranger with whom he has boldly initiated contact by means of a strategy or method? "Boldness must necessarily run roughshod over a sensitive dialogue grounded in trust," it is reasoned.

The relational evangelist thus ascribes the qualities of impatience and insensivity to boldness. Boldness in evangelism would be "confrontational and intrusional," forcing a monologue, rather than dialogue. It would provide little or no platform on which to begin a true conversation touching on sensitive spiritual issues. Thus, initiating contact with strangers and attempting to communicate the gospel outside of a relational context is considered inherently insensitive and less than biblically effective communication.

Once again, it is not as simple as that. We can be *both* bold *and* sensitive, for sensitive, authentic and effective communication *does* happen outside of a relational context. As C. E. Autrey stated, "Every experienced soul winner has seen men, women and children make decisions for Christ the very first time they were ever approached on the matter. These decisions were genuine and the life lived afterwards proved it."[9]

A true biblical boldness, as we have discussed from the life of Paul, is committed to sensitive interaction with the hearers. The relational approach has not "cornered the market" on sensitivity. As we will discuss later, anyone committed to relevance, sensitivity and listening can achieve effective communication regardless of his relational status with the listener.

Calling the Part the Whole

The third error in relational reasoning might be termed "calling the part the whole." Such thinking is grounded in the assumption that one's attitudes and presuppositions encompass *all* that is relevant to a particular topic. Such thinking usually leads one to reason, "If it is different, or beyond my experience, it is wrong, or at best, suspect." This mindset is at odds with the spirit of comprehensiveness, which believes that one's opinion and experience are not the final word, but only part of a bigger picture.

Many from the relational-incarnational approach fail to recognize that there is indeed effective and sensitive evangelistic life beyond its borders. Of course, I am not calling for a comprehensiveness with no limits. As I have argued, one's practice of evangelism must be grounded in an appreciation of the ethical and theological limits set by Scripture. But biblical theology and practice is the *only* limit to be placed on our philosophy and practice of evangelism. I would, therefore, reserve the term "comprehensively biblical" only for the comprehensive-incarnational approach to evangelism.

It is not that the relational school and its resulting philosophy and practice are unbiblical; there is ample evidence in the New Testament to support this approach. But the relational approach cannot bear the weight of the label "biblically comprehensive." As a philosophy of evangelism, grounded in a presuppositional base, it has a tendency to confine legitimate and effective evangelism to a range of practice that is limited by its relational, ethical and communication concerns. Thus, it errs in calling the part the whole. This error in logic is what lies behind the rejection and/or lack of appreciation for the broad range of evangelistic approaches that find their rationale in the comprehensive mindset. Even more serious, however, the relational-incarnational school finds little room for some crucial theological considerations.

Lack of Urgency

The issue of urgency is not often seen in the relational scheme of things. One author writes that the relational-incarnational method is effective in that it "frees the Christian from unnecessary (and often unbiblical) pressure." This results in a strategy that is "low pressure and long range."[10] Earl Palmer states, "Evangelism, like sanctification, takes time. Threfore, we must take the time it takes. When we relate to people, we must remind ourselves that we are on a long journey together. The idea that this is my only chance to talk to this person is a great detriment."[11]

While it is true that we would not want our sense of urgency in communicating the gospel to be expressed at the expense of sensitivity and an appreciation for developing relationships, we must realize that we are dealing with matters of heaven and hell in evangelism. A biblically grounded sense of urgency carries with it the concerns of time, intensity and comprehensiveness.

Paul wrote, "Behold, now is the 'acceptable time,' behold, now is the "day of salvation'" (2 Corinthians 6:2). Paul is saying that the new age is here in Christ. The gift of forgiveness of sins and the Holy Spirit are available. There is no such thing as "business as usual" now that Jesus has died and has risen from the dead. One's *eternal destiny* is at stake. What could be more urgent?

Paul, understanding the urgency of the hour, exhibited a corresponding intensity in his evangelistic appeal. He wrote that God is "*entreating* through us; we *beg* you in behalf of Christ, be reconciled to God" (2 Corinthians 5:20). The hour is urgent; therefore, my evangelistic appeal must manifest a corresponding intensity.

Paul, grasping the scope of the evangelistic task, also wrote, "I have become *all* things to *all* men, that I may by *all* means save some" (1 Corinthians 9:22). Paul's concern was not limited only to those he could reach with a minimum of inconvenience. He was committed to doing whatever it took to "save some." The idea that for evangelism to be effective, it must be done in the context of personal relationships, or in the context of the nonbelievers' exposure to a living fellowship of the body of Christ, cannot bear the burden of the theological elements of time, intensity and the scope of the evangelistic enterprise.

There are just too many people who need to know Christ as soon as possible to insist that effective evangelism must be relational in approach. Not everyone is blessed to have Christian friends who can "flesh out" the life of Christ. Not everyone is fortunate enough to witness the life-changing power of the gospel and new life in Christ as it is manifested corporately in the local church.

Thus, a philosophy of evangelism that insists on the presence of a relational element (as a normative practice) will unfortunately exclude those not privileged to have meaningful exposure to Christian friends or the corporate witness of the church. This is why many groups practice initiative evangelism and employ strategies that encompass masses of people. It is not that they are against the relational element in evangelism, but they do not allow it to determine the scope of their outreach. Let's reach our friends. Let's do whatever it takes to communicate authentically to them. But let's not forget that others also need to hear the gospel.

The Identification Factor

It is obvious from our discussion of New Testament evangelism that the early church sought to cultivate a conducive context for the preaching of the gospel. They worked hard to identify with their audience, even to the radical extreme of Paul who desired "to become all things to all men."

We need to go where the lost are, engage them on their own ground, speak to them in their own language, understand their concerns, hopes and dreams. We are reminded that "Jesus Christ was crucified not in a cathedral between two candles, but on a cross between two thieves on the town garbage heap; at a crossroad so cosmopolitan that they had to write His title in Hebrew, and in Latin and in Greek; at the kind of place where cynics talk smut and thieves curse and soldiers gamble."[12] Jesus ate with prostitutes and sinners. He walked in the heat, filth and disease of the first-century world. He confronted demons, cried when a close friend died and participated in the joy of a wedding party. He stretched out His hand to bless children and to cleanse a leper. Jesus identified with us, that we might receive His grace and love. He came to call sinners, and to call them it was necessary to be in contact with them. Thus, to follow in Jesus' footsteps is to "seek the lost," to identify with those whom we must reach. But what does this mean in terms of a philosophy and practice of evangelism?

Does identification with one's audience necessarily place the burden of the relational factor on the evangelist? I believe not. As Figure 3 shows, identification with one's audience includes, but is not limited to, the relational context. A knowledge of cultural thought patterns, language and the human condition from a biblical perspective are all facets of the broad concerns of identification. The core of identification is our common humanity. As one person created by God in His image and sharing in the certainties of the human condition (death, fear, guilt, alienation, loneliness), I have a right to speak to another person, created by the same God and sharing in the same human predicament. If our common humanity served as the *only* point of contact, I would still have significant identification with my listener.

FIGURE 3
DIMENSIONS OF IDENTIFICATION

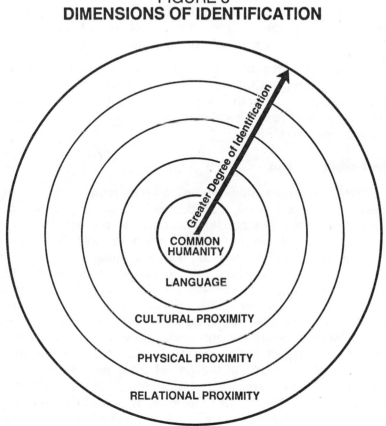

Common Humanity—our shared image of God and the human situation.

Language—the ability to verbalize the gospel to the listener in words he can understand clearly.

Cultural Proximity—insight and empathy into the listener's cultural operating assumptions (secular, misdirected religious and nominalist) that influence response to the gospel.

Physical Proximity—our availability to interact with the listener on a regular basis.

Relationship Proximity—our level of intimacy with the listener, leading to insight into his personal decision-making process, his spiritual preparedness and his general response pattern to the gospel.

Of course, language identification is also necessary for the effective communication of the gospel. At Pentecost, many people heard the gospel for the first time in their own language, and they became the first converts to the church (Acts 2:5-12).

The first two identification categories, common humanity and language comprehension, are *essential* to the effective communication of the gospel, but the categories of cultural values, physical proximity, and relational proximity are matters of degree of *effectiveness,* not necessities.

The Gospel Content

Relational-identification is ideal, and therefore to be heartily pursued in the communication process whenever possible, but it is not theologically mandatory in order to present the saving truth of the gospel effectively. Nor is it a *prerequisite* for effective communication of spiritual truth. This reasoning is grounded in the New Testament teaching on the nature of the gospel and work of the Spirit. The real issue is, does effective evangelism *require* an authenticating human context? Most in the relational school answer yes. One author states, "Christians are to be good news before they share the good news. The words of the gospel are to be incarnated *before* they are verbalized. Let me put it another way. The music of the gospel must *precede* the words of the gospel and prepare the context in which there will be a hunger for those words." This music of the gospel is "the beauty of the indwelling Christ as lived out in the everyday relationships of life"[13] (emphasis added). I believe, however, that this emphasis on the life and relationships of the messenger, while in one respect is quite healthy, at the same time does not give due credit to the truth of the self-authenticiating nature of the gospel.

Acts 17:1-4 and 1 Thessalonians 1:1-6 give us the context of Paul's proclamation of the gospel in Thessalonica. Paul walked into town a total stranger, but soon the gospel itself began to create its own context of authority, relevance and power. 1 Thessalonians 1:5 states, "For our gospel did not come to you in word only, but also in power and in the Holy Spirit and with full conviction; just as you know what kind of men we proved to be among you for your sake."

Here we have the three key ingredients of context, which took the gospel message from the realm of "word only" (or the word of men) and authenticated it as "the word of God, which also performs its work in you who believe" (1 Thessalonians 2:13).

(1) The first ingredient is the power of the Holy Spirit. In 1 Thessalonians 1:5, Paul probably was referring to the fact that his gospel preaching was validated by the Spirit's powerful work in the midst of the Thessalonians. Romans 15:19 says that Paul preached the gospel "in the power of signs and wonders, in the power of the Spirit."

In Acts 14:3, Luke says of Paul's witness in Iconium, "Therefore, they spent a long time there speaking boldly with reliance upon the Lord, who was bearing witness to the word of His grace, granting that signs and wonders be done by their hands." Whatever these attesting miracles were, it is clear that the awe-inspiring presence of God was evident as Paul delivered the gospel. (See also 1 Corinthians 2:4.) The Spirit's witness is necessary if the gospel is to be perceived by the audience as the message of God.

(2) The second ingredient is the gospel's ability to bring "full conviction" as it is preached. The gospel has the power to convince. It is the truth. The gospel penetrates the "thoughts and intentions of the heart." It is "living and active and sharper than any two-edged sword" (Hebrews 4:12). It "performs its work in those who believe" (1 Thessalonians 2:13), and the result is "full conviction" (1 Thessalonians 1:5). As the Holy Spirit convicts men of their sin, the possibility of right standing with God, and judgment if they refuse Christ's offer of salvation, a need is created in their hearts that the gospel alone is designed to meet. It is the perfect cure for the now-revealed illness. The hearer finds himself with a mind convinced of the truth of the gospel message because of the "ring of truth" and self-evident authenticity of the message.

(3) The third ingredient in the gospel context is the evidence of the lives of Paul, Silas and Timothy, the "kind of men we proved to be among you for your sake." Paul was convinced that effective communication was grounded in two factors, truth and

personality. He shared not only the gospel, but also his own life with the Thessalonians (1 Thessalonians 2:6).

But the real issue is the relationship of the gospel to one's life, and the priority of each in the spiritual communication process. This is the point of contention between the relational and comprehensive schools.

The relational school suggests communication of the gospel through two channels of *equal* priority, the gospel and the evangelist's life. But I would suggest an analogy from the world of music: the relationship between a song's melody and harmony. The melody is the organized succession of tones, the musical structure that makes one song recognizable from another and memorable to the listener. As such, the melody stands on its own. The harmony is a set of additional notes whose sole purpose is to enhance the musical beauty of the melody. It is meaningful only in relationship to the melody and, of course, cannot stand on its own. In the same way, the gospel is the melody. It can stand on its own; it is recognizable and memorable. Our lives are the harmony, enhancing and beautifying the gospel, but meaningful only as they relate to it. Paul's life did not *produce* the power and conviction experienced by his converts; only the Spirit and Word could do that. But his life was in *harmony* with the "melody" of the gospel.

Thus the Spirit and the Word produce the power and conviction necessary or a context of authentic communication and true understanding leading to conversion. The gospel creates its own platform for effectiveness. It calls attention to itself; it earns its *own* right to be heard.

We have now covered the errors of using rhetoric and false dichotomy, and calling the part the whole. The last area of improper reasoning in this approach is what I call false comparison.

The False Comparison

Many in the relational-incarnational school suggest a one-to-one relationship between Christ's ability to incarnate the life-changing power and moral character of the gospel and our ability, as His children, to do so. Jesus' very presence is said to have been evangelistic. He did not just *bring* the word of truth; He *was* the word of truth. He did not just preach the gospel; He was the gospel and, of course, still is the gospel. Therefore, *my* presence (life, character and service) could also be termed "evangelistic" since I bear witness of Jesus as I live out a lifestyle that reflects His presence. By implication then, living the Christian life in character, fellowship and service is as valid a form of evangelism as is sharing the gospel. In line with such reasoning, one author wrote, "Perhaps we don't have a big enough definition of evangelism. When I say 'evangelism' I mean not only verbal proclamation but visual proclamation as well: the whole disclosure of God in the world."[14]

Joe Aldrich, an articulate spokesman for this position, has written, "In the truest sense, evangelism is displaying the universals of God's character — His love, His righteousness, His justice and His faithfulness through the particulars of my everyday life. Therefore, evangelism is not a 'special' activity to be undertaken at a prescribed time. It is the constant and spontaneous overflow of our individual and corporate experience of Christ." He concludes that "even more specifically, evangelism is what Christ does through the activity of His children as they are involved in (1) proclamation, (2) fellowship, and (3) service."[15]

Thus, true evangelism is seen as not only the communication of the gospel, but also the "fellowship" and "service" of the saints. As we can see, the one-to-one comparison of a person's life to the life of Christ would lead logically to a one-to-one comparison of that life (fellowship and service) to the gospel of Jesus Christ (proclamation). *Both* are presumed to be efficient conveyors of good news and, therefore, evangelistic in nature. As Aldrich states, "Evangelism, then, is stereophonic. God speaks to His creatures through two channels: the written word and you, His 'living epistle,' His 'good seed.'"[16]

But what are we to make of such a comparison? I believe that this reasoning errs in two major areas. First, it is grounded in a misunderstanding of the technical, biblical definitions of *witness* and *evangelism* which leads to an artificial distinction between those terms. It is reasoned that "as long as a man simply tells another about Jesus, he is a witness. But the moment he tries to get that person to do something with Christ, he leaves the realm of witnessing and enters the province of soul winning, i.e., one who seeks to 'manipulate a prospect into doing anything with Christ.'"[17] Thus, "witnessing and soul winning are two different specialities," and the teaching that "evangelism equals soul winning" can lead only to unhealthy evangelistic models to the hurt of the evangelistic enterprise.[18]

I believe that such reasoning misses the point of the New Testament teaching on the nature and activity of the witness and of evangelism. It is technically incorrect to broaden, and therefore dilute, the New Testament meaning of witness by including a nonverbal, nonpersuasive ministry of "being light to the world" and/or a verbal testimony to Christ with no emphasis on the decisive nature of the gospel.

To be a witness, in Luke's terminology, means "to bear witness in the sense of proclaiming Christ" (Acts 4:33; 23:11). Luke 24:48 and Acts 1:8 indicate that the apostles were witnesses, having been "commissioned by the Lord with the proclamation of the message of the kingdom."[19]

In Acts, the verb (to witness) is used in solemnly declaring and attesting the apostolic preaching in order to win a favorable verdict from the hearers (Acts 2:40; 8:25; 20:24).[20]

Thus, Luke uses this word in the sense of giving "the full proclamation of the message of Christ," the "testimony to Jesus as the Christ (Acts 18:5), the proclamation of the grace of God (Acts 20:24), [and] the urgently wooing address of the gospel of Christ."[21]

It is not surprising that in this context of bearing witness (Acts 28:23), Paul also saw fit to "convince" or "persuade" nonbelievers to come to Christ. "The term witness suggests something of the atmosphere of a trial, a lawsuit between Christ and the world, in which the apostles are witnesses."[22]

Thus, the role of the biblical witness to Christ and the gospel is (1) to acquaint himself thoroughly with the facts of the case, i.e., the historical gospel information; (2) to deliver the facts faithfully, regardless of the circumstances or unpopularity of the facts, i.e., to be ready to suffer unjustly; and (3) to describe the meaning and significance of the facts to others with a passionate persuasiveness. The concept of a biblical witness is placed firmly in the context of persuasive proclamation of the gospel and is to be identified biblically with soul winning — asking someone to do something with Christ. The apostolic witness was intended to elicit a response. They preached, as Bunyun put it, what they "smartingly did feel." Our witness can do no less.

In looking at the second error of this false comparison, it is plain from our previous discussion on the definition of both "gospel" and "evangelism,"[23] that neither of these terms allows for the nonverbal/nonpersuasive "service" and "fellowship" of the saints to be included under the technical definition of evangelism. While the methodology of first-century evangelism was indeed flexible, the definition of what constituted true evangelism was narrow and precise. Evangelism *is* soul winning. It is the proclamation of the gospel with a view to persuading lost men and women to come to Christ. Anything less is not evangelism.

Divine Channels?

The one-to-one comparison assumes that both one's life and the gospel are divine channels through which the living Christ is communicated with saving benefit to the nonbeliever. While I would never want to minimize the crucial role of the quality of life of the one bearing witness to the gospel, we must ask, "Is the one-to-one comparison valid?" I believe the answer is no.

Jesus was the perfect, sinless Word of God incarnate. In Him all the fullness of God dwelt in bodily form (Colossians 1:19). He was the gospel itself. In like manner, the gospel is the light of the glory of Christ (2 Corinthians 4:4), and the power of God for salvation (Romans 1:16). But we fall far short of this. True, we are in the process of being renewed into His image (2 Corinthians 3:18), and we will manifest, *to a degree,* the character and service given us by Christ.

But we must keep in mind that we are limited in our reflection of the glory of God in the face of Christ, due to our continued fallenness. Our lives, character and service do not bear witness to the glory and saving presence of Christ on a level equal to that of the self-authenticating power and authority of the gospel. Our lives do not do justice to the nature and intent of true evangelism. Here are some reasons.

Our lives, in the process of sanctification, cannot bear the burden of purity, truth and glory inherent in the gospel. As Alan Walker commented, "A serious fallacy has spread through the church today. It is the so called presence concept. While valuable as a protest against too great a trust in merely verbalizing the gospel, the presence concept is a danger as a half truth. The presence idea is the reappearance of one of the worst features of the liberal era of theology. It claims that it is only necessary to be kind and good, to be concerned. The presence idea is filled with pharisaism, a pharisaism which claims that quality of life can be so transparent that Christ shines through. It is a denial of the evangelical faith which believes that a man must, through repentance and faith, be brought to a saving knowledge of Jesus Christ."[24]

The idea that "I don't speak, I let my life do the talking" or "I shouldn't speak until my life has done some talking" forces us to ask, "Whose life is good enough for such an assignment?"

Samuel Shoemaker once said, "I cannot by being good, tell men of Jesus' atoning death and resurrection, nor of my faith in His divinity. The emphasis is too much on me, and too little on Him. Our lives must be made as consistent as we can make them with our faith; but our faith, if we are Christians, is vastly greater than our lives. That is why the 'word' of witness is so important."[25]

This subtle shift toward the life of the messenger and away from the content of the gospel is noted by another author: "Relational evangelism, in spite of its good intentions, does not put its emphasis on the hearing of the word ot truth as the necessary kindling which the Holy Spirit ignites in regeneration (Romans 10:17). Relational evangelism's approach can neglect the theological content of the gospel by shifting the focus to the personality and experience of the evangelist."[26]

The "stereophonic" approach (God speaking to the lost *equally* through two channels — you and the gospel) is confusing for the non-Christian. Instead of being exposed to the clear witness of the self-authenticating power and authority of the gospel, he is exposed to its dim reflection in a fallen human life. True, this life *should* be different from that of the unregenerate. But understanding the source of this distinction becomes a burden of spiritual discernment that the non-Christian cannot bear.

How is he to tell the difference between the solid and attractive lifestyle of the Mormon family across the street and that of the evangelical family next door? Both husbands go to church on Sunday with the entire family, treat their kids and wives nicer than does anyone else on the block, are faithful to their wives and are very friendly. They are both against abortion, don't drink or smoke, and are continually mentioning Jesus Christ and their activities at church. How is a spiritually blind, unregenerate man to distinguish between the truth of the gospel and the lie of a cult? Between that which brings eternal life and that which leads to death and destruction? If the lost are to "tune in" on the character and lifestyle of the messenger *before* they hear the gospel, and if this channel is considered to be on a par with the gospel message channel, then I must argue that the lost will not have access to the clear information they need on which to base any sort of eternal decision. At best, they will pick up "static" when the life of the messenger falls short (which is inevitable for all of us) and contradicts his perfect message. How can we expect the non-believer to know that we are a reflection of the good news until they know what the good news is?

Even the most perfect life ever lived was radically misunderstood by many in His audience. Jesus manifested the very life of God, yet was rejected and put to death by His own countrymen. The pagan neighbors of Peter's audience unjustly slandered the Christians as "evil doers." This should convince us of the limits of letting our lives speak for the gospel or of placing the testimony of our lives on a par with the gospel. The gospel is too important to be left to the uncertainties and insufficiencies of human character and behavior. It must be allowed to speak for itself in all its power and authority.

The Difference It Makes

The relational school in general has a built-in aversion to methodology, technique, tools and systematic strategy. The practical result of this, I believe, is illustrated in a story told about D. L. Moody. One evening after a crusade meeting, Moody was confronted by an irate man who challenged his methods in bringing the gospel to non-Christians. Moody calmly asked him, "Tell me, what methods do you use in doing evangelism?" "I don't do evangelism," responded the man. To which Moody replied, "Well, I think I like the way I do it better than the way you don't."

Moody's experience is still common today. Usually those critical of methods offer none as a better alternative. Carl Henry observes, "Every method of not evangelizing is wrong — and many methods of evangelizing are right."[27] As Benjamin Disraeli once said, "It's easier to be critical than correct."

The avoidance of methods can lead easily to the inactivity of paralysis. It is no accident that where you find an emphasis on *how* to do evangelism, there you will also find people *doing* evangelism. The reason is that it has been made easier through the availability of a simple strategy and method. The questions, "How do I start, and how do I communicate the gospel clearly?" have been answered. The usual doubts and fears about sharing the gospel have been substantially resolved, enabling the once inactive believer to take his first concrete steps in evangelism.

It is also no accident that, generally, where you do not find a method, there you will not find the widespread practice of evangelism. Only those who are by nature creative and outgoing will find the resolve to overcome their fear and inertia and engage in evangelism. The rest will be paralyzed by the simple question, *How* do I go about doing this?" Evangelism may be much discussed and positively reinforced but, in the final analysis, little is done. While we need to be flexible in our methods and avoid building a monument to any one approach, we also need to realize that a method is often the difference between doing evangelism and just talking about it.

The Relational Short-Circuit

While it is not the intent of those who lead the way in relational evangelism, emphasis on the evangelist's quality of life and his relationships with non-Christians can be misapplied easily to the practice of evangelism.

First, the emphasis on sharing the gospel in the context of a warm, ongoing relationship is easily misinterpreted by the one overcome by the cultural undertow of convenience and comfort to mean that no initiative need be taken to verbalize the good news. To fulfill our calling as ambassadors, we only need to engage in a friendly relationship with a non-believer and point generally to Jesus. But the claim that everything we do is evangelism, or that developing relationships is evangelism, is often a cover-up for a witness that is so vague that *nothing* we do is evangelism. Such thinking can degenerate easily into a philosophy of evangelism that elevates the cultivation of relationships above the theological concerns of the urgent and crucial nature of the gospel.

The spirit of convenience can creep in here. If evangelism is hard, creates tension and is subject to rejection, such a "rocking of the boat" is to be avoided, lest it jeopardize the relationship. What is sacrificed is a clear presentation of the gospel and the call to decision. The end result is inactivity and/or verbal reticence in the name of sensitivity and relationship building.

Second, this reasoning severely limits the scope of evangelism to encompass only those non-Christians to whom the evangelist can relate in an atmosphere of ease and harmony and in a convenient manner. The majority of non-Christians will be excluded from one's realm of witness.

In summary, a lack of a comprehensive mindset leads to an unfamiliarity with, if not rejection of, theological concerns and practical methodology that encourage the *doing* of evangelism. Evangelism is nothing if it is not done. The gospel is powerless to change lives if left untold.

CHAPTER 15

Putting the Go in the Gospel

T he New Testament data on the theology and practice of evangelism should serve notice to the Christian that these truths must be incorporated into one's life. Such is the task of developing a personal philosophy of evangelism.

We might define a philosophy of evangelism as a *consistent, biblically informed pattern of communicating the good news to those outside of the kingdom of God.* We are commanded to be faithful to our Master and bring glory to His name by bearing much fruit in the work of evangelism. Therefore, a philosophy of evangelism is not a luxury reserved for those given to theological contemplation. It is a necessity for every Christian.

I believe that there are three essential questions we must ask, for their answers form the foundation for a biblical philosophy and practice of evangelism:

(1) *Does the New Testament teach it?* Is my approach to evangelism grounded in theological convictions regarding salvation, the gospel and evangelism? Is it grounded in the certainties of God's plan to redeem a lost creation, the lostness of man and responsibilities of our ambassadorship?

(2) *Did the first-century church demonstrate it?* Has my philosophy and practice of evangelism been modeled by the

first-century church? Have the theological realities that drove the first-century church to proclaim the gospel with boldness and sensitivity caused me to develop similar patterns for communicating my faith?

(3) *Does it work?* Does my philosophy and practice of evangelism make me effective in getting the gospel out to as many as possible, as soon as possible and as clearly as possible?

Our personal approach to evangelism must be grounded in a concern for biblical theology, biblical practice and biblical effectiveness.

Boldness in Evangelism

I believe that a biblical philosophy of evangelism will compel us to commit ourselves to boldness and to taking the initiative. What does it mean to be bold in evangelism? Does it mean to drive through the streets of your town announcing the gospel through a bullhorn? Should you stand up on a table in your cafeteria at work and challenge the audience to repent and believe the gospel? Is it modeled by someone like John the Baptist crying in the wilderness, or Stephen just before he was stoned, or Paul before he was run out of the synagogue?

Unfortunately, the mental images conjured up by the words "bold" or "aggressive" are usually associated with conflict and confrontation, or with awkward social situations that offend nonbelievers. But the concept of aggressive evangelism deserves better. It must be lifted out of the pit of misunderstanding and emotional considerations and placed in its proper biblical context.

Biblical Boldness

The Greek word for boldness is *parresia,* meaning "outspokenness, frankness, plainness of speech that conceals nothing and passes over nothing".[1] The verb *parresiazomai* means "to speak boldly" and is always used in the New Testament in connection with speaking the gospel message.

This word is used in Acts 9:27,28; 13:46; 14:3; Ephesians 6:19,20; and 1 Thessalonians 2:2 to describe Paul's courage and confidence as he preached the gospel at the risk of great personal harm. This same word is used in Acts 18:26 and 19:8 to describe the great openness and clarity with which the gospel is meant to be spoken. Thus, to be bold in evangelism means to speak the gospel courageously, confidently, openly and clearly, free from the constraints of shame and the fear of opposition.

Paul's ministry to the Thessalonians is a perfect example of boldness in action (1 Thessalonians 2:1,2). His visit to Thessalonica, with Silas, had been preceded by great personal suffering in Philippi, where both men had been beaten, flogged and jailed for their proclamation of the gospel (Acts 16:12-40). As one commentator puts it, "Still staggering from these injuries and indignities, the two came to Thessalonica. Under such conditions most people would have refrained from repeating a message that had led to such violent treatment, but not these men. With God's help, they mustered sufficient courage to declare in this new city their gospel from God."[2]

The New International Version translates 1 Thessalonians 2:2: "With the help of God, we *dared* to tell you this gospel in spite of strong opposition." This verse teaches us two things about boldness:

(1) Their boldness led Paul and Silas to action (telling the gospel) in the midst of opposition. Biblical boldness will always lead to the courageous action of telling the gospel no matter what the circumstances might dictate.

(2) This action, however, is not grounded in the emotional makeup or raw courage of the evangelist. Neither is it the boldness of pride or self-assuredness. Rather, it is "with the help of God" or, as the Revised Standard Version states, "We had courage in our God to declare to you the gospel of God." God is the author of such boldness. Boldness is not so much a great act of courage as it is a confidence placed in God's great ability to strengthen the evangelist and confirm the gospel message in the midst of trying circumstances.

Paul knew that God was committed to bearing witness to the truth of the gospel by the confirming work of the Spirit (1 Thessalonians 1:5; see also Acts 4:29; 14:3; and Hebrews 2:4). He also knew that the gospel was God's instrument to produce eternal results in the lives of those who believed (1 Thessalonians 2:13; see also Acts 20:32).

Paul had a profound appreciation of his role and God's role in the work of evangelism. He was to step out in the confidence that God would indeed act on behalf of the messenger and the message, taking the initiative to share the gospel even in the midst of difficult circumstances. God would grant him the courage to do so, and would bring lasting results from Paul's obedience in the form of lives changed by the gospel message.

Boldness and "Aggressive Evangelism"

Aggressive evangelism is grounded in the biblical concept of boldness. I believe that the word *aggressive* aptly characterizes Paul's courageous, confident, clear and open evangelistic ministry. To be aggressive means to be disposed to vigorous activity. The one who is aggressive is the determined initiator, the one on the offensive, the risk taker. The aggressive evangelist is the one who, like Paul, is unhindered by the concerns of personal risk and opposition and, in the proper context of sensitivity and propriety, makes sure the gospel is clearly communicated to all who will listen.

To paraphrase Bill Bright, aggressive evangelism is taking the initiative to share Christ in the power of the Holy Spirit and leaving the results to God. We take the initiative to share Christ with others: we do not wait for them to come and ask us about Christ.

Let us evaluate aggressive evangelism in light of the three criteria for a biblical philosophy of evangelism. Is it grounded in theology? Is it demonstrated in practice? Does it work?

Aggressive Evangelism and Biblical Theology

A biblically informed theology of evangelism compels us to practice aggressive evangelism. There are at least four reasons for this:

(1) Aggressive evangelism is grounded in the principle of the cruciality of the gospel and the urgency of evangelism. The gospel is good news, not nice views. There is a heaven, there is a hell, there is only one Savior, and there is an eternal choice confronting every man and woman on earth. Those who practice aggressive evangelism take this truth seriously, knowing that the gospel is a crucial, urgent and, therefore, relevant message to all people at all times.

(2) Aggressive evangelism is grounded in the very nature of the gospel. As Paul so clearly understood, the gospel has a self-authenticating quality. Upon its proclamation, hearing and acceptance, it "performs its work" in those who believe (1 Thessalonians 2:13). It comes not "in word only" as a mere "word of men" (1 Thessalonians 1:5; 2:13), but "in power and in the Holy Spirit and with full conviction" (1 Thessalonians 1:5).

The gospel is God's instrument, designed to effect the response of repentance and faith in the heart of the nonbeliever. When it is faithfully and simply communicated in the power of the Spirit, the "word of the cross" is the power of God for salvation (1 Corinthians 1:18; Romans 1:16).

It is crucial to note that the Word of the gospel, as it is presented to sinners, never stands alone; the Spirit of God bears witness to it. The Word is "the sword of the Spirit" (Ephesians 6:17) and as such is said to penetrate the human heart as a living, active, piercing power to effect God's intended result (Hebrews 4:10). Paul knew that the success of his evangelistic ministry was due to the power of the Spirit bearing witness to the truth of the gospel and to its ability to save the lost (Romans 15:19; 1 Corinthians 2:4; 2 Corinthians 6:6; Acts 14:3).

The gospel, as God's Word, is power. It is more than a cognitive message or symbol of ultimate reality. The gospel is more than just instruction. God's spoken Word is invested with the power to bring order out of chaos, light out of darkness (Genesis 1:1,3) and life out of death in the physical realm (John 11:43,44). Similarly, the gospel, as contained in God's written Word, is able to bring spiritual life out of spiritual death (John 5:24-29) and light out of darkness in the realm of the human heart (2 Corinthians 4:6).

Aggressive evangelism takes these theological truths to heart as it majors on taking the initiative to bring lost sinners into contact with the gospel. The evangelist is confident that he delivers the gospel, not as a mere competitor in the marketplace of ideas, but as an ambassador entrusted with the most powerful message ever unleashed on mankind. The evangelist is confident that the gospel is capable of creating its own hearing and platform of relevance in a sinner's life. As such, the primary role of the evangelist is simply to turn the message loose.

(3) Aggressive evangelism is grounded in the saving activity of the Holy Spirit. The ability of the gospel to save sinners is dependent on the fact that God is the ceaseless seeker who sends the Spirit to seek out the lost. As we have just seen, one aspect of this work is that the preaching of the Word of the gospel is always accompanied by the confirming work of the Spirit.

But a second dimension of the Spirit's saving activity is often unnoticed: His work of "unblinding" and convicting the lost to prepare them to accept the gospel when it is communicated. John 16:8-11 tells us that the Spirit is at work enlightening and freeing men and women who are spiritually blind and bound in Satan's domain. Whenever the seed of the gospel falls on fertile ground, it is evidence that the Spirit has gone ahead of the evangelist to cultivate and water the soil (John 4:34-38; Acts 16:14).

Aggressive evangelism is tuned into the theological reality that, wherever we go, the Spirit has prepared "many people" (Acts 18:10) to embrace the gospel. Thus, the question must always be asked, "How do we know who is in the process of being unblinded, unbound and convicted by the Holy Spirit? How can we recognize God's many people?" The answer is quite simple. We gain insight into a nonbeliever's spiritual state only as we take the initiative to inquire by means of a sensitive presentation of the gospel.

Think for a moment how difficult it is for us who have been given our spiritual sight to take the initiative to talk to the lost about the gospel. I have everything going for me, and it is still a monumental struggle. Now think of how difficult it is for those still in an unregenerate state to initiate a conversation with us.

Aggressive evangelism takes this very practical concern to heart and reasons, "How can I expect him to take the first step toward me, given his spiritual condition? I must, out of theological necessity, take the first step toward him." We, the spiritually sighted, must, by reason of our sight, *move first.* We cannot expect the spiritually blind to make the difficult trip to our front door.

(4) Last, aggressive evangelism is grounded in the authority of Jesus Christ. The Great Commission is an authorized work. By that I mean that Jesus both commands that it be done and ensures the success of our venture. Very simply, the aggressive evangelist, like Paul (2 Corinthians 5:11), holds the conviction that to be obedient is to "go," as Jesus commanded, and to expect that the power, authority and presence of Jesus Himself will ensure the success of his mission. We go, therefore, out of obedience and in an attitude of expectancy.

The aggressive evangelist realizes that at its most foundational level, evangelism is obedience. As such, circumstances or emotional predisposition do not determine one's philosophy of evangelism. As Charles Spurgeon once stated, "He does not sit in the arm chair and catch fish. If we never do any work for Christ except work we feel up to the mark, we shall not do much." Christianity is a missionary religion. It asks not why men are not coming to us, but why we are not going to men.

Thus, aggressive evangelism is grounded in biblical theology. An appreciation for the crucial nature of the gospel, the urgency of evangelism, the lostness of man, the power of the gospel to save, the saving work of the Spirit and the authoritative command of Christ to take the gospel to the world all lead the evangelist to one inescapable conclusion: The faithful execution of my role as an ambassador for Christ requires that I take the initiative to ensure that the good news is communicated to all who will listen, as soon as possible, so that they might comprehend the gospel as clearly as possible.

Aggressive Evangelism and Biblical Practice

The biblical evidence of the evangelistic practice of the first-century church indicates that aggressive evangelism was the typical approach. It was demonstrated as a way of life. The reason is quite simple: the first-century Christians were gripped by the same theological realities we have discussed. Thus, Jesus initiated a conversation with the woman at the well, Philip with the Ethiopian eunuch (Acts 8:26ff), Paul with Lydia (Acts 16:13), and Peter with the Jerusalem Jews (Acts 2:14). Having a personal philosophy and practice of aggressive evangelism puts us in good company.

It Works!

I am committed to the practice of aggressive evangelism primarily because it is theologically demanded and biblically demonstrated. But the final reason is that I have seen its practical benefits, both in my own life and in the lives of those with whom I have shared the gospel.

The Initiative Factor

A commitment to aggressive evangelism has benefited me greatly in the area of developing my personal motivation to share my faith. By nature, I am not an outgoing person. If left to myself, I would prefer to keep to a small circle of close friends. In terms of a ministry I would prefer to be a keeper of the aquarium rather than a fisher of men.

But I have found that taking the initiative to share my faith is like exercising a spiritual muscle. The more I put myself in a position to see God work through the sharing of the gospel, the more confidence I gain in the power of the gospel to save and in the ability of Jesus Christ to support me with His supply of courage and strength.

The adage is true that we more easily *act* our way into thinking than think our way into acting. It has been freeing to me to realize that God desires to use me as I step out in obedience, and that I need not wait for my emotional makeup or circumstances to dictate when evangelism ought to be done. The issue is never whether or not to go. The command to go has already been given. The only issue is whether I will obey.

The Wisdom of the Initiative Approach

The initiative factor also brings practical benefit to the lost. In all the years I have been a believer, only a handful of unbelievers have taken the initiative with me to discuss spiritual things. Usually this happened because they had seen me aggressively sharing the gospel with others and knew that I would be a "safe" person to ask some spiritual questions. But I have seen hundreds of others, who never would have taken the initiative with me, respond positively to my attempt to share the gospel with them. Some of these came into God's kingdom as a result. These experiences have taught me some practical lessons that underscore the "why" of aggressive evangelism.

One afternoon as I was visiting a young man, we were discussing the gospel and his relationship with Christ. He was very interested, and a few days later he trusted in Christ as his Savior as a result of our time together. A week later I had a similar conversation with one of his close friends. It turned out that he had been a Christian for quite some time. As I told him about his friend's newfound faith in Christ, he could hardly believe it. "Him?" he asked. "I'll believe it when I see it".

I asked him if he had tried to communicate the gospel to him lately. He replied, "There's no way he is interested in the gospel."

"How do you know he isn't interested?" I asked.

"Well, he drinks, smokes and doesn't go to church", he replied. (In other words, he acted like a non-Christian.)

The new believer's Christian friend had taken upon himself the burden of deciding whether or not his friend was ready to "do business" with Christ. His criteria were based purely on external and superficial concerns. He really had no way of wisely discerning his friend's level of spiritual preparedness. Only by taking the initiative to communicate the gospel with him could he have known his interest.

A philosophy of aggressive-initiative evangelism is simply a wise way of interacting with a spiritually blind world. The Christian committed to taking the initiative relieves himself of the burden of determining another's spiritual receptivity.

This wisdom of the initiative approach was brought home to me through my experience with a young man with whom I initiated a spiritual conversation a few years ago. As we were discussing the personal implications of the gospel, our time drew to a close, and he invited me to return the next day and continue our conversation. We had taken an hour to establish the relevance of Jesus Christ to his life and the possibility that God really loved him. The next day, after seriously studying passages in the Scriptures, he became convinced that he indeed had a personal sin problem. He invited me back a few days later to discuss the gospel further. We talked about Jesus Christ, His death for sin and the necessity of making a personal decision to trust Christ. The spiritual light finally dawned on him, and he placed his faith in Christ.

If I had asked this young man, "Why didn't you seek out Christians to talk about this? Why did you wait for me to come to you?" he probably would have answered, "I didn't even know I had a spiritual problem before you talked to me. I never knew the solution was to be found in Christ, so why should I seek out Christians?"

This young man was living proof of the theological reality of man's spiritual blindness. Sin, due to its blinding nature, dulls a nonbeliever to his spiritual problem and its solution in the gospel. Only as the gospel was shared did the Holy Spirit begin the unblinding process so that the gospel could grab hold of this young man. By taking the initiative, we place ourselves in God's hands as His tool to effect spiritual change in the lives of the lost.

Misconceptions of Aggressive Evangelism

At this time you might be reasoning, "If this is all so clear, why aren't more Christians committed to aggressive evangelism?" Often a Christian's reluctance to become involved in aggressive evangelism is grounded in misconceptions concerning its nature and implications in practice.

"Confrontational" Evangelism

Aggressive evangelism has been unfairly stereotyped in recent years. The most common misconception is that aggressive evangelism is inherently a pushy, confrontational, socially awkward and generally insensitive practice.

We all have seen or heard of people who "turned others off" by their aggressive methods. I once took a new believer to a football game, only to find that another believer was there wearing a sandwich sign proclaiming "Christ is Coming" on the front and "Repent or Go to Hell" on the back. Many in the crowd ridiculed him, and fellow believers were shocked and dismayed at our brother's insensitivity.

John the Baptist may not have struggled with this method, but my new believer friend had some problems with it. Needless to say, he threw out the baby with the bathwater and refused to have anything to do with taking the initiative to share the gospel. "Why put myself in the same camp with the sandwich-board crowd?" he reasoned. Since this new believer had not developed any personal conviction on the practice of evangelism, he was essentially neutralized as a witnessing Christian.

I have witnessed the efforts of many street preachers who major in bringing the crowd to an angry confrontation, often resulting in physical blows being inflicted upon the evangelist. I have overheard people in the crowd saying things like, "If this is what real Christianity is all about, leave me out." Many witnessing Christians cringe, realizing that the nonbelieving world often fails to distinguish between them and others who use some of the more radical methods to proclaim the gospel.

The last thing I want to do here is criticize the methods of others. I have been on the other end of such criticism, and I know what it feels like. I am thankful for any way that the message is proclaimed and for fruit that comes of it. I admire the boldness of these believers and their willingness to suffer for the gospel. But the fact remains that certain methods of sharing the gospel may erect emotional barriers that inhibit those who are struggling with their own role in evangelism.

But aggressive evangelism need not be offensive. Taking the initiative to share Christ with someone need not be confrontational or socially awkward. There is no reason in the world that I cannot *both* take the initiative *and* be sensitive in communicating the gospel. Disassociating a warm heart and zealous commitment from a sensitive and culturally relevant approach to evangelism usually betrays the acceptance of a false dichotomy. Such thinking says that if I'm aggressive, nothing need stand in my way to get a hearing for the gospel — not social propriety, or even the sensitivities of the hearer. On the other hand, such reasoning continues, if I am really committed to being a sensitive person, I will respect another's personal space, right to privacy and spiritual sensitivity, and I will refrain from taking the initiative.

Boldness and Sensitivity

The first-century church knew no false dichotomy between boldness and sensitivity in their evangelistic practice. In fact, they found it impossible to extricate one from the other. They realized that the message of the gospel traveled along the two-lane highway of boldness *and* sensitivity. With no boldness, the gospel would be silenced by persecutors, suffering, inconvenient circumstances and the fears of the evangelist. It would never reach the ears of unbelievers.

Without sensitivity, the gospel might be heard, but not truly understood. The goal of the first-century Christians was not merely to get unbelievers within earshot of the gospel, but to help them truly understand its content and personal implications. Therefore, they boldly took the initiative — in a spirit of sensitivity.

Paul modeled this combination in Thessalonica. He was bold enough to preach the gospel to potentially hostile strangers, even after he had been physically attacked only days earlier in Philippi.

But note, in the context of this boldness, Paul took great care to manifest a deep sensitivity. He states that he behaved gently, as "a nursing mother tenderly cares for her own children" (1 Thessalonians 2:7). Paul adds, "Having thus a fond affection for you, we were well pleased to impart to you not only the gospel of God but also our own lives, because you had become very dear to us" (1 Thessalonians 2:8). As Paul boldly proclaimed the gospel to them, he was sensitive enough to work "night and day so as not to be a burden to any of you" (1 Thessalonians 2:9). Paul was so sensitive that he did not want the Thessalonians to think for a moment that he was in the gospel preaching business for profit. He was willing to endure "labor and hardship" (1 Thessalonians 2:9) so that they would receive the gospel.

Paul's sensitivity also manifested itself in great patience in his evangelistic ministry. In the context of bold proclamation, he "reasoned," "explained" and "gave evidence" to his hearers (Acts 17:2,3). Paul was willing to flex and do whatever it took to see men and women come to Christ. While some were probably saved at the first preaching of the gospel, others had to return again and again, discussing the message with Paul and slowly coming to grips with the truth of Jesus' identity as the Messiah. Like a patient farmer, Paul was content to plow the field, plant the seed, and wait for the spiritual harvest of new believers.

It is obvious then, that there is only a surface contradiction between boldness and sensitivity. Aggressive evangelism by no means implies a lack of sensitivity on the part of the evangelist, or a socially awkward experience for the nonbeliever. Let us pray as Jim Elliot prayed, "Lord, give me firmness without hardness; steadfastness without dogmatism; love without weakness."[3]

"Inflexible" Evangelism

A second, and closely related misconception is that aggressive evangelism is inherently inflexible due to its insistence on taking the initiative and its embracing of various strategies and tools to communicate effectively with nonbelievers. Thus, it is off limits for those committed to creativity and a natural way-of-life witness. But, grounded in a concern for sensitivity, aggressive evangelism takes on a flexibility that its critics usually ignore.

Tony, Marcus, and Taking the Initiative

I like watching football running backs like Tony Dorsett and Marcus Allen. They like to line up deep in the I-formation. For you less informed fans, that means that they are a good seven to eight yards behind the line of scrimmage where their blockers are to arrange for holes to appear in their opponents' defensive line. What does it mean for a runner to be aggressive as he is handed the ball? Does it mean that he should simply put his head down, churn his legs and drive forward until he is tackled? Obviously not. To be aggressive in this situation certainly means to move ahead. But it also means to pick the spot in the line that looks like the best place to break through the defense. It could even mean to give ground while running around the end. It could also mean to run straight ahead if that is where the hole is. It could mean to adjust speed, even to slow down momentarily in the hope that a blocker can make a hole in the defensive line. The runner is aggressive, fighting for every yard he can get, but at the same time he is constantly looking for blockers and open field. His goal is not just to run hard, but to gain yardage, and he will do whatever it takes to accomplish this within the rules of the game.

We might say that the good runners manifest a "flexible, controlled aggressiveness." This combination is necessary to gain yardage. He must not only be able to drive ahead but also, at any given moment, be able to adjust his course and speed to take advantage of opportunities as they open.

This example illustrates aggressive evangelism. "Aggressive" does not mean that we become bulls in a china shop, our heads down, trying to make a point by our boldness. Rather, we take the initiative because we are constrained by the theological realities, biblical models and our concern to communicate effectively to the lost.

Thus, aggressive evangelism will differ from situation to situation, person to person, social context to social context. But at its core is the principle, "I must do anything within the bounds of biblical ethics to initiate effectively and communicate the gospel to all who will listen." This is the common denominator of all aggressive evangelism, and applies not only to our witness to strangers, but also to our witness to friends and family.

"Offensive" Evangelism

A third misconception is that aggressive evangelism is inherently intrusive or offensive to non-Christians. Did the first-century Christians, even in the context of great sensitivity, evoke the offense of nonbelievers? Of course they did. Paul's contemporaries called him a "real pest." People sneered at him (Acts 17:32). He made people angry and resentful (Acts 17:5). But here we need to make a crisp distinction between the manner of the evangelist (boldly taking the initiative) and the actual message of the gospel.

Paul did not offend people because he took the initiative. Rather, when others were offended, it was by the gospel message itself. We do not find his audiences saying, "Away with this man who has the gall and insensitivity to speak to us before we came to him. How dare he initiate spiritual conversation with us." No, we find the offended responding as they do because the message itself was so upsetting. Just as there is sure to be thunder and lightening as a warm air front meets cold, so there is bound to be emotional and spiritual "thunder and lightening" as the gospel of the kingdom of God confronts those who are in the kingdom of darkness.

The gospel pierces the heart. It yanks the rug out from under the spiritual pride and complacency of its hearers. Jesus is very clear that we should expect a built-in "offense factor" as we present the gospel to the lost. Those who are aligned with the world's system — whose identities and presuppositions are bound up in the pursuit of the lust of the flesh, the lust of the eyes and the boastful pride of life — will, unless the Holy Spirit convicts them, have a difficult time with the message and, as a result, reject both the message and the messenger (Luke 12:49-53).

In John 15:15-25, Jesus tells us that this offense taken against the gospel is grounded in the world's aversion to dealing with Him. This reaches such emotional proportions that Jesus calls it "hate" (John 15:18,19,23). We must take sober note of Jesus' warning that the world's hatred for Him will inevitably manifest itself as a hatred for those who bring His message.

Therefore, conflict with the nonbelieving world will always be a possibility due to the reality of the spiritual battle that rages over the souls of men. While it is true that some offense may at times be due to the insensitivity of the evangelist or his method (and we should do all we can to avoid this), it would be wrong to assume that all of the sparks are caused by aggressive methods used in evangelism.

Aggressive evangelism, once freed from these three misconceptions, can be appreciated as a biblical and effective approach to getting out the good news. There is no basis for assuming that the negative traits of insensitivity, inflexibility and offensiveness are inherent to its nature and practice. An informed aggressive evangelist is concerned with one thing: communicating the gospel boldly in such a way that it is understood clearly by the hearer in order that Jesus Christ might be glorified in the lives of both speaker and hearer.

CHAPTER 16

A Philosophy of Training, Tools and Techniques

T he setting was my dorm room one spring evening. A group of my friends had gathered to relax, talk and listen to records. During the last month my life had changed radically as my conversion to Christ began to take hold. A couple of my friends had noted that I no longer ran around with them on their weekend drinking nights, and they demanded an explanation.

I soon had my first opportunity to witness of my new faith in Christ. Every eye in the room was fixed on me as I tried to explain how Christ had forgiven me and was changing me.

Then the questions, and sparks, began to fly. For the next two hours I learned everything I did not know about sharing my faith. "Oh, you're a Jesus freak?" "Are you too good for us now?" "What about those who have never heard about Jesus?" "Will God send me to hell if I don't believe like you?"

As the questions kept coming, I realized that I did not have many answers. My friends seemed to be having a good time, but I was just barely hanging on. It was the lions versus the Christian, and I was eaten alive by their questions. Each time I tried to explain the gospel, I found myself off the track, stumbling for my next thought and failing to center the discussion on Jesus.

After the room cleared out, I evaluated the time. Sure, I had succeeded in letting everyone know that I was now different and that this difference stemmed from what Jesus had done in my life. But not one of them left with the faintest idea of what the gospel was or how he could become a Christian. I felt I had missed a golden opportunity and soon realized that I could not adopt a fly-by-the-seat-of-my-pants philosophy if I was to comunicate the good news effectively. I needed some training!

The next week I met with the local Campus Crusade for Christ director, and he agreed to train me in the basics of evangelism. Since that day my training has been an ongoing process. I am thankful that God took me through that painful experience because I came to realize the great importance of training in evangelism. Knowing the how to's has opened up countless opportunities for me to communicate the gospel that otherwise, I am sure, would have gone unnoticed or have been beyond my capabilities.

The Problem Raised

I became excited about being trained in the how to's of evangelism, but I soon realized that not all of the Christians on campus shared my enthusiasm. In fact, as I began to share the gospel with my non-Christian friends, neighbors and anyone else who would listen, I was criticized for my efforts — not by them, but by the believers on my dorm floor. Their criticism revolved around two philosophical issues.

The Stifled Personality

Training, as we shall see, is inseparably related to the use of techniques and tools. As such, training in evangelism asks a Christian to submit himself to the use and mastery of at least one tool for sharing the gospel (in my case, the tool was the Four Spiritual Laws). This approach usually limits the range of styles a person can choose to put the training into practice, at least *initially*. However, it may grow into a variety of styles later.

Some have a hard time with this approach. They see this insistence on the use of a particular evangelistic tool or technique as stifling to personality, creativity and the desire to be "natural." They want to meet the particular needs of an evangelistic situation as "God should lead," free to interject their own personalities and preferences without the straitjacket of a "canned approach." A rigorous training approach using tools and techniques is not only considered "not my cup of tea" but is also seen as detrimental to Christians who seek to share the good news.

The "Canned" Gospel

A common argument goes something like this: "How can one tool or tract be used in a variety of situations with a variety of people who have a variety of different felt needs? Won't the use of one tool be so narrow as to make your presentation of the gospel meaningless to your listeners? Won't this stifle the Holy Spirit as He seeks to apply the gospel creatively and individually to the heart of the nonbeliever? After all, Jesus dealt with no two seekers alike, why should I? The disciples did just fine without being taught the how to's, so why should I submit to such training?" Many Christians shy away from training in how to use a tool to share their faith because of these concerns.

In addition to these philosophical barriers to training, techniques and tools, there are other concerns. I call them practical barriers.

The Fear of the Actual

By its very nature, training demands practice and experience. True training is more than just the storage tank theory: "Listen up, you might need this some day." Rather, it necessitates the actual doing of the task for which you are being trained.

When I asked to be trained in how to share my faith, I knew that I would actually have to go out and do it.I would be asked to put some shoe leather to my good intentions. Many realize this close association between training and going and, frankly, it is a scary proposition. For some it is too scary, so they refrain from being trained. It is a challenge to their comfort zone, that built-in protective barrier that shuns any risky activity. We resist anything that makes us go out on a limb and trust God to make us adequate to handle a situation (like witnessing). Training necessarily leads to action, and that thought may make us uncomfortable.

The Pride Barrier

A few years ago I was watching some 8- and 9-year-olds play foosball, the tabletop game approximating field hockey. I am one of the worst foosball players in the world. I took on one of those kids and got clobbered. My pride was hurt, and it did not help matters when one of the kids watching the game said to me, "Want some tips?" My first thought was, *Listen, kid, who do you think you are? What can you teach me?* Of course, the answer was, *a lot.* I swallowed my pride and took a lesson.

Training benefits only those with a teachable attitude, a willing submission to the training concept. To be trained, I must admit a few things:

(1) I could do better than I'm now doing. I've got room to improve.

(2) There are other people who, by reason of their experience and study, know more than I do and could help me to be more effective.

(3) I've got to start sometime, so I'll break out of this inertia and my personal comfort zone and get some practical experience.

(4) I've got to start somewhere, and this means beginning with the basics.

The concerns of inertia and pride are easily addressed, but what of the philosophical barriers? Are they valid? Might training, methodology and tools be a detriment to our service for Jesus Christ? Would Jesus approve of such an approach? As I have thought through these questions and spoken to many who oppose this sort of systematic training, I have, I hope, found some helpful answers. They fall into two categories, biblical and practical considerations.

Biblical Considerations

We get an idea of the biblical concept of training from Hebrews 5:11-14. The author of Hebrews wrote to encourage and exhort a group of sluggish Christians who had grown weary and lost heart in their commitment to Jesus. He held up a picture of where they ought to be to convict them of their complacency and indifference toward spiritual growth. In essence, He contrasted maturity with immaturity. Hebrews 5:14 says that mature men are those "who because of practice have their senses trained to discern good and evil." It is no coincidence that the words *practice* and *training* appear in the same sentence defining mature men.

Practice (*hexis*) denotes a habit or experience. The New International Version translates it "constant use." The King James Version reads "by reason of use." *Practice* literally translates "having been exercised." It is set in sharp contrast to the description of the immature man, who is "not accustomed" to the Word (Hebrews 5:13). Maturity demands experience — performance on the playing field of real-life.

Closely related is the world *trained*. The Greek word is *gymnazō*, from which we get our English word *gymnasium*. In the ancient Greek world, this word meant "to exercise" and generally was used to describe training the body or mind or disciplining oneself toward a greater end. The word is used in 1 Timothy 4:7 to describe disciplining oneself toward the end of godliness.

Hebrews 5:14 speaks strongly of maturity being a matter of great effort. There is no instant road, no magic formula, no easy way out. The words *exercise, practice* and *training* suggest strenuous, consistent pursuit of a goal, involving hard work, practical application and commitment of time and energy.

Thus, when we speak of training in evangelism, we are talking about a single-minded pursuit of becoming the most effective evangelist possible, no matter what it takes. We are talking about a process of maturing. This process cannot be confined to classroom lectures, but will necessarily branch out into practical situations. It will demand much time logged in these experiences. A half-hearted, let-the-chips-fall-where-they-may attitude does not do justice to the Word. Nothing less than a rigorous, practical approach can do justice to the biblical goal of evangelistic training, which is to equip workers, who are few, for the harvest, which is plentiful.

Jesus and Training

Jesus placed a premium on training His disciples to equip them to form the nucleus for His church and take the gospel to the world. To this end, the disciples were trained continually in the essentials of godly character, prayer, forgiveness, discipleship and evangelism — all, I might add, in the context of real-life experience.

So far so good. But would Jesus, who, out of His great sensitivity, dealt with no two people alike, have approved of His disciples using an aggressive strategy — rather than a relationship — to initiate contact with nonbelievers? Would He have given His blessing to using a tool or "canned" approach to sharing the gospel rather than letting it flow "naturally" from their lives?

Before we answer no, let us turn to Matthew 10:5-23, Luke 9:1-6, and Luke 10:1-16, where Jesus gives instructions to the twelve and the seventy before He sends them out as apprentice evangelists. These passages clearly indicate that Jesus provided His disciples with specific guidelines for their evangelistic mission. He told them exactly what to say: "The kingdom of God has come near to you" (Luke 10:9), "the kingdom of heaven is at hand" (Matthew 10:7). He told them to whom they should and should not speak: not to Samaritans or Gentiles, but to Jews only (Matthew 10:5,6). He told them how to divide up: two by two (Luke 10:1); what to take or, more specifically, what not to take (Matthew 10:10, Luke 9:3); whom to stay with to establish a base for ministry (Luke 10:5-7, Matthew 10:10,11); how to be supported (Matthew 10:10, Luke 10:7); what to do in case of rejection (Luke 10:10; 9:5, Matthew 10:14); and what to expect in terms of opposition (Matthew 10:16-23).

It is quite likely that these instructions were used by the early church as normative guidelines for evangelistic work.[1] What are we to make of Jesus' apparent inflexibility and specificity in these instructions? As Tom Hanks perceptively observes, "Does this mean that we are confronted with a contradiction in the Bible that the Jesus who dealt with no two seekers alike also sent out the seventy with a canned program?" Hanks answers, "No, not if we distinguish between our Lord's example as an *evangelist*, and His example as a *trainer* of evangelists."[2]

Hanks goes on to say, "Programs we have labeled 'canned evangelism' have grasped (at least intuitively) that if you are going to train great numbers of evangelists, you've got to put the cookies on the lower shelf, at least to start with." He adds, "Contemporary movements involving canned programs have often been characterized by this biblical sense of urgency — not only to evangelize, but to train evangelists — keenly aware that the 'harvest is plentiful but the laborers are few' (Luke 10:2). Is it any wonder that the Holy Spirit has been pleased to bless them?"[3]

It is obvious that Jesus appreciated the power of basic training to mobilize His disciples by helping to overcome the inertia of their uncertainty, fear and lack of experience. Nothing less than these specific instructions would get them out into the harvest field.

Practical Considerations

Training, strategy, tools and methodology are inseparably linked to the concept of biblical effectiveness. I am aware that many see the concerns of effectiveness as an Americanized, 20th-century, Madison-Avenue intervention onto the pages of Scripture. Effectiveness has been likened to raw pragmatism, to a preoccupation with quantity at the expense of quality, to an emphasis on results at the expense of ethics, and to glorification of methods over and above the man, message and manner of evangelism.

I believe that the word *effectiveness* needs to be rescued from these accusations. After analyzing the New Testament church's practice of evangelism, I am convinced that effectiveness, properly defined, was at the heart of their evangelistic ministry.

The church's appreciation of the theological realities touching on the work of evangelism (the urgency of the task, the necessity that the gospel be communicated to as many as possible as clearly as possible, the readiness of the harvest field), compelled them to adopt whatever strategies and methodologies, within the framework of biblical ethics, that they thought would accomplish their task of bringing Christ to the world. Thus, effectiveness is not mere pragmatism, because it is grounded in theological concerns and conformed to biblical standards.

Neither is effectiveness a shallow preoccupation with numbers. Rather, it is grounded in the conviction that three thousand or five thousand souls added to the church bears mentioning (Acts 2:41; 4:4), because they are numbers of individuals for whom Jesus died. A desire for effectiveness drives the evangelist to maximize the impact of the gospel. Just as Paul's use of strategy on his missionary journeys reflected a desire that a maximum number could come to know Jesus Christ, and just as Jesus' emphasis on basic training served to mobilize His men for a solo mission, so the evangelist will utilize training, tools, methodology and strategy to reach as many individuals as possible for Christ.

Training and Effectiveness

To train means to "render skillful, proficient or qualified by systematic instruction." The two components of this definition are (1) the goal — a person is made skillful, proficient or qualified to perform a particular task; and (2) the means — this skill or proficiency is imparted by systematic instruction.

My high school football coach was a fanatic about training, as are most coaches. To him, systematic instruction was the name of the game. We would practice the same things hour after hour until we got it right. I can remember having to tackle a runner ten times in a row until I did it correctly. It is reasonable to conclude that anything worth doing is worth being trained in. If it is important, it is worth doing correctly, with the greatest efficiency. Proficiency and skill are not accidents. They require hard work and careful instruction in mastering the basics.

Methodology, Technique and Creativity

A technique is "the manual or bodily skills necessary to accomplish some end or result; the manner or methods by which certain details are handled or problems solved; any method for accomplishing something." A method is a "way, means or manner of proceeding." Thus it is a regular, systematic or orderly way of doing anything. Where you have true training you have, by necessity, a methodology or technique. This is just another way of saying that the instruction is orderly and purposeful and moves logically toward the end of making one skilled. Training cannot be a hit-or-miss proposition. There is a way of proceeding, an orderly way of training and applying that training that will lead to maximum effectiveness for a maximum number of people. It will provide a solid foundation for further growth, personal creativity and enjoyment of the skill.

A medical student learns skills based on this principle. He must take the required courses and learn specified techniques and procedures. We would not consider him sufficiently trained if he had been to a medical school that said, "Learn what you think you need, it's up to you. Just be yourself, be creative. We don't want to stifle you by making you do things our way." Even though a particular operation could be performed a couple of different ways, the student is never told to go ahead and do it any way he wants. He must learn the basic skills before progressing to the level of proficiency where he could have the privilege of making a choice. Creativity and personal preference cannot be introduced to a skill-related task until quality and effectiveness are ensured. Thus, true training requires a methodology to help accomplish its aim of making a person skilled.

Tools

Tools are any instrument or means necessary to the efficient implementation of one's trade or task. They are generally "anything designed to effect a purpose." Tools are the extension of our training. They enable us to implement what we have learned. They help us put our systematic training into action. Without an effective tool, the evangelist is like a surgeon without a scalpel or a hitter without a bat. The lack of a tool can render our training useless.

The Necessity of Methodology and Tools

Do we really need methods to be effective in the work of evangelism? If a method is described as a "systematic or orderly way of doing anything" then I would say yes. The alternative to having methods is trifling with the concerns of effectiveness, and in the area of evangelism that is a serious matter.

A method that is truly grounded in a desire for effectiveness represents much trial-and-error experience of those who have gone before us. Popular methods are popular because they have brought consistent results in the past. They can, therefore, be embraced as the fruit of others' successes and failures, intelligent thought and hard work. Thus, an evangelist would be foolish to ignore the storehouse of wisdom reflected in evangelistic tools like the Four Spiritual Laws and strategies like James Kennedy's Evangelism Explosion. Since good methods are affirmed by past experience, the evangelist using these methods will be traveling wise, well-paved paths of successful, effective ministry.

Some Cautions

Correctly understood, training, tools, methodology and strategies offer a powerful contribution to our effectiveness as evangelists. But this effectiveness can be limited severely or short-circuited if we fail to grasp two factors. We must view training and all that it offers in light of the elements of flexibility and progress.

Flexibility

The first-century church sought to spread the gospel by any ethical method that worked. In the name of effectiveness, they were ready to flex, to change strategies in order to take advantage of all open doors for the gospel. Thus, when large group meetings became dangerous and counterproductive to the spread of the gospel, and they needed something better suited for the tense social environment, they adopted a home evangelistic strategy (Acts 5:42). When they were forced to leave Jerusalem and their "household strategy" and were scattered into the rest of Judea and Samaria, they went about proclaiming Christ to strangers in an unfamiliar social context (Acts 8:4ff). They were ready through public proclamation or personal persuasion to reach out to friends, family or total strangers. They understood that "flexibility, variety and openness become important if evangelism is to be comprehensive and effective."[4]

Therefore, effective methods must never be allowed to degenerate into an end in themselves. To "absolutize" any one method, strategy, technique or tool as the only way to go about doing the work of evangelism would violate the spirit of flexibility required to implement our training effectively in a variety of ministry contexts. By all means, use all means!

Progress

Just as methodology can degenerate into an end in itself, so can training. Evangelistic training is the *means* to an end — effectiveness in communicating the gospel — and this is a subject that takes a lifetime to learn and can never be mastered.

We dare not fall into the "sophomore" (Greek: *wise-fool*) trap of getting a little training and failing to realize it is no more than just that — a *little* training. Even the most trained among us must acknowledge that we are lifelong learners who are only beginning to come to grips with what it means to be an effective witness for Christ.

Therefore, do not allow your training to box you in to doing evangelism only one way. Do not assume that just because you have mastered an evangelistic tool, you need no more input on the how to's of clearly communicating the gospel. Remember, training in the basics is a foundation from which we can go on to greater effectiveness. Do not short-circuit training by fossilizing. You will only serve to discredit the very training, tools and methodology that were intended to propel you into a lifelong maturing in evangelism.

Training — The Bridge to Action

My personal experience has taught me that I am less likely to do something if I am not sure how to do it, especially if I see it as a high-risk area. I guess I am not the kind of person who enjoys taking risks. I even get a queasy feeling going to a new restaurant simply because I have no idea what to expect. A few years ago I had a chance to go on a camping/mountain climbing expedition. It sounded great, but I did not go. As I evaluated why, I came up with two reasons: I didn't have any camping equipment, and I didn't know how to climb mountains. I felt the experience would endanger my personal comfort zone. I felt bad about not going, but not bad enough to break out of that comfort zone. Inexperience and fear of failure dominated my decision.

I think this is how many people feel about evangelism. The problem is not that they do not want to do it, but they are held back by the nagging thoughts of *I've never done it before. I don't know how. What if this happens or that question is asked?*

They may balk also because they do not have the proper equipment (tools) to do the job. "Sure, I could show a person some verses in the Bible, but that's a far cry from making the issue of trusting Christ clear and staying on the subject of Christ's offer of love and forgiveness." Here is where training, techniques and tools step in to get us "over the hump." An easy-to-use tool can give us confidence to venture out of our comfort zones and try a new, perhaps even frightening experience. Then, as we undertake challenging tasks, gain experience, and see ourselves succeed, we actually can feel our confidence rising.

Our local newspaper ran an article entitled, "When the Pressure's Really On, They're at Their Best." The article featured interviews with professionals who had to deal with "major league, weak-in-the-knees, life-or-death pressure." As I read it, I thought how relevant their comments were to the high-risk situation of witnessing. Those interviewed were a major league relief pitcher, a fireman and an emergency room doctor. They all agreed that the predominant emotion facing them in the demands of their job was the fear of failure, but the common antidote was the factor of preparation.

The emergency room doctor stated, "A lot of the ability to deal with whatever situation will arise comes from training . . .

making sure that you have the tools, the skills, the techniques and the knowledge so that when you are confronted with a sudden situation, you immediately know what to do and how to do it."

The firefighter added that from preparation comes confidence. "We have confidence because of our training programs and because we keep our physical skills up and maintain our equipment so that we know that whatever situation arises we will go into it prepared and capable."[5]

I think these comments are relevant to the witnessing experience. A necessary factor in getting us over the barriers of fear and lack of confidence is training in the use of an evangelistic tool. It may sound too simple, but a little training in how to make contact with nonbelievers and how to use a simple tool to share your faith can make the difference between stepping out and actually getting your feet wet and staying on the sidelines talking about it.

It is no accident that where strategy, training and tools are emphasized, people are out *doing* evangelism. They have found the how to's sufficient to get them over the hump of inertia.

CHAPTER 17

An Interpersonal Communication Model

C ommunication is a tricky business. We often are attempting to hit a moving target. Words seem to disappear into thin air, and we wonder if they have touched the listener's heart. Hendrick Kraemer asks some tough questions of the Christian communicator: "Where and how do I live? In a ghetto or in living contact with the world? Does the world listen when I speak to it, and if not, why not? Am I really proclaiming the gospel, or am I not? Why has such a wall of separation risen between the world and what I must stand for? Do I know the world in which people live, or do I not. . . . How can I find a way to speak again with relevancy and authority, transmitting the 'words of eternal life' entrusted to me?"[1]

These are disturbing questions for the conscientious communicator. How can we begin to get a handle on the skill of communicating Christ to an ever-changing audience that is often typified by spiritual misconceptions and apathy toward the issues of the gospel?

Models Can Help

Models can help give us insight into what is going on in the world of communication as we share the gospel. A word of caution however: no model is perfect. No model takes into consideration all the possible variables and their relationship to the communication process. We must not confuse the model with the real situation. Let us look at two models that shed helpful light on interpersonal communication and make some applications to our task of communicating Christ.

The Shannon-Weaver Communication Model

The Shannon-Weaver model (see Figure 4) can be applied readily to all conversations and, in our case, is very helpful in understanding the dynamics of the evangelistic encounter. This model is especially helpful in two areas. First, it is concerned with message fidelity — the degree to which a message is received and interpreted as it was intended. Second, it addresses the role of "noise" or static that may interfere with the fidelity of the message.

FIGURE 4
THE SHANNON-WEAVER MODEL

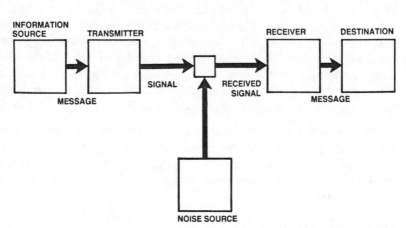

This model was originally devised by the Bell Telephone Laboratories to help examine the accuracy (fidelity) of message transmission. See Claude E. Shannon and Warren Weaver, *The Mathematical Theory of Communication* (Urbana, Illinois, University of Illinois Press, 1949), p. 9. Used by permission.

It is obvious that such a model can be helpful to the evangelist who desires to communicate the gospel accurately and clearly. He wants to avoid any barriers that might prevent the gospel from taking root in the heart of the listener.

The Basic Model of the Communication Process

This model (Figure 5) is also quite helpful in providing a simple overview of the mechanics of the communication process. In combination with the Shannon-Weaver model, it can teach us much about the practice of communicating the gospel with maximum clarity. Here are six components of the communication process.

FIGURE 5
BASIC COMMUNICATION MODEL

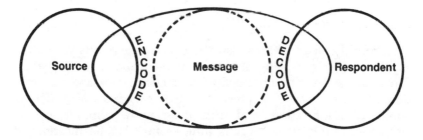

From David Hesselgrave's *Communicating Christ Cross Culturally* (Grand Rapids: Zondervan Press, 1980), p. 29. Used by permission.

1. The Information Source

The information is, of course, the gospel and we, the Christian communicators, are the source. There is a sense in which we are only a secondary source, God being the primary source/initiator of the entire process of communicating the gospel. Thus, we communicate only because He has first communicated through Christ. As He communicates, He continually seeks the lost through the convicting ministry of the Holy Spirit.

2. Encoding (Transmitting) The Signal

The source "encodes" the message. This means to put the message into some kind of coded system for the benefit of the respondent (listener).[2] We will limit our discussion to the encoding of the message into words, written and spoken.[3] The source must package and present the message in a manner that offers the best chance of reaching and influencing the listener. That is, the communicator puts the gospel into his or her own words, or presents someone else's words (such as by using a tract or other gospel presentation), keeping in mind the listener's ability to understand the message.

3. The Message

For us, this is the content of the gospel itself. It is the specific information concerning the death and resurrection of Jesus Christ and His offer of love and forgiveness to sinners.

4. Noise Source

Probably all of us have had the experience of answering the telephone and not being able to hear our caller over the static. The issue here is one of "fidelity" or accurate message transmission. Static or "noise" is present in the mechanics of phone-to-phone communication, and it is even more common in the mechanics of interpersonal communication. It has been estimated that even in the best of situations, communication is only 80 percent effective. Part of the reason is noise.

Noise could be defined as "unwanted signals that can disrupt message fidelity." In the arena of interpersonal communication, there are at least four sources of noise that hamper the transmission of the gospel from person to person.

(1) Cultural noise. This comes in the form of cultural misconceptions and negative input that directly distort the understanding of the gospel by the listener. As a result, he is not able to hear accurately what we are saying. For instance, the listener may be influenced by the secular view of man as independent from and not responsible to God. Thus, he perceives the gospel to be

irrelevant and quite possibly nonsense. The nominalist might be influenced by cultural noise that says, "Jesus is nice but not necessary." Thus, he could easily misinterpret the gospel as the cure for "whatever ails you" rather than as a message of forgiveness.

(2) Theological noise. Our message of Jesus Christ as the substitute for sin may be muffled by the theological static of "I'm O.K., you're O.K., so who needs to throw himself on the mercy of Christ?" Or the misdirected religious person may perceive that what one believes does not really matter as long as he is sincere.

(3) Personal noise. This static comes in the form of personal experiences and attitudes that hinder the listener from appreciating the ramifications and benefits of the gospel to himself. For instance, He may have had a negative experience with some"Christians" or have been turned off to the gospel by past religious experiences. He may reason, "I know some Christians and I wouldn't want to be one," or "I've tried to be religious and it didn't work."

(4) Spiritual noise. The Bible is quite clear that Satan has blinded the minds of the unbelieving (2 Corinthians 4:4). The world system is designed to tell the nonbeliever a set of lies concerning his eternal destiny and Jesus Christ.

Only the Holy Spirit can counteract the debilitating effects of this noise. Only he can graciously enable the listener to operate on a frequency that overrides his spiritual blindness, freeing him to see the light of the gospel and its power for salvation.

The sure presence of noise is the very reason that the wise Christian communicator will do his homework so he can get in touch with his listener's heart. Noise levels and patterns differ greatly from person to person, but the unchanging gospel must be clearly communicated so that all can hear and have an opportunity to believe.

5. Decoding

Upon hearing the message, the listener must interpret or decode it (Figure 5) so that he mentally grasps the message in terms that are meaningful to him. Remember, listeners decode, or understand, messages only in the framework of the presuppositions and assumptions of their personal world. The source must encode and transmit the message with this is mind.

The meanings are not so much in the words as they are in the people. "We do not transmit meaning, we transmit words. Words stimulate the meaning the other person has for them."[4] As the Chinese proverb says, "90% of what we see lies behind our eyes."

I became painfully aware of this truth as I attempted to share the gospel with a Mormon. He heartily agreed with my presentation. He said he had been "saved" by the "grace of Jesus," was "born again" and was going to "heaven." While our wording was the same, however, we were using a different dictionary. He agreed with me because he interpreted my words from his own framework, which provided the same words but with different meanings. I am afraid that the noise and perils of decoding got the best of our conversation.

The combination of noise and decoding can take its toll on the fidelity of the message. Therefore, the communicator must work to ensure that the message is received and understood with the highest degree of accuracy possible.

6. Feedback

How does the communicator know if his message has broken through the noise, been decoded correctly and penetrated the heart? The answer is to cultivate an atmosphere that encourages feedback. As Figure 6 indicates, feedback is the process by which the listener becomes the source, encoding the information he has just received from you, then giving a message back to you that reflects the degree of his understanding. Feedback is vital in evangelistic communication for at least four reasons.

FIGURE 6
FEEDBACK MODEL

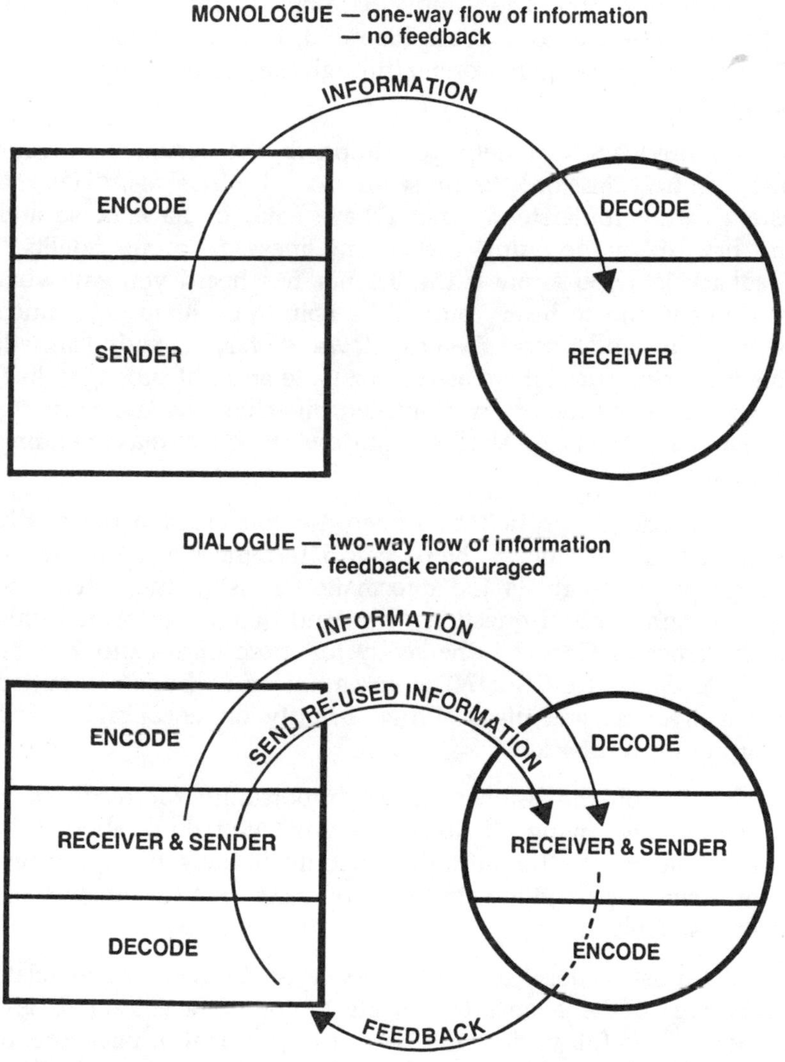
MONOLOGUE — one-way flow of information
— no feedback
INFORMATION
ENCODE
SENDER
DECODE
RECEIVER
DIALOGUE — two-way flow of information
— feedback encouraged
INFORMATION
SEND RE-USED INFORMATION
ENCODE
RECEIVER & SENDER
DECODE
DECODE
RECEIVER & SENDER
ENCODE
FEEDBACK

This chart was adapted from a chart used in classroom lectures by Dr. Herb Klem, professor of missions at Bethel Theological Seminary, St. Paul, Minnesota. Used by permission.

(1) An emphasis on feedback ensures a dialogue, a two-way process of honest interaction, instead of a monologue, a one-way flow of information. The listener becomes part of the communication process and, as a result, his mind, heart and will are more likely to be engaged in reasoning through the personal implications of the gospel.

(2) Feedback can help you improve the accuracy of your message transmission. We must always ask ourselves, "Has the listener truly understood what I have said, or have noise and the hazards of decoding robbed my message of its fidelity?" Feedback lets you know if the listener has heard you say what you meant him to hear. You will be able to evaluate how much he has truly understood the gospel. As we have already learned, this matter is crucial if we are to persuade and not propagandize, if we are to call clearly for Spirit-led, life-changing decisions for Christ and not settle for shallow, spurious responses masquerading as saving faith.

(3) Feedback can help you keep the conversation personally relevant to the listener. It helps you determine his receptivity to the gospel message. Is the information causing the listener to ask the right kind of questions, the kind that are answered only in the cross of Christ? Is he ready for more information? Is he ready to decide for Christ? The communicator who is committed to effectiveness will place a high priority on encouraging and interpreting feedback.

(4) To rob the listener of the opportunity for feedback is tantamount to saying, "I don't care what you think about this, just let me talk." This attitude not only hinders the evangelist from accurately handling the word of truth, but also insults the listener's personhood.

We must respond to the listener as an individual and relate the value of the gospel to his life situation, speaking to any barriers to his full understanding of the personal implications of the gospel. Feedback is essential in this process.

Lessons From the Model

The cycle is now complete. Source has become listener, and listener has become source. In a very real sense, we become listener and source simultaneously. As we deliver the message, we are tuned in to the listener's feedback, evaluating whether our message has fallen on hard, rocky, thorny or good soil (Mark 4:1-20). Source, encoding, message, noise, decoding and feedback are the necessary components of true communication. A proper understanding of each is essential to an evangelistic conversation in which the truth of the gospel is clearly and sensitively communicated so that an informed decision for Christ is possible.

A Decision-Making Model

Dr. James Engel, director of the Billy Graham graduate program in communications at the Wheaton College Graduate School, has given us a model of the spiritual decision-making process (see Figure 7).

This helpful model depicts the roles of God, the communicator and the listener in the process of communicating the gospel. Everyone we talk to falls somewhere on this scale in terms of his spiritual decision-making process and receptivity to the gospel.

This scale is helpful to us as communicators of the gospel in four ways. First, it shows us that apart from the convicting ministry of the Holy Spirit, no listener can understand or respond to the gospel. Only the Spirit can neutralize the spiritual noise caused by Satan's blinding and binding efforts and free the listener to appreciate the grace and truth of the gospel.

Second, it shows that the Spirit of God and the communicator work in harmony to bring the listener to an understanding of the gospel and to the point of personal decision. As Hendrick Kraemer points out, "The communication of the gospel, which is necessarily incumbent upon the church and its members, is neither primarily nor ultimately dependent on our human ability to communicate." Kraemer maintains that although we are called to a constant sharpening of our communication skills, "the primary author of the effective transmission of the message is the Holy

FIGURE 7
DECISION-MAKING MODEL

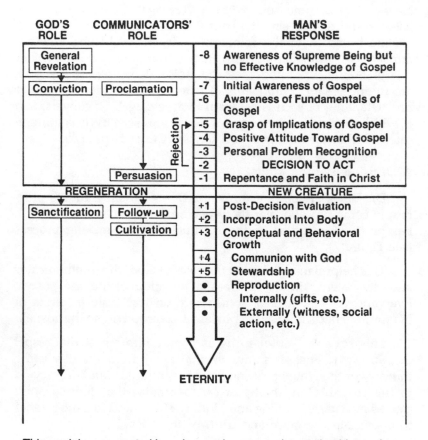

GOD'S ROLE	COMMUNICATORS' ROLE		MAN'S RESPONSE
General Revelation		-8	Awareness of Supreme Being but no Effective Knowledge of Gospel
Conviction	Proclamation	-7	Initial Awareness of Gospel
		-6	Awareness of Fundamentals of Gospel
		-5	Grasp of Implications of Gospel
		-4	Positive Attitude Toward Gospel
		-3	Personal Problem Recognition
		-2	DECISION TO ACT
	Persuasion	-1	Repentance and Faith in Christ
REGENERATION			NEW CREATURE
Sanctification	Follow-up	+1	Post-Decision Evaluation
		+2	Incorporation Into Body
	Cultivation	+3	Conceptual and Behavioral Growth
		+4	Communion with God
		+5	Stewardship
		●	Reproduction
		●	Internally (gifts, etc.)
		●	Externally (witness, social action, etc.)

ETERNITY

This model as presented here has undergone an interesting history. In rudimentary forms, it was first suggested by Viggo Sogaard while he was a student in the Wheaton Graduate School. It later was revised by James F. Engel and published in such sources as *Church Growth Bulletin* and elsewhere during 1973. Since that time, modifications have been introduced as others have made suggestions. Particularly helpful comments have been advanced by Richard Senzig of the communications faculty at the Wheaton Graduate School and Professors C. Peter Wagner and Charles Kraft of the Fuller School of World Mission. (From *What's Gone Wrong With The Harvest,* Grand Rapids: Zondervan Press, 1975, p. 45. Used by permission.)

Spirit," the invisible third partner in the communication process.[5] Without His witness, ours is futile. But with His witness, ours can be a tool in His powerful hand to effect spiritual results in the life of the listener.

Third, this chart shows us that different people have different levels of spiritual understanding and interest in the gospel. While some are ready to respond today, some are not. While many are ready to take the next step toward accepting Christ, some are stalled in their decision-making process or are headed away from Christ.

Finally, this chart gives us insight into the sequence of decision steps leading to the actual event of conversion/regeneration. The listener must have an awareness of the fundamentals of the gospel before he can grasp its personal implications, and he must grasp those implications before he can recognize his problem.

The Application to Personal Evangelism

This model lends strong support to the proposition that "success in witnessing is simply sharing Christ in the power of the Holy Spirit and leaving the results to God."[6] The New Testament is full of examples of the gospel being presented and received with a wide range of responses. When Paul preached the gospel in Athens, the crowd divided into three camps (Acts 17:16-34). Some sneered at the thought of the resurrection of the dead and rejected his message. Some joined him and believed. Others said, "We shall hear you again concerning this." They were not yet ready to believe, but their curiosity had been sufficiently stimulated for them to return for more information.

Since not everyone is at the same level of spiritual preparedness, we need to ascertain as best we can at what point the listener is on the scale, then help him move as far toward trusting Christ as is appropriate. This model underscores the importance of encouraging feedback to determine the spiritual preparedness of the listener, enabling us to respond with the appropriate information.

To be sure, many are ready to receive Christ, and it would be a tragedy to deny them the opportunity. Some are struggling to gain a grasp of the personal implications of the gospel. They need to receive information and encouragement from us to take that next step in the decision-making process and move closer toward receiving Christ.

I always pray for two things in light of this model: first, that God would lead me to people who are ready to decide, so that I might help them to enter His kingdom; second, that God would grant me the wisdom to determine where my listeners are in the decision-making process, so that I might speak to their point of need with relevance and with the gospel's authority. Regardless of one's position on this scale, I can have an eternal impact on his life and fulfill my role as an ambassador for Christ.

Tools and the Communication Process

Perhaps you are wondering how tools like the Four Spiritual Laws, Billy Graham's *Steps to Peace With God* and James Kennedy's *Evangelism Explosion* fit into these communication models. As I have mentioned in a previous chapter, some believe that the use of tools is inherently inflexible and insensitive. But I believe that tools are as flexible as the people using them. Rigidity is imposed not by the tool but by the attitude of the communicator.

Three Communication Attitudes

I would like to suggest three different attitudes toward the communication process (see Figure 8) and discuss how they relate to the use of tools in communicating the gospel.

The Source-Centered Attitude

Communication is a learned art. It is easier for some of us than for others. Some of us are naturally outgoing and can tune in to others' feelings more easily. Some of us are withdrawn and fearful of making contact with others, even on a superficial level. But regardless of our personality type and gifts (or lack of them)

FIGURE 8
THE ROAD TO OTHER-CENTERED COMMUNICATION

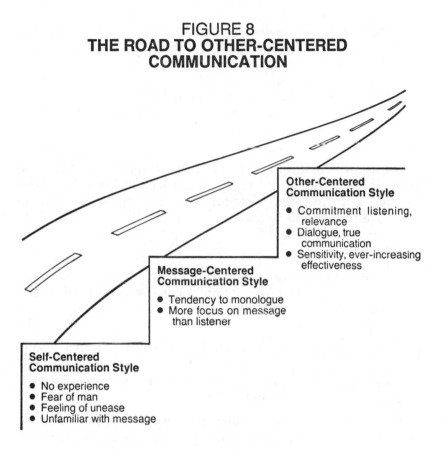

Other-Centered Communication Style

- Commitment listening, relevance
- Dialogue, true communication
- Sensitivity, ever-increasing effectiveness

Message-Centered Communication Style

- Tendency to monologue
- More focus on message than listener

Self-Centered Communication Style

- No experience
- Fear of man
- Feeling of unease
- Unfamiliar with message

in the area of communication, most of us start out on the bottom rung of the ladder as "source-centered" communicators.

A source-centered communicator is one whose attention is focused on himself. Most of us find it difficult, if not impossible, just to be ourselves and act naturally when another person is present and we sense that he may be evaluating us. What happened the last time you were told, "Just act natural, I want to take your picture"? Did your attention automatically turn inward as you asked yourself, *How is my hair? Is my best side showing?* Did you become self-conscious to the point of discomfort?

We find ourselves dealing with the same tendencies in our first attempts to witness to others about Christ. The fear of being rejected, the lack of experience, and the discomfort that comes from doing something new all force us to turn our attention inward and ask, *What does this person think of me? Does he think I'm strange, talking about Jesus like this? Lord, help me get through this conversation. I hope my mouthwash is still working.*

The result of this inward focus is communication with limited effectiveness. With all our energy and attention focused on these questions, there is little left for dealing with the concerns of message fidelity and feedback.

To the Rescue

Don't despair: there is help. While most of us must put in our time as a source-centered communicator, we need not languish in this mode. Here are three ways we can break out of this communication style.

First, realize that although this self-centered style comes naturally to all of us, we need not remain in its grip. Purpose in your heart to do anything necessary to escape its negative influence on your communication.

Second, realize that training in the use of a good evangelistic tool, as well as experience in using it, are the means to escape the source-centered attitude. I am convinced that many Christians are so overwhelmed by fear and the inertia of inexperience that they avoid witnessing situations like the plague. Who wants to go through the discomfort of the source-centered communication experience? This is where a tool like the Four Spiritual Laws can help in a couple of ways. It gives you the assurance that once you are in an evangelistic conversation, you will actually have something of spiritual significance to say. Regardless of your prior training, personality and level of communication skills, you can intelligently communicate the gospel by using such a tool. It is a great way to get started and will provide the assistance you need to communicate confidently.

This is why I recommend that everyone, no matter how spiritually mature, no matter what personality type, participate in a training program that equips him to break through the fear and experience barriers and actually get involved in *doing* evangelism. Such training can help you know how to introduce the gospel, communicate it and close an evangelistic conversation. Even more important, training can help you shorten the amount of time you have to struggle with the deficiencies of the source-centered attitude, for the fear and inadequacies of this phase are overcome only as experience is accumulated.

I have seen these principles work in my own life. As I first learned that sharing the gospel was for everyone, I decided to try it out with the help of a friend. At first I just watched him and prayed, but the time soon came for me to go solo. I was scared to death and felt so self-conscious that I am sure I did nothing more than read through the Four Spiritual Laws booklet as fast as I could. If any of the pages had been stuck together, I would not have noticed. After I finished and my trainer evaluated the time, my first question was, "Is it always this hard and unpleasant? I thought sharing the gospel was a great joy." He replied that as I gained more experience and training, I would feel more natural. He was right.

What About Effectiveness?

You might be asking, "If the source-centered communication style is such a negative experience, will the gospel get through?" I have to answer this question with a qualified yes. I have seen people come to Christ in spite of the most awkward of communication attempts. The reason is that God is committed to validating the authority and relevance of the gospel message to the listener's heart regardless of our clumsy attempts to share Christ. God is more concerned with our availability than our ability. So if you are struggling with the pitfalls of source-centered communication, do not despair. God will still use you.

On the other hand, it would be a mistake to presume upon the grace of God to make up for our lethargy and lack of commitment to improve our communication skills. God will use you, but He desires to use you as a sharpened tool in His hands. There is no place for mediocrity here. If there is one area in which to pursue excellence, it is in the communication of the gospel.

Thus, if you are in the source-centered stage, possibly just learning how to overcome your fears and get out there to do evangelism, congratulations. But there is much more ground to cover in the name of being the best ambassador possible for Jesus Christ.

The Message-Oriented Attitude

Congratulations! You have graduated from the deficiencies of the source-centered phase. Your heart no longer beats wildly, your self-consciousness no longer consumes your attention. You are free to concentrate on a higher concern — the message of the gospel.

The message-oriented communicator asks himself, "Am I doing justice to the content and intent of this message? How am I doing in terms of fidelity?" But as Figure 7 shows, this phase still falls short of true other-centered communication. The communicator's energies are focused on the message, not on the listener.

What is the best way to free yourself to invest your emotional energies in the listener? The answer is to master the message to such a degree that it becomes second nature to you. Only then can your communication energies be focused on the listener. This is why concentrating on a particular format for sharing the gospel is so important, for the sooner I master the message, the sooner I can move into the most efficient realm of communication, the other-centered style.

Other-Centered Attitude

The goal of all tools and training should be to move the Christian communicator through the source and message stages and into the other-centered style.

At this point I want to discuss two divergent approaches to evangelistic training, both of which can be barriers to progressing toward other-centered communication.

"I've Arrived"

The "I've arrived" attitude keeps many trained Christians from the joys and challenges of the other-centered phase. They reason that overcoming their fears and inertia and mastering the message is all there is to being an evangelist.

But this is a tragic attitude because communication, as we have mentioned, is not just delivering a message. It is also ensuring that the message is understood. The goal of evangelism is to give the listener an opportunity to make an informed decision for Christ. But such a decision may be hampered by noise (cultural, theological or personal), which makes an informed decision sometimes difficult. The Christian who has stagnated in the message-centered style is ill prepared to deal with these concerns.

"I'm a Natural"

On the other extreme is the instant-expert syndrome. The Christian reasons that he can bypass the deficiencies and pitfalls of the self- and message-centered styles and become an other-centered communicator because it is easy for him to "just be natural." Therefore, he need not bother with tools and training.

A positive side to this thinking is that the communicator really wants to be other-centered. He is usually conscious of the need for genuine communication.

But the shortcomings are serious. First, while some very gifted people may indeed be "natural" other-centered communicators, most of us must admit that we are not so inclined. As a result, we must deal with the fears and inadequacies inherent in the self- and message-centered styles. Telling someone to "just be natural" does not help him overcome these barriers.

Second, this person usually views tools and training as stifling and inflexible factors. After all, how can I be trained in how to be myself? I do not need a tool for "sharing from my heart" what Jesus has done for me. With tools and training out of the picture, the Christian is then left to himself to navigate the tricky waters of other-centered communication. The result is that often no true evangelism takes place, or the evangelistic encounter is not typified by a clear presentation of the gospel.

The Joy and Challenge of Other-Centered Communication

The other-centered communication style does not happen by accident. It is the result of hard work, experience and training. In a real sense it is a privilege, reserved for those who have mastered their message and overcome the fears and inertia that would otherwise rob them of life-changing conversations about Christ with their friends, neighbors and anyone else who will listen. We will discuss this level of communication more fully in the next chapter.

CHAPTER **18**

The Art of Other-Centered Communication

T he evangelist is a persuaded person persuading others. So we approach an evangelistic opportunity without apology and quite purposefully, to persuade. David Hesselgrave writes, "Missionary communication does aim at response. When the desired response is well thought out and specific, communication will likely be more effective."[1]

There is much more to effectively communicating the gospel than merely penetrating physical ears with the sound waves of our voice. Rather, we must speak the gospel in a way that is meaningful to the hearers. It must speak not only to the mind but also to the heart, for this is where the seeds of the gospel take root, germinate and bear the fruit of eternal life.

Not surprisingly, the first-century church was a persuasive, communicating church, for those Christians were convinced that God had authoritatively and finally spoken to the world through His Son (Hebrews 1:2). Therefore, they went about the task of making this truth known to a spiritually illiterate world by confounding (Acts 9:22), proving (Acts 1:29), reasoning (Acts 18:4), persuading (Acts 18:4), admonishing (Acts 20:31), informing (Acts 21:21, 24), begging (2 Corinthians 5:20), reproving (2 Timothy 4:2), rebuking (2 Timothy 4:2) and urging (1 Peter 2:11) to the end that all who would listen might have the opportunity to respond intelligently to Christ.[2]

The Challenge of Other-Centered Communication

Norman Geisler writes, "The Christian accepts as axiomatic that his task is to communicate Christ to the world. That sounds simple enough, but in fact is very complex. It is complex for at least three reasons: first, there are many views of 'Christ'; secondly, there are many ways to 'communicate'; and thirdly, there are many 'worlds' to which Christ must be communicated."[3]

The ambassador's role carries with it a twofold burden. On the one hand he must be faithful to his sending sovereign power and the messages that power wishes to transmit. On the other hand, the ambassador carries the burden of effectiveness. His job is not merely to transmit messages, but to make sure they hit their mark — that they get to the ears of the right people and are understood from the heart. John Stott describes this balance well, "We have to engage in the continuous struggle to relate the given gospel to the given situation. Since it comes from God, we must guard it; since it is intended for modern men and women, we must interpret it."[4]

Such is the challenge of communicating to persuade. We must straddle two worlds. We speak to the lost (secular, misdirected religious and nominalist alike), who live in their world of illusions, misconceptions and misperceptions of spiritual truth, about another world, that of Jesus and His kingdom. And while we seek to bridge this gulf, we must ensure that the message not only reaches the ears but also pierces the heart.

How can the Christian communicator fulfill this ambassadorial task? An understanding of the concepts of identification and sensitivity will take us far toward learning the art of other-centered communication.

Maneuvering for the Gospel

I was sailboating one day with two friends in San Diego Bay. We had rented our boat, a model that was extremely slow and unmaneuverable and was slowed even further by our inexperienced crew. More than once we found ourselves headed on a direct course for another boat. Fortunately, the other boat, usually a sleek fiberglass model manned by an experienced pilot, would turn away to avoid a collision. The other boat's pilot understood the principle that the more maneuverable boat must be the one to change direction.

The world of communication operates along the same lines. The word *communication* comes from the Latin word *communis*, meaning "common." Thus, the communicator is the one who establishes common ground with his audience, for communication is a meeting of minds, not a knocking of heads. In order for two parties to experience this common ground leading to a meeting of their minds, at least one party must maneuver to avoid colliding head-on or, just as unfortunate, having their message run aground on the rocks of misunderstanding.

Identification is the process of finding this "common ground." It means to take our message to the listeners, to meet them on their own "turf," not only geographically but also culturally, intellectually, spiritually and personally. Identification means to take the life situation of our listening audience seriously, to understand what motives, presuppositions and experiences lie behind their world views and how these influence their response to the gospel. We must listen through their ears and see life through their eyes so that any barrier to their hearing the gospel and seeing the saving grace of the cross might be, by God's grace, removed. As an experienced missionary once said, "I never found a man I couldn't talk to about Jesus if we were walking down the same road together." This is the goal of identification.

Thus, the bearer of good news must seek to be in touch with his audience by gaining the greatest degree of familiarity possible with their life situation: their language, personal values, cultural operating presuppositions, subculture affiliation, personal experiences, personality type and decision-making styles.

First-Century Maneuvering

Paul understood that, while the gospel is self-authenticating and earns its own right to be heard, we as wise stewards of this powerful message must do everything in our power to ensure that it is heard *and* understood. To get his audience to hear and understand the gospel, Paul reasoned that he would need to maneuver and at times inconvenience himself to overcome barriers to the gospel.

Paul writes in 1 Corinthians 9:19-23, "For though I am free from all men, I have made myself a slave to all, that I might win the more. And to the Jews I became as a Jew, that I might win Jews; to those who are under the Law, as under the Law, though not being myself under the Law, that I might win those who are under the Law; to those who are without law, as without law, though not being without the law of God but under the law of Christ, that I might win those who are without law. To the weak I became weak, that I might win the weak; I have become all things to all men, that I may by all means save some. And I do all things for the sake of the gospel, that I may become a fellow-partaker of it."

Paul's reasoning is clear: The good news is both for hearing *and* understanding. Paul would do anything in his power to ensure that no barrier existed between his audience and Christ except for the stumbling block and foolishness of the cross. Paul's persuasive intent "that I might win the more" compelled him to find the common ground that served as a platform from which the self-authenticating gospel could be turned loose in all of its saving power.

The Ghetto Gap

A ghetto could be defined as an "ethnic enclave," a group of people who so closely identify with one another that their contact with those of other groups is severely restricted. Ghettos need not be geographically defined. In fact, they are more likely culturally determined. People usually live, work and play together because they have a shared ethnic, religious or national identity that gives them common points of reference, a common world view and sense of community. We are more likely to be comfortable with "one of our own" and less comfortable with those of other "ghettos" or subcultures.

This sociological phenomenon applies directly to the evangelical Christian experience in the United States and, indeed, worldwide. Christians naturally enjoy being around one another. This is not wrong, for fellowship is a wonderful experience. But the ghetto phenomenon is a good thing gone haywire. Fellowship was never meant to exert an all-encompassing claim on the Christian's life or build a wall between us and the nonbelieving world.

A Case Study

Joe and Janet are a typical suburban couple. They are non-believers. Their social life revolves around their small circle of friends who all enjoy frequenting a local night spot. Alcoholic drinks are served (that's why they go there) and good conversation takes place (the non-Christian equivalent of fellowship). They have no friends who are believers, though some in their circle of friends are nominalists. Joe and Janet are preoccupied with making house payments, saving for a summer vacation and keeping their two teenagers out of trouble.

To their friends' surprise, Joe and Janet come to Christ through watching a Billy Graham Crusade on TV. (They turned the channel to what they thought would be *Magnum, P.I.,* but it had been pre-empted.) They are soon contacted by a local evangelical church couple, Bob and Linda, who help them take their first steps of growth in the Christian life.

At first Joe and Janet feel uncomfortable with these new "friends." They don't seem to be interested in the same things. Bob and Linda's kids go to a Christian school. Bob and Linda go to church three times a week and do not own a TV. Joe and Janet went to church three times last year and watch TV every day. Bob and Linda would never dream of going to Joe and Janet's favorite night spot; in fact, they have lobbied their state representative to take away the bar's liquor license. It is safe to say that Bob and Linda and Joe and Janet are from two different cultures, even though they share in the demographic profile of white, middle-class, suburban, middle-age Americans.

As Joe and Janet begin to grow in Christ, they become more comfortable in church and with Bob and Linda, and less comfortable with their old friends and social activities. As the months pass, Joe and Janet spend less time with their old crowd. Their "common ground" no longer exists. As Joe and Janet drive by their old favorite night spot on their way to their children's Christian school, they offer a prayer of thanksgiving to God that He has delivered them from their old lifestyle. But then a sad thought tugs at their hearts. What about their old friends? It is not that they are all that bad; there's just nothing much left to talk about with them; they have lost their common interests. The spark has gone out of their relationship. It is a little sad, but their new Christian friends have filled the void.

Joe and Janet have come full circle. Only a year ago they were essentially cut off from any meaningful interaction with believers. The only way the gospel could have reached them was through the bridge of their TV set. Now they find themselves with no bridges to meaningful interaction with nonbelievers, even their old friends. The thought of sharing the gospel with them is scary. "Why should they listen to us?" Joe and Janet reason. "We don't talk anymore; we have nothing in common. We're not sure they even like us. In fact, come to think of it, we haven't seen any of the old gang for over six months. It would be awkward to talk to them about Christ now."

Bridging the Gap

Why is identification so crucial to our role as communicators? I hope this common case study has hinted at the answer.

Identification is the practice of staying in touch with our hearers, physically, culturally and intellectually. It means to stay in geographic proximity by continuing to spend time with them. It means to be able to sympathize with how they think — their personal values, cultural presuppositions, hopes and fears. But most of all, it means to bring Jesus Christ into their world so that they can come into His.

The identifying communicator will relate Jesus Christ to the real world of his listeners. He will see his audience as God sees them (lost without Christ), meet them on their own turf, and help them to see their real need and Jesus' ability to meet it.

God never intended for us, as new creatures in Christ, to lose touch with those yet to believe. John Stott states this well: "Conversion must not take the convert out of the world, but rather send him back into it, the same person in the same world, and yet a new person with new convictions and new standards. If Jesus' first command was 'come!', His second was 'go!', that is, we are to go back to the world out of which we have come, and go back as Christ's ambassadors."[5]

Summary

The other-centered communicator must speak with the authority of the one who commissioned us to go and with the sensitivity and relevance of the one who came to us, took on the form of a bondservant and lived among us. We must study both our message and audience so that we fulfill our role as faithful ambassadors of the sovereign King.

The choices are three. We can insist they come to us, which very few are willing to do. We can ask them to meet us halfway. Or we can go to them, meet them on common ground and assist them in reading the roadsigns to the kingdom. The last choice is the burden of the other-centered communicator.

CHAPTER **19**

Communication in Action: The Art of Salty Speech

Over three-hundred years ago, Blaise Pascal wrote these observations on mastering the art of eloquent, relevant communication: "Eloquence is an art of saying things in such a way (1) that those to whom we speak may listen to them without pain and with pleasure; (2) that they feel themselves interested, so that self-love leads them more willingly to reflection upon it." Pascal noted further, "This assumes that we have studied well the heart of man so as to know all its powers, and then to find the just proportion of the discourse which we wish to adapt to them."[1]

The Art of Salty Speech

Colossians 4:5, 6 provides a biblical framework for such eloquent, relevant and effective communication of the gospel. Paul wrote, "Conduct yourselves with wisdom toward outsiders, making the most of the opportunity. Let your speech always be with grace, seasoned as it were with salt, so that you may know how you should respond to each person."

Let us take a closer look at this passage to learn some principles of "salty" communication. First, Paul says to "conduct yourselves with wisdom toward outsiders" (pagans). To be wise means, in Paul's words, to "make the most of the opportunity."

Paul is saying that we are to be alert for every opportunity to present Jesus Christ to those with whom we make social contact. Our friends, neighbors, business associates and anyone else we meet in our daily routine are prime candidates for such opportunities. As Proverbs 11:30 states, "He who is wise wins souls." Time is a precious commodity; it belongs to the Lord and should therefore be used to further His aims. His aim in this case is that the believer will enter into social contact with the nonbeliever with eyes wide open to gospel opportunities. The opportunities are always there. Most of the time it is simply a matter of seeing them.

Whether these social contacts are regular and highly relational or sporadic and superficial, they can be "sanctified" by serving as a platform to introduce others to Christ.

Second, Paul's use of the word "grace" to define our speech shows us God's concern that we approach others in the same manner in which He already has approached us in Christ. Grace here means charm, winsomeness and attractiveness, relevance and sensitivity. Grace always loves, always accepts, always tells the truth and always points to the power of the Holy Spirit to bring about change. Our speech must exhibit these same qualities.

Grace in our speech also brings with it a humility of spirit. God has dealt with us in grace, and God wants to deal with this "outsider" in the same way. We are just one beggar telling another where the bread line begins. Grace leaves no room for a haughty, superior spirit, for the ground is level at the foot of the cross.

Third, Paul uses a common kitchen metaphor as he relates our speech to adding the appropriate amount of salt to food to suit each person's taste. Wisdom in communicating the gospel is more than just seizing the opportunity; it is tailoring the opportunity to meet the needs of the individual nonbeliever. Thus, Jesus salted His communication with the woman at the well by presenting Himself as the giver of "living water."

A pastor tells the story of two secretaries talking at the office paper-shredding machine. The Christian was sharing the gospel with the nonbeliever, who was troubled by her guilty conscience. The Christian secretary said a "salty" word to her friend as she compared the ability of God to forgive and forget her sins to the shredder's ability to make short work of a piece of paper. The nonbeliever got the point: God has taken our sins and run them through His shredder, the cross of Christ.

Paul's use of the salt analogy points to the truth that God desires His gospel to appeal to the spiritual palate of each person. The implication is that the Christian communicator actually can make difference as to whether the gospel is perceived as a "bland," irrelevant message, or spiced just right to make it the most relevant, joyful news the listener has ever heard. Thus, being wise is a matter of initiating with boldness and following through with the sensitivity of gracious, salty speech. We are not to violate our audience by insensitive pontifications, nor are we to bore him with dull, irrelevant conversation.

Salty Speech in Action

As Proverbs 15:23 states, "A man has joy in an apt answer, and how delightful is a timely word." Proverbs 15:2 says, "The tongue of the wise makes knowledge acceptable, but the mouth of fools spouts folly." The burden of salty speech is to make the gospel acceptable, palatable good news to the nonbeliever. I would like to suggest two ingredients necessary for the practice of using salty speech: a listening ear and a commitment to sensitivity.

The Priority of a Listening Ear

An authority on communication estimates that poor listening skills could cost the American economy a billion dollars a year. He suggests that a great many of the three million divorces per year are related to the simple inability or unwillingness of one or both parties to listen. The sinking of the Titanic and the attack on Pearl Harbor are tragedies that might have been avoided — if people had listened.[2]

An absence of a listening ear can have just as tragic effects on the task of evangelism. The evangelist must affirm with the Lausanne Covenant that "our Christian presence in the world is indispensible to evangelism, and so is the kind of dialogue whose purpose is to listen sensitively in order to understand."[3] We must listen in order to understand, for discernment is invaluable as we seek to gain common ground with our listeners so that they may hear and understand our message.

The late Lyndon Johnson was fond of a sign that hung in his office: "You ain't learning nothin' while you're talking." It would be wrong to assume that the sole challenge of communication is to talk correctly. One must listen attentively. As we have noted, a message delivered without feedback may become irrelevant to the listener and fail to fulfill its persuasive intent.

The Challenge of Listening

Listening is a rare art. In *The Listeners*, Taylor Caldwell has one character, wise old John Godfrey, express a universal lament as he tells a reporter, "Nobody really listens." The Roman poet Seneca wrote, "Listen to me for a day — an hour — a moment! Lest I expire in my terrible wilderness, my lonely silence! Oh my God, is there no one to listen?"[4]

Why is it so hard to listen? One reason is that we think much faster than we talk. As one person speaks his 125 words a minute, the other person's mind is racing ahead, figuring out what he wants to say. This is not listening, for the second person's attention is focused on plotting his next move, not on giving feedback to the speaker. The second person is a "foot tapper," just biding his time until his turn to speak. The effective other-centered communicator must give the other person his undivided attention, and this does not come easy to self-centered humans.

Listening and Discernment

Discernment is the process of taking note of the concerns that are important to my audience. This involves listening to the feedback and then analyzing it in light of what I just said. Note that feedback can be words, body language, or even silence. As I discern feedback, I am able to speak wisely as the gospel conversation progresses. How do I know what to say next? How can I more effectively zero in on and speak to the listener's felt needs, erroneous assumptions and any other barriers that keep him from seeing the cross of Christ? In other words, how can I season my speech with grace and salt (Colossians 4:5, 6)? The answer lies in listening with discernment.

God places a high premium on listening with discernment. Proverbs 29:20 states, "Do you see a man who is hasty in his words? There is more hope for a fool than for him." Proverbs 17:28,29 says, "He who restrains his words has knowledge, and he who has a cool spirit is a man of understanding. Even a fool when he keeps silent, is considered wise; when he closes his lips, he is counted prudent."

We need to work at the art of listening in silence if we are to be effective persuaders for Jesus Christ. A "cool spirit," ready to listen for comprehension, slow to interrupt with a barrage of words, quick to discern the right amount of salt to add to one's speech to satisfy the spiritual palate of the listener is what God is looking for in His ambassadors.

Learning Listening

It is estimated that most of us listen at an average of only 25 percent efficiency.[5] How, then, can you become a better listener?

First, be responsible to make your conversation a dialogue, not a monologue.

Second, practice "listening alertness" by asking yourself questions about your listener's feedback. Use Figure 6, the feedback model on page 221, to zero in on significant factors that influence his reception of the gospel. For example, does he understand your terminology? Has his response to the gospel been affected negatively by his nominalist, religious or secular assumptions?

Third, and most important, pray for the godly discipline of listening. Proverbs 18:2 states, "A fool does not delight in understanding, but only in revealing his own mind." Proverbs 18:13,15 reads, "He who gives an answer before he hears, it is folly and shame to him. . . . The mind of the prudent acquires knowledge, and the ear of the wise seeks knowledge."

To listen is to be wise; to give an answer before he hears is the way of the fool. The art of listening is mastered only by those who have been taught by God to overcome the tendencies of their self-centered communicating style and have replaced them with the "cool spirit" of discernment.

Saying It Sensitively

Sensitivity is the prize commodity of insight gained by listening to feedback. If communication is composed of three elements — what you say, how you say it and to whom you say it — then sensitivity is the thread that binds these three components into an effective communication experience.

Feelings are powerful factors in our decision-making process. They can shape our attitudes and responses to people and concepts, and information in general. To further complicate the communication process, our words have a powerful influence on others' feelings. Words are verbal arrows that always find a way to penetrate the heart. As Proverbs 18:21 states, "Death and life are in the power of the tongue."

Imagine for example, a friend saying to you with great sincerity and feeling, "You are one of the most enjoyable people I have ever met. Your life is a constant source of encouragement to me. There are days when I think I cannot go on, but then I think of you and life seems worth living again." What a lift such remarks would give! You would be encouraged. Your heart would respond with thanks.

But suppose an hour later another person tells you, "You absolutely disgust me. You are a sorry excuse for a human being. I never want to talk to you again." Your spirit would be crushed, your vitality drained. You would be hurt. As the author of Proverbs realized, words carry an impact that penetrates to the very core of our being.

The Christian communicator must take note of *what* he says and *how* he says it. How we deliver the gospel can affect whether or not our message is heard and embraced, for how a person *feels* about the message will be a crucial factor in its acceptance or rejection.

The sensitive communicator *delivers* the message, *listens* to feedback, *takes note* of message fidelity, noise factors and feedback, and *continues to present* the gospel in light of these factors. Thus, sensitivity is essential to facilitating a true dialogue.

People want to be communicated *with*, not *at*. Not only do we need to know what our listeners are thinking, but *they* must also know that we know what they are thinking.

The sensitive communicator will create an atmosphere in which the listener feels the freedom to raise questions or even to disagree. If barriers to the understanding of the gospel exist, they need to be dealt with. The communicator cannot afford to gloss over them in the hope that they will take care of themselves.

Sensitivity in Action

Every Christian communicator must reckon with the barrier of hostility toward the gospel. This hostility may be grounded in the listener's misconceptions about the gospel, his negative experiences with other Christians, or his own rebellious, sin-darkened soul. Often the sensitive spirit of the Christian communicator can defuse this hostility.

The writer of Proverbs says, "A soft answer turns away wrath" (Proverbs 15:1). One spring day at a midwestern university, I had the chance to put this truth to the test. A crowd had gathered outdoors to hear a Christian singer. After the concert, many of us attempted to talk to those in the audience about Christ. I asked a young woman what she thought of the concert, and she responded, "I liked the music, but I don't like the message behind it." When I asked her why she felt this way, she said, "Christians make me mad. I just can't understand why they make such a big deal about Jesus." As she spoke I could sense her deep-seated bitterness.

At this point I could have turned away and approached another person, or I could have taken out my Four Spiritual Laws booklet and asked her if she would be interested in hearing the gospel. Neither alternative seemed wise. Instead, I decided to see whether it was true that a "soft answer turns away wrath." I said, "It seems that you've had an unfortunate experience with Christianity. I'm interested in knowing why you feel this way."

I'll never forget her expression as it changed from bitterness to curiosity. "You really want to know why I feel like this?" she asked.

"Sure," I said.

"No one has ever asked me how I felt about Christianity before," she said. "Are you sure you're interested?"

I assured her that I was, and she proceeded to tell me the story of how her high school friends had "rejected her" because of their faith in Christ and the fact that she was not a believer. She felt that Jesus had taken away her best friends. She was still deeply hurt by this experience, even though it had happened more than three years earlier.

After listening for about twenty minutes, I asked her if she had ever understood exactly what it meant to be a Christian. She replied that she was not sure, but then she had never wanted to know until now. I invited her to go through the Four Spiritual Laws booklet with me, and she said, "If you had asked me twenty minutes ago, I would have said no, but I now think I'd really like to." She did not trust Christ, but for the first time she understood the gospel and was genuinely touched by the experience.

There are so many who, for various reasons, have hostility barriers that hinder their ability to understand the gospel. Be sensitive to these opportunities. Remember, "If you want to gather honey, don't kick over the beehive."

Saying It Salty

Sensitivity means knowing how to respond to a given person in given circumstances so that all barriers to understanding can be addressed and, by God's grace, removed. The writer of Proverbs underscores the communicator's need for sensitivity: "Like one who takes off a garment on a cold day, or like vinegar on soda, is he who sings songs to a troubled heart" (Proverbs 25:20). "There is one who speaks rashly like the thrusts of a sword, but the tongue of the wise brings healing" (Proverbs 11:8). "Like apples of gold in settings of silver is a word spoken in right circumstances" (Proverbs 25:11).

As Lord Chesterfield said, "Learning is acquired by reading books, but the much more necessary learning, the knowledge of the world, is only to be acquired by reading men, and studying the various editions of them." The evangelist must be a student of the people with whom he intends to communicate. One cannot read the gospel accounts of Jesus' dealings with men and women without being struck by one truth: Jesus dealt with every person in a way that perfectly matched the need of that person's heart.

As Jesus addressed the woman at the well (John 4), He was able to expose her sin without crushing her spirit, that she might see her need for Him. Jesus spoke uplifting words to the down-trodden, the outcasts, and the poor in spirit, that they might see Him as the answer to their deepest need. Jesus also spoke words of sober warning and judgment to those blinded by their pride, self-sufficiency and complacency.

The other-centered communicator is committed to the proposition that if Jesus is to be accepted or rejected, let it be the *true* Jesus and not a Jesus made of the misconceptions and ignorance of the audience. If the gospel is to be presented, let it be communicated in simplicity, clarity and power, unhindered by noise in the heart of the listener.

Figure 9 illustrates various barriers that can be erected to prevent a person from coming to the Savior. But we must realize that if there is to be any barrier at all between a nonbeliever and a proper understanding of the gospel, it should be only the one beyond our ability to remove — that of a sin-blinded heart. Only God can remove that barrier through the supernatural intervention of the Holy Spirit's convicting ministry.

FIGURE 9
BARRIERS TO RESPONDING TO THE GOSPEL

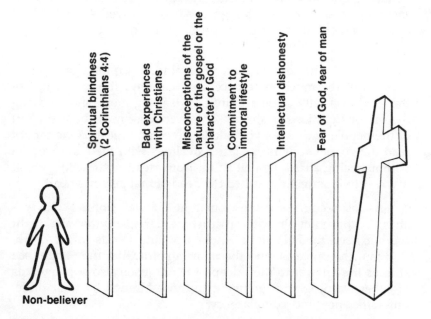

NOTE: This model was first suggested to me during a lecture by Tim Downs, a traveling speaker with Campus Crusade for Christ.

CHAPTER 20

A Strategy for Every-Member Mobilization

Every-member mobilization means that every member of Christ's body must be motivated and equipped to "go" with the gospel, taking the good news to all who will listen. As John Stott put it, "Evangelism is a responsibility laid by Christ upon His whole church and every member of it. So the people of God must be both mobilized and trained."[1] The Lausanne Covenant states: "In every nation and culture there should be an effective training program for pastors and laymen."[2] C. Peter Wagner affirms, "All Christians at all times should be prepared for that moment when God brings them into contact with a person prepared by the Holy Spirit for accepting Christ."[3] Every-member mobilization is crucial if the church is to fulfill its mandate to take the gospel to all nations (Matthew 28:18-20).

The Priority of Every-Member Mobilization

Every-member mobilization is crucial to the very life and witness of the local church. As George Peters observed, "Evangelism will be perennial and effective to the degree that it will succeed to mobilize, train, and actively involve the total 'priesthood' of God, the total 'body' of Christ. This is an axiom of the Scriptures that can be neglected only at the peril of the church."[4]

The growth of any movement, secular or spiritual, is based on its ability to mobilize its membership in effective, continuous, expansion-related activity. The church is no exception to this rule in its calling to the work of evangelism.

In my thirteen years of doing evangelism, however, I have come to a painful truth: After all is said and done, there is usually more said than done. Evangelism is much discussed, encouraged and "taught," but seldom demonstrated. Evangelism is nothing if it is not done. For to fall short of *doing* evangelism is to remain neutral in the spiritual battle. The proof of our spiritual convictions is in the doing. So, how can we bridge the gap between intention and action, discussion and demonstration?

I have observed that the doing of evangelism will flourish only when certain factors are present in the corporate life of a church or any community of believers, as well as in the lives of its individual members. Only then will the motivational and structural barriers to every-member evangelism be surmounted.

Overcoming Motivational Barriers

Ah, the feet. Home of ingrown toenails, corns, calluses, strange odors and fallen arches. There is nothing glamorous here. These things were not glamorous to the average Middle Easterner in biblical times, either. As the victims of dusty roads, sandals and a lot of walking, feet were surely the dirtiest and most undesirable part of the body.

In this context Isaiah surprisingly declared, "How lovely on the mountains are the feet of him who brings good news" (Isaiah 52:7). Now, why did Isaiah single out the feet for praise? Why not sing the praise of the messenger himself, or his tongue or radiant face?

Perhaps the feet — mundane, hardworking, and absolutely necessary — are the most fitting symbols of those qualities God sees as praiseworthy in the evangelist. God knows that the spreading of the good news is hard work. It will bring the evangelist in contact with the filth and grime of the world. It is very rarely a glamorous, limelight activity. But, I might add, this is good news for most of us who consider ourselves average people. If you do not mind hard work, and a little dirt under your spiritual toenails, you are certainly qualified to be a messenger of the good news.

I think Isaiah praised the feet because they stood in the "doing gap." The feet must take the good news to the mountaintop where it can then be proclaimed. Our feet must move us to those who need to hear before the tongue can speak and the good news is shared, heard and believed.

The praises of the feet turn our attention to the necessity of putting shoe leather to our heartfelt theological convictions. In this sense, our feet are a measurement of the depth and intensity of our convictions. The question we need to ask ourselves every day is not whether we grasp the crucial nature of the gospel, but whether it has grasped us — by the feet.

As I write this, my thoughts turn to a young Christian college woman whose feet regularly carried her more than a mile through snow, sometimes up to her knees, to a state university student center. Why? So she could share Christ with students who needed to hear. I think of the feet of the great missionary Hudson Taylor, as they marched up the plank to board the ship Dumfries in Liverpool, England, for a five and one-half month voyage. It was his theological convictions which led his feet to China. He reasoned, "I would never have thought of going out to China had I not believed that the Chinese were lost and needed Christ." Or consider the feet of martyred Jim Elliot, compelled to go to the Auca Indians out of the conviction that simple obedience to his Master must direct his steps.

These are the "beautiful feet" of which Isaiah speaks, the feet God loves to see in action. There is a direct link between our convictions and our feet. Therefore, the church or Christian community must do everything in its power to develop and strengthen biblical convictions of the nature and necessity of evangelism.

Structures for Involvement

How are the seeds of conviction planted? How are they watered and cultivated? And most important, how do they translate into action?

I believe the answer is twofold. First, as we discussed in an earlier chapter, we must allow the teaching of God's Word to sink into our hearts. This is foundational to the church's work of evangelism. Second we must put ourselves in situations where we can act on our convictions.

We must expose ourselves to both biblical content and real life context, to knowledge and experience, to training and practice. Too often, there is an overemphasis on content and knowledge at the expense of practical experience. We will do well to pay heed to the words of nineteenth-century English philosopher Herbert Spencer who said, "The great aim of our education is not knowledge but action." So don't fall into the trap of thinking that if your conviction level is lagging, you must *first* work on building your convictions *before* you go out and do evangelism. No, the best way to build convictions about evangelism is to go out and do it *as* you are processing the biblical information which fuels your convictions.

It is a psychological truth that we are more likely to act our way into thinking, than to think our way into acting. In *Ethics,* Aristotle addressed the issue of how one gains a particular virtue. He maintained that virtues are habits of the will, built up act by act, not intrinsic capacities dependent on personality type. How does one become a builder? he asks. "By building," is the simple answer. A man becomes brave by being brave, and self-disciplined by being self-disciplined.[5]

The application to the realm of evangelism is obvious. We become experienced and therefore effective, "natural," sensitive and bold communicators of the gospel by *doing* evangelism.

Reality Exposure

If I had to choose between a lecture or discussion on evangelism and an actual evangelistic experience, I would choose the experience. It's been said that "one specific is worth a hundred generalities." I also believe that one personal experience is worth a hundred lectures on evangelism. Why? Because of the principle of reality exposure.

Applied to evangelism, this principle states: "If you want to develop a burden for the lost, go out and talk to the lost and find out how lost they really are. If you desire to have the crucial nature of evangelism branded on your heart, go out and do it, and you will become convinced of just how crucial it is. If you want to develop the conviction that Jesus does indeed change lives, take His life-changing message to others and see if this isn't true."

If you want to experience the power of the Spirit, the boldness that comes only from God, then you must move out in obedience. His provision of power and confidence is granted in the context of your obedience, *as* you go. As one author puts it, "The Spirit is not a guide and a helper for those on a straight way perfectly able to manage on their own. He comes to assist men caught up in the thick of battle, and tried beyond their strength."[6] The fruit is at the end of the limb. The kind of convictions that translate into action aren't lectured or discussed into our heads. They are hammered into our hearts on the forge of personal, front line experience. This is the principle of reality exposure.

Strategies for Personal Action

These truths lead me to recommend a strategy for every-member mobilization that is structure-, training- and accountability-oriented.

Frankly, my recommendations will cut across the grain of most recent thinking on how to get yourself and others doing evangelism. Most of the contemporary writing on this topic has revolved around the evangelistic philosophy of the relational-incarnational school, which we discussed in Chapter 14. It is an established fact that some of the most fruitful evangelism is that done with friends and acquaintances, and I have no argument here. But, in addition, many in this school suggest that the work of evangelism will simply "happen" as the spontaneous, way-of-life overflow of a spiritually healthy, vital body of believers who are in tune with their spiritual giftedness.

The elements of tools, and training and accountability are seen as at best useless, and at worst an unnecessary intrusion into the free-flowing evangelistic life of the church; a programmatic substitute for spiritual vitality.

We wholeheartedly affirm that all effective evangelism must have Christ at the core of the life of both individual evangelist and Christian community, and that the presence and fellowship of the church is foundational to the success of any group's evangelistic effort. Yet it must not be erroneously concluded that structural elements are incompatible with this truth and are, therefore, unnecessary or obtrusive. As we have noted before, it is a both/and, not an either/or, proposition. Of course, not all of those who affirm the superiority of relational evangelism ignore the benefit of structural elements. Joe Aldrich helpfully suggests many types of what he calls "harvest vehicles," i.e., evangelistic dinners, seminars, home Bible studies and many others.[7]

But a popular concept rooted in the relational approach has become almost axiomatic: Only a certain minority of believers can and should be mobilized to participate in strategic/initiative evangelism. This minority is usually placed at around 10 percent of the local body of Christ, i.e., those with the gift of evangelism. C. Peter Wagner has suggested this figure, not so much to set a limit on what sort of evangelistic training should be offered, but rather to encourage the church that there are more potential evangelists out there who should be trained than are presently stepping forward. He notes that of the 10 percent whom he believes have the gift of evangelism, only one half of one percent are actively using it. He wisely argues that the first step in mobilizing the church in evangelism is to call those with the gift of evangelism to accountability and action.[8]

However, the thinking that these figures should limit the numbers of those involved in strategic/initiative evangelism is the prevailing attitude in the church today. Joe Aldrich articulates this position as he states, "I doubt that 10 percent of the body of Christ will ever be effective in this type of evangelism." He adds that while the initiative approach or, as he calls it, the "confrontational/intrusional" approach, is legitimate, 95 percent "are either incapable of such a ministry or feel they have no ministry in evangelism because the only visible model offends their sensitivities toward people. As a general rule, the confrontational approach should be a methodology reserved for the abnormal rather than the normal witness experience."[9]

In his response to inquiries concerning his paper "Contemporary Practices of Evangelism" submitted to the Lausanne Congress on World Evangelism, Dr. George Peters followed similar reasoning. He stated that as a church was mobilized to do evangelism, we could expect only 10 to 15 percent to be involved in what he called "active, confrontational" evangelism. He went on to conclude that 20 to 30 percent of a congregation could be expected to be trained in a friendship or relational approach to evangelism. The rest would be encouraged to pray for the work of evangelism.[10]

I certainly do not mean to disparage such gifted and experienced men committed to the task of world evangelization, but I must ask, "Do they report what *is* or what *should* be the state of the church in its evangelistic function?" The heart of the issue is whether a church ought to develop a strategy for training *all* willing believers that utilizes a structure to help mobilize *all* believers to take advantage of *all* possible bridges between them and the nonbelieving world. Is not the goal *maximum* mobilization to equip and mobilize every possible member for the New Testament calling to "be ready in and out of season" (2 Timothy 4:2); "to make the most of every opportunity," even with outsiders (Colossians 4:5); and to take the gospel to all nations? If it is, then we need to put the necessary training and evangelistic opportunities within the reach of every believer.

This desire for maximum mobilization should lead to an appreciation for the structures which provide training, tools, accountability and a comprehensive approach to building bridges of contact between the church and the lost. These structures will also enhance the spiritual vitality of the church as its members put themselves in a position to experience the Spirit's enabling power and boldness. Thus, structures are a two-way street, carrying the life of the church from its vital core to the thirsty world, *and* replenishing and strengthening this core with the returning flow of spiritual vitality that comes only from a front-line ministry experience. I believe that a structured approach to the church's evangelistic mandate, properly understood and implemented, will serve as a conductor, not an inhibitor, of the communication of the life and presence of Jesus Christ. Without such structures, I believe that the church's ministry to a lost world and even her very spiritual vitality will be severely hampered. The barriers of inexperience, fear and inertia will keep believers from making contact with the lost and thus obeying God's mandate to take the gospel to the world.

Suggestions for Every-Member Mobilization

The goal of every-member mobilization is to involve as many believers as possible in a maximum ministry of effective, ongoing personal evangelism. Here are three suggestions, which, if integrated into the motivational and structural environment of a church or Christian organization, will greatly enhance the flow of our spiritual wealth to a world in need of Christ.

Suggestion 1: Make it easy for any member of your group or congregation to be trained in the use of an evangelistic tool.

I am convinced that many Christians lack the confidence to share their faith regularly simply because they lack an effective method to communicate the gospel adequately. Fear grounded in lack of training and experience can cut the feet out from under even the most well-intentioned believer. A simple evangelistic tool and basic training, however, can replace this fear with confidence, leading to the first steps of active involvement in evangelism. The use of such a tool is often the difference between doing evangelism and just talking about it.

Suggestion 2: Encourage commitment to an accountability structure.

Accountability will help members overcome barriers of fear and personal inconvenience. All of us struggle with breaking through our comfort zone. For most of us, evangelism is not a comfortable activity. Here we often face the "chicken and the egg" dilemma. We reason, "I don't want to do evangelism unless it feels natural." This feeling is quite understandable. But what we really are saying is, "I'll do it when it's in my comfort zone." And how does any activity get to the point where it "feels natural"? You guessed it, by *doing* it. Only personal experience broadens the boundaries of our comfort zone.

The only way out of this dilemma is to come to grips with the fact that the Christian life is full of "faith barriers" that must be broken. This experience is never easy or painless. But we walk by faith, not by sight (2 Corinthians 5:3), and we must acknowledge that the Christian life is strenuous effort, often involving spiritual conflict (1 Corinthians 15:58, Colossians 1:29, Eph. 6:10-20). We must make sure we are mentally prepared, filled with the Spirit and meditating on God's Word as we face these challenges.

To help your members broaden their comfort zone, suggest that each one place himself in a position of mutual accountability with another member to embark on a faith venture that takes each of them outside the safe borders of his comfort zone.

This accountability structure can take many forms. Some lay people have found accountability study-prayer groups to be an encouragement to their ministry of evangelism. These groups meet weekly to study the Scriptures and to pray specifically for friends, family members and acquaintances and for the lost in general. This group holds each member accountable to make the most of opportunities throughout the week to share the gospel with those in their natural sphere of influence. These people are prayed for by name and the group prays for "divine opportunities" to share the gospel with them. Each week a report is given on how God answered these prayers. Some take this accountability structure one step further and set aside a time every week (or however often they have determined) to go out in pairs to engage in an actual evangelistic conversation.

Why a specific time? Isn't this a bit rigid or artificial? Why not just leave it to a way-of-life approach?

First, this commitment to accountability in no way negates one's commitment to way-of-life evangelism. In fact, a specific, regular time of evangelism will greatly enhance our way-of-life ministry. The more evangelism you *do,* the more *natural* it will feel. The more natural you feel, the more *confident* you will become, and the more confident you become, the more *convinced* you will be that the doing of evangelism is crucial to the unfolding of God's love plan for a lost world. The end result is that evangelism will become a conviction and a way of life and the more evangelism you will *want* to do.

Second, and closely related, the accountability approach takes seriously the fact that just as prayer, worship, meditation and Bible study are spiritual disciplines, so is evangelism. Are prayer, worship, meditation and Bible study to be way-of-life experiences for the believer? Of course. But does this fact hinder us from setting aside specific times during our week to concentrate solely on one or more of these activities? Of course not. We meet at a specific time and place every week for worship and prayer.

Our commitment to spiritual disciplines is the very means by which we ensure that they become all the more rich and meaningful as a way-of-life experience. Evangelism is no exception.

As Figure 10 indicates, there is a wide spectrum of attitudes and involvement in personal evangelism. The point I would like to make from this chart is that while many are positive about evangelism (-5 to -2), they have yet to decide to become personally involved in witnessing (point 0), and have not actually begun to witness with any degree of confidence ($+1$ to $+4$). As beneficial as talks and training classes are, they will not get us from -2 to $+1$. Only the support of a personal accountability structure, coupled with training in how to use a tool and an ongoing strategy for making contact with interested non-Christians will translate the would-be evangelist's good intentions into actions. As Jesus sent out the disciples two by two, each person should find someone who will be accountable with him as he practices the discipline of evangelism.

Suggestion 3: Organize a comprehensive strategy to contact the maximum number of the lost with the gospel.

FIGURE 10
HOW PEOPLE BEGIN TO WITNESS

INPUT		ATTITUDES

Holy Spirit	HUMAN	
	Sermons, talks, books.	-7 Opposed to or ignorant of opportunities for witness.
	Influence of friends, models.	-6 Aware of responsibility to witness, aware that others witness.
Illuminates Word to raise our conviction level.		-5 Think that witnessing is a good thing.
	Lectures, classes and talks specifically on evangelism. Begin speaking of evangelism with personal, biblical conviction. Training in the how to's of evangelism.	-4 Think that witnessing is good for self.
		-3 Realize barriers to personal witnessing, i.e., fear, no training, no experience.
		-2 Pursue active study and training.
Grants us boldness to witness.		-1 Participate in watching others witness, pray for the witness of others.
	Opportunity for involvement in accountability structure.	0 Decide to witness personally.
Brings fruit as we witness.	Ongoing "front line" experience.	+1 Witness only with the support of others.
	Continued training and experience.	+2 Witness with the support of an accountability structure.
	Way-of-life emphasis.	+3 Witness with intrinsic motivation and boldness.
		+4 Witness as a way of life with enjoyment.

This chart is adapted from a chart used by Dr. Herb Klem, professor of Missions at Bethel Theological Seminary and is used with his permission. This chart is adapted originally from a chart devised by Dr. James Engel.

As we learned from our New Testament survey of evangelism, the first-century church used all means available to reach all people for Christ, for they were convinced that the Heavenly Father was intent on a maximum finding of the lost. But their comprehensive, flexible, initiative-taking approach to getting out the good news has come upon hard times in the American church. Training the laity to take the initiative with anyone who will listen is out of style. In its place, an approach which limits our gospel outreach to our personal sphere of relational contacts, using "natural," (usually non-tool oriented way-of-life) means to make contact, is recommended.

This emphasis is one of the sad by-products of falling prey to the assumption that the majority (90 percent plus) of the church can be expected to do *only* "friendship evangelism" or pray for the success of the outreach of others. As a result, little or no training will be offered beyond the scope of helping the evangelist learn how to be more natural and sensitive or how to start a gospel conversation with their nonbelieving neighbor. While this is, of course, helpful information and should be made available to all in the body of Christ,[11] it certainly does not pave the way for a maximum involvement of God's people in making evangelistic contact with all who need to hear.

Rather, the believer should be offered the opportunity for training and involvement in a wide variety of evangelistic strategies. For the sake of simplicity, I have chosen to describe two categories of such strategies, the "strategic/initiative" approach and the "initiative/way-of-life" approach.

Strategic/Initiative Evangelism

This type of outreach is so named because it combines the elements of strategy and initiative. It is strategic in that it employs a conscious and wise organization and distribution of resources for bringing trained Christians into evangelistic contact with interested non-Christians in the most advantageous way. It is initiative-oriented in that it asks believers to take the first step to initiate the contact and boldly yet sensitively communicate the gospel to all who are interested.

The question is sure to arise, why not just let the Spirit lead? Why impose a strategy on what should be a natural and spontaneous overflow of the church's vital core of spiritual life? While it is true that the Holy Spirit cannot be programmed, He does operate according to order. Strategy is not a foreign concept to His work of bringing the gospel to the world. We see the Spirit leading Paul to Macedonia (Acts 16:6-10) where he preached the gospel (always going first to the synagogues), and to strategic cities like Philippi (a seat of Roman government) and Thessalonica (on a strategic trade route conducive to the rapid spread of the gospel) (1 Thessalonians 1:7,8).

Paul understood that strategic/initiative evangelism is an exercise in wise, Spirit-led stewardship of the church's most valuable possession, the gospel. Used correctly, this approach is a channel of blessing to those outside of the kingdom. As such, strategy is always the servant, never the master, of our highest priority — to put trained, concerned Christians in touch with as many people as are drawn to Christ by the Spirit.

There are many varieties of strategic/initiative evangelism, but they all have one common objective, to enable the evangelists to make evangelistic contact with non-believers.

The Evangelist's Waterloo

Making contact is the spiritual Waterloo for many a well-meaning evangelist. After many years of doing evangelism, I still suffer from spiritual lockjaw. It often seems hard to start a gospel-oriented conversation. The incredible spiritual inertia that must be broken through should come as no surprise, for we are in a spiritual battle. The enemy knows our weakness and fear and is a master at exploiting these to render us silent in the face of evangelistic opportunities.

Overcoming Inertia

Strategic/initiative evangelism comes to our rescue by helping us in our struggle to break the ice and make contact with an interested nonbeliever. The following list of methodologies is not exhaustive, but it will give you some ideas of the comprehensive nature of the strategic/initiative approach.

1. Meetings as a bridge. This strategy, using meetings as common ground, puts Christians in touch with nonbelievers in a context where the gospel can be discussed openly. Such meetings can range from church worship services to evangelistic home studies to prayer breakfasts. Two of my friends have seen incredible results with a Christmas party theme. They invite neighborhood friends to attend "coffees" where the true meaning of Christmas is presented.[12]

Our church recognizes that our Sunday morning worship services provide such a point of contact. As Christians bring friends, family members and neighbors, or as the spiritually curious walk in off the street to attend a service, they are duly noted (through a church friendship register) and are put in touch with trained people from our congregation who arrange a meeting to share Christ with them within the week.[13]

Some of my friends have begun a neighborhood home Bible study. Couples from the block are invited to participate in an open Bible study where all are made to feel comfortable, and no question is too ridiculous to be considered seriously and given a sensitive answer. People in their neighborhood who might never consider attending a church feel welcome. This strategy has provided a rich network of relationships that have proven to be effective in opening opportunities for gospel conversations. These Bible studies can be geared to discuss the claims of Christ, or may revolve around issues of relevance to nonbelievers, issues which find their resolution in Jesus Christ. Topics such as successful marriages, child-rearing, or apologetic issues are just a few of the categories that could work for you.[14]

2. Surveys and evangelistic tools as a bridge. The use of surveys can be a helpful bridge to make contact with nonbelievers. They can be used in a neighborhood door-to-door strategy, or randomly in parks, shopping centers or other appropriate public places. I have found surveys to be helpful not only in breaking the ice with nonbelievers, but also in discerning their spiritual

interest level so that I might better communicate the gospel to them.

The evangelist must be very careful to avoid two profound abuses of such a strategy. First, we must not see the survey only as a foot-in-the-door technique, a mere device to ease a potential contact into a gospel conversation. We must be up front about our purpose being both to get the person's opinions on a survey *and* to share the gospel with him if he is interested. To withhold our true intentions from him is nothing less than manipulation. We have nothing to hide.

Second, we must not see the survey as a mere formality to get us to our "real purpose" of sharing the gospel. Rather, we must use the survey as a tool to gain insight into the spiritual preparedness of the nonbeliever. We must listen to their responses and take note of their level of spiritual preparedness and how it will touch on their response to the gospel. Used correctly, surveys can be a great asset in helping us to make contact and to communicate after contact is made.

In addition to surveys, tools like the Four Spiritual Laws or other theologically sound tracts can help break the ice and get a gospel conversation started.

Not long ago, two of my friends joined in a conversation with two other Christians who were trying to introduce the gospel to another student. These two Christians, steeped in the relational-incarnational approach to evangelism which discouraged the use of tools, were finding it quite difficult to steer the conversation toward the gospel.

To their frustration, the conversation ended without a mention of Christ. They then asked my friends how they directed the conversation toward the gospel. One of them took a Four Spiritual Laws booklet from his pocket and explained, "I just ask them if they've ever heard of the Four Spiritual Laws, explain that it tells how to have a personal relationship with Christ and ask them if they are interested. If they are, we have a great chance to talk. If they aren't, I thank them for their consideration and go about business as usual."

C. Peter Wagner states that "an ingenious device like the Four Spiritual Laws is an invaluable tool, and the more Christians who know how to use such a tool in conjunction with their role of witness, the better."[15] If done in a sensitive, nonthreatening manner, this simple, direct approach enables you to determine who is interested in the gospel and gives you an incredible opportunity to explain the good news clearly and concisely.

Meetings, surveys and tools all serve as effective means to put believers in touch with the nonbelieving world — friends, acquaintances and strangers alike.

This list of bridges is only the beginning. There are many creative ways to talk to nonbelievers in an attractive, nonthreatening and relevant manner. What is important is that nonbelievers are brought into contact with Christians who are ready and willing to share the gospel. Therefore, Christians should have readily accessible bridges to the nonbelieving world so they can share the gospel on a regular basis. Only a comprehensive, flexible, initiative-taking strategy will ensure this.

The Way-of-Life/Initiative Approach

This approach is so named because our daily lives provide the arena of contact. Our friends, neighbors, relatives and potential friends (i.e., acquaintances and sometimes even strangers) are the sphere of evangelistic activity. We approach them in a more spontaneous relational manner because we are normally and naturally in contact with them as a "way of life."

This approach, although more casual and less structured, still places the responsibility of initiative on the evangelist. Indeed, many who advocate and practice the way-of-life approach, even to the exclusion of the strategic-initiative approach, are firmly committed to taking the initiative to share Christ with all who will listen.

You As the Bridge

The way-of-life approach is a most effective form of evangelism. It affords a built-in relationship of intimacy and trust and provides a ready bridge for further involvement in the church if the friend or acquaintance should come to Christ. Here are some practical suggestions to aid you in a ministry of way-of-life evangelism.

1. Make sure that you always have a list of friends who do not know Christ. Pray for them daily. Identify with them so that you might present the gospel to them with sensitivity, relevance and power. Pray that God would open their hearts to the gospel and that He will give you boldness as He provides the opportunities for you to communicate Christ.

A practical question often raised in this type of approach is, what do I do if I have no non-Christian friends to share with? Or, what do I do if I have shared with all of my nonbelieving friends and they aren't ready or willing to hear more about the gospel? Let's discuss these questions one at a time.

If you have few close non-Christian friends, join the crowd. As we have discussed, this is a major problem in the body of Christ. If you want to resolve it in your own life, it is really quite simple. Go out and meet nonbelievers on their own terms. There is plenty of common ground between us if we would only look for it.

Your common interests might include a back yard that borders on that of a nonbelieving neighbor. Maybe you both enjoy gardening, root for the same sports team, have children going to the same school or work for the same company. There are plenty of activities and causes that would prove to be a comfortable point of contact for both you and the nonbelieving world. Taking the initiative is the key. Don't count on your neighbor joining the PTA so he can meet Christians. You need to be the one who takes the first step. Here is where participation in an accountability group can benefit you greatly. Seek out a person or group who will hold you accountable to pray for and seek out those in your natural sphere of influence.

What do you do if your nonbelieving friends have heard the gospel and for whatever reason don't desire to continue to talk with you about Christ? First, continue to relate to them as friends. It is important not to allow a crust of evangelical subculture to form over your life so that you quit relating and listening to them. Stay in touch, and keep praying.[16]

A decision though, must be made as to whether a new bridge will be pursued. If you are committed to the New Testament spirit of comprehensiveness, you will find a way to get in touch with others, even strangers, who do not know Christ and who will be willing to listen to the gospel. Just as the first-century church did not limit their witness to Jerusalem, but spread the gospel to the far-off and foreign, so we are compelled to find a way to get the gospel out to listening ears and open hearts — even if they are reachable only by bridges other than natural friendship.

As Figure 11 shows, the strategic/initiative and way-of-life approaches, though different at certain points, are not mutually exclusive. Each approach carries certain strengths and weaknesses that highlight the necessity of combining the two in the church's outreach strategy.

While the strategic/initiative approach ensures a maximum impact in terms of numbers reached and provides for the discipline and accountability crucial for the training of effective evangelists, it must not be allowed to box us into an emphasis that fails to take advantage of our most likely mission field, those closest to us.

Also, while the way-of-life/initiative approach is quite effective in bringing the gospel to a limited sphere of people on a regular basis, it can be a problem for Christians who are not naturally outgoing or who have never received training in the "how to's!!

Although these two approaches are mutually reinforcing, I believe that, *sequentially,* priority must be given to the strategic/initiative approach. Why? Because the strategic approach is foundational to the implementation of a successful way-of-life emphasis. As already noted, if convictions are forged in the context of personal experience, if training is required to help the would-be evangelist overcome the inertia of fear, lack of confidence and lack of experience, if strategic points of contact help us to break the ice and engage in actual evangelistic encounters, then the strategic/initiative approach is the training ground for the effective pursuit of a way-of-life ministry. Without learning the lessons offered by the strategic/initiative approach, one could find the

FIGURE 11
STRATEGIES FOR INVOLVEMENT

Strategic/Initiative	Way-of-Life Evangelism
1. Makes contact through relationships or strategies.	Makes contact through relationships and daily routine.
2. Confined to limited number of hours per week.	Ideally, can take place as often as believer is in touch with nonbelievers.
3. Will happen consistently due to built-in accountability structure.	Will happen to degree that believer is intrinsically motivated.
4. Provides for ongoing training in use of tools and communication skills due to presence of trainer or other believer, i.e., two-by-two strategy.	By definition, allows for no trainer/trainee experience due to spontaneous nature.
5. Crosses relational boundaries to insure comprehensive scope of witness.	Limited in scope by relational element or sphere of daily routine.
6. Lower percentage of valid conversions and numbers added to visible expression of Christ's Body.	Higher percentage of conversions seen and numbers added to visible expression of Christ's Body.

challenges of relational evangelism overwhelming. While the church indeed owes a great debt to those who have written to equip the church in a relational approach to evangelism, much more needs to be written concerning how to overcome the difficulties in this approach. This fruitful form of evangelism is, I believe, also the most challenging to practice on a regular basis.

The difficulties of relational evangelism are vastly underrated. The challenge of overcoming fear and of breaking the ice without a strategic bridge or accountability structure, and thus on the sheer force of our intrinsic motivation, it taken too lightly. The same could be said of the difficulty of cultivating the friendship and trust of our unsaved neighbors. The tricky business of using friendships as a platform for evangelistic encounters without succumbing to the ethical pitfalls of the "hidden agenda" is rarely discussed. While these difficulties should not discourage us from practicing friendship evangelism, they should serve notice to the evangelist taht successful way-of-life evangelism is grounded in communication and interpersonal skills which are greatly enhanced through training and actual evangelistic experience. This is why, at least in sequence, the strategic/initiative approach should be given priority.

Comprehensiveness Reconsidered

I hope it is obvious that a great degree of overlap exists between the way-of-life and strategic approaches. Both place the burden of initiative on the evangelist. Also, in a very real sense, our friends, relatives and potential friends are the most strategic people to reach. We must not forget our Jerusalem on the way to the uttermost parts of the world. Both approaches benefit greatly from the use of an evangelistic tool. Both require the qualities of boldness and sensitivity on the part of the evangelist. There need be no final tension between these various methods. The issue is not whether strategic/initiative evangelism is superior to relational evangelism or vice versa. The church obviously needs to practice both. Rather, the issue is whether the church is fulfilling her evangelistic mandate by sharing the gospel in the most effective way possible, with the boldness, urgency and sensitivity that the crucial nature of the gospel demands. Will as many as possible hear as soon as possible, as clearly as possible, with every possible opportunity to go on in the faith? This is the issue.

Ideally, every Christian would have *both* a circle of friends for whom he prays daily and to whom he seeks an opportunity to present the gospel, *and* a strategy that offers ongoing training and holds him accountable to share the gospel. Beware of any imbalance that finds you sharing with strangers but not with your friends and those in your natural sphere of influence. Beware also of an approach to evangelism that has you building relationships as a bridge to the few, resulting in a barrier between you and the rest of the nonbelieving world.

We need to be open to being used by the Lord in the lives of anyone and everyone. Any strategy for contact, no matter how effective, can become both a bridge and barrier — a bridge to those of your target group and a barrier to the rest of the world. Only a commitment to comprehensive, flexible outreach can keep this from happening.

Donald McGavran communicates this balance well. "Of all the factors which influence church growth, none is more immediately available to all Christians than to evangelize the natural fringes of the existing church. This is where most growth occurs. These are the nearest of the fields white to harvest. These are the people who already have some knowledge of Christ and the Christian life. Evangelizing each network of social connections out to its fringes is always sound procedure. True, it must always be supplemented by deliberate attempts to go to the Samaritans among whom Jews have no relatives and few friends. The huge numbers of unreached peoples of the world warn us not to limit evangelism to networks of friends."[16]

Summary

Every-member involvement has two ingredients: first, theological convictions leading to action; second, commitment to a structure that provides training and flexible strategies to equip and mobilize as many believers as possible for a fruitful, ongoing ministry of taking the gospel to all who will listen. While allowing for the fact that some will be more comfortable and better suited for certain styles of evangelism than others, I would strongly urge every believer to be trained to take the initiative to share Christ with anyone who is interested and to remember that the strategic/initiative approach is the best place to start. This evangelistic approach should not be limited to a minority of the body of Christ.

If you are already involved in the great adventure of evangelism, keep it up. Your ministry will undoubtedly prove to be a blessing to believers who are encouraged by your commitment, and to nonbelievers who hear the gospel through you. If you are not yet involved in evangelism, don't despair. It is within your reach. Seek out someone to train you. Find a group of people who have biblical convictions in this area and who are active in evangelism regularly. Get involved in their training, structures and strategy. You will be blessed by God as you align your life with His great purpose of bringing Christ to the world.

References

Chapter One
1. James Denney, *The Death of Christ* (Chicago: InterVarsity Press, 1951), p. 157.
2. D. P. Thomson, *Aspects of Evangelism* (Barnoak, Scotland: The Research Unit, 1968), p. 10.

Chapter Two
1. Colin Brown, ed., *The New International Dictionary of New Testament Theology, Vol. 2,* English language translation (Grand Rapids: Zondervan, 1976), p. 111.
2. Michael Green, *The Meaning of Salvation* (Philadelphia: Westminster Press, 1965), p. 237.
3. Brown, *New Testament Theology,* 3:200.
4. Ibid., p. 205.
5. James Orr, gen. ed., *The International Standard Bible Encyclopedia,* 4 vols. (Chicago: The Howard Severance Co., 1929), 4:2541.
6. Frank Gacbelein, ed., *The Expositors Bible Commentary, Vol. 10* (Grand Rapids: Zondervan, 1976), pp. 448-49.
7. Colin Brown, ed., *The New International Dictionary of New Testament Theology, Vol. 3* (Grand Rapids: Zondervan, 1978), p. 357.
8. James Orr, gen. ed., *The International Standard Bible Encyclopedia, Vol. 4* (Chicago: The Howard Severence Co. 1937), p. 2591.

Chapter Three
1. James Denney, *The Death of Christ* (Chicago: InterVarsity Press, 1951), pp. 156-57.
2. Frank Gaebelein, ed., *The Expositor's Bible Commentary, Vol. 10* (Grand Rapids: Zondervan, 1976), p. 282.
3. Denney, *Death of Christ,* p. 187.
4. Ibid., p. 189.
5. Gaebelein, *Bible Commentary,* 9:157.
6. George W. Peters, "Contemporary Practices of Evangelism," *Let the Earth Hear His Voice,* ed. J. D. Douglas (Minneapolis: World Wide Publications, 1974), p. 194.

7. C. S. Lewis, *Mere Christianity* (New York: MacMillan Co., 1943), p. 38.
8. DeVille Jard, *The Psychology of Witnessing* (Waco, Texas: Word Books, 1980), p. 99.
9. *Minneapolis Star and Tribune,* May 28, 1984. See also *Christianity Today,* October 21, 1983, p. 41.
10. Karl Menninger, *Whatever Became of Sin?* (New York: Hawthorne Books, Inc., 1973), p. 13ff.
11. A. H. Strong, *Systematic Theology* (A compendium of 3 vols.) (Chicago: Judson Press, 1907), p. 647.
12. Deville, *Witnessing,* pp. 99-100.
13. Jonathan Edwards, "The Warnings of scripture are in the best manner adapted to the awakening and conversion of sinners," *The Works of President Edwards,* 4 vols. (New York: Robert Carter and Brothers, 1864), 4:330.
14. Ibid., p. 331.
15. Denney, *Death of Christ,* p. 171.
16. Ibid., p. 170.
17. Richard Lovelace, *Dynamics of Spiritual Life* (Downers Grove, Illinois: InterVarsity Press, 1979), p. 109.
18. Robert Ferm, *The Psychology of Christian Conversion* (Westwood, New Jersey: Revell, 1959), p. 128.
19. James Denney, *Studies in Theology* (London: Hodder & Stoughton, 1895), p. 128.
20. Otto Betz, *What Do We Know About Jesus?* (Philadelphia: The Westminister Press, 1968), p. 40.
21. George Jackson, *The Fact of Conversion* (New York: Eaton & Mains, 1908), p. 225.

Chapter Four

1. The terms *keerusso* — preached (Mark 1:14; 14:9; 16:5,20; Luke 24:47; Acts 8:5; 9:20; 19:13; 20:25; 28:31; 1 Corinthians 1:23; 15:2; Galatians 2:2; Colossians 1:23; 1 Thessalonians 2:9; 1 Timothy 3:16; 2 Timothy 4:2) and *martureo* — witness (John 1:7,8; 15:32,27) are used to speak of the spreading of the good news of Jesus Christ in the New Testament.
2. "The Lausanne Covenant," *Let the Earth Hear His Voice,* ed., J. D. Douglas (Minneapolis: World Wide Publications, 1975), p. 4.

3. D. P. Thomson, *Aspects of Evangelism* (Barnoak, Scotland: The Research Unit, 1968), p. 37.
4. Paulus Scharpff, *The History of Evangelism* (Grand Rapids: Eerdmans, 1964), p. 3.
5. This is not to say that true evangelism has taken place only if a decision is made. This would confuse the *definition* of evangelism with the *goal* of evangelism.
6. Colin Brown, *New International Dictionary of New Testament Theology*, 3 vols. (Grand Rapids: Zondervan, 1978), 3:48.
7. Ibid., 2:107.
8. William Barclay, *Turning to God: A Study of Conversion in the Book of Acts and Today* (London: Epworth, 1963), p. 101.
9. David Hesselgrave, *Communicating Christ Cross Culturally* (Grand Rapids: Zondervan, 1978), p. 406.
10. Billy Graham, *A Biblical Standard for Evangelists* (Minneapolis: World Wide Publications, 1984), p. 57.
11. Augustine, *On Christian Doctrine IV,* 12, quoted in Hesselgrave, *Communicating Christ,* p. 437.
12. Richard Lovelace, *Dynamics of Spiritual Life* (Downers Grove, Illinois: InterVarsity Press, 1979), p. 106.
13. John Stott, *The Lausanne Covenant* (Wheaton, Illinois: The Lausanne Committee for World Evangelization, 1975), p. 12.
14. Evangelism via the radio, TV, movies and tapes would be an exception to this statement.
15. "Salt," *The Encyclopedia Brittanica Macropaedia,* 30 vols. (Chicago: Encyclopedia Brittanica Inc., 1977), 16:192.
16. J. Rendel Harris, *The Newly Recovered Apology of Aristides* (New York: James Pott & Co., n.d.) pp. 56-57, 60-61.
17. John Hendrick, *Opening the Door of Faith* (Atlanta: John Knox Press, 1977), p. 96.

Chapter Six
1. J. D. Douglass, gen. ed., *New International Dictionary of the Christian Church* (Grand Rapids: Zondervan, 1974), p. 976.
2. Michael Green, *Evangelism in the Early Church* (Grand Rapids: Eerdmans, 1970), p. 274.
3. Billy Graham, *A Biblical Standard for Evangelists* (Minneapolis: World Wide Publications, 1984), p. 65.

4. J. B. Phillips, *The Young Church in Action* (New York: MacMillan, 1956), p. vii.
5. J. B. Phillips, *Letters to Young Churches* (New York: MacMillan, 1952), p. xiv.
6. Ibid.
7. For a further discussion of these barriers, see Green, *Evangelism,* pp. 38-47; and A. H. Strong, *Systematic Theology* (a compendium) (Chicago: Judson Press, 1907), pp. 191-92.
8. Green, *Evangelism,* p. 47.
9. Elisabeth Elliot, *Shadow of the Almighty* (New York: Harper & Brothers Publishers, 1958), p. 79.
10. Jim Elliot, *The Journals of Jim Elliot,* ed. Elisabeth Elliot (Old Tappan, New Jersey: Fleming H. Revel Co., 1978), p. 216.
11. Phillips, *Letters,* p. xiv.
12. Elliot, *Shadow,* p. 79.
13. Phillips Brooks, *Twenty Sermons* (New York: E. P. Dutton & Co., 1894), p. 330.
14. Donald Guthrie, gen. ed., *New Bible Commentary* (Grand Rapids: William B. Eerdman's Publishing Co., 1973), p. 1157.
15. Ronald Enroth, "The Power Abusers," *Eternity* (October 1979), p. 26.
16. D. T. Niles, *That They May Have Life* (New York: Harper and Brothers, 1951), p. 96.
17. Leon Morris, *I Thessalonians* (Grand Rapids: William B. Eerdman's Publishing Co., 1959), p. 44.
18. Green, *Evangelism,* p. 199.

Chapter Seven

1. James I. McCord, "Know Thyself: The Biblical Doctrine of Human Depravity," *The Nature of Man,* ed. Simon Doniger (New York: Harper and Brothers, 1962), p. 28.
2. Blaise Pascal, *Pensees,* Number 81.
3. *The Compact Edition of the Oxford English Dictionary,* 2 vols. (Oxford, England: Oxford University Press, 1971), 2:2704.
4. C. F. Keil, and F. Delitzsch. *Commentary on the Old Testament,* 10 vols. (Grand Rapids: William B. Eerdman's Publishing Co., 1981), 1:120.
5. Ibid., p. 174.

6. Karl Menninger, *Whatever Happened to Sin?* (New York: Hawthorne Books, 1973), p. 221.
7. C. F. H. Henry, *Faith at the Frontiers* (Chicago: Moody Press, 1969), p. 21.
8. Harry Blamires, *The Secularist Heresy* (Ann Arbor, Michigan: Servant Books, 1956), p. 35.
9. Ibid., p. 34.
10. Ibid., p. 13.
11. Deitrich Bonhoffer, *Letters and Papers from Prison* (New York: MacMillan 1971), p. 311.
12. Blamires, *Secularist Heresy,* p. 13.
13. Pascal, *Pensees,* Number 213.
14. Pascal, *Pensees,* Number 194.
15. Jonathan Edwards, "Man's Natural Blindness in the Things of Religion," *The Works of President Edwards,* 4 vols. (New York: Robert Carter and Brothers, 1864), 4:26; idem, "Vain Self-Flatteries of the Sinner," ibid. 4:323.
16. "In His Own Words," *People Magazine* (November 28, 1983), vol. 20, no. 22, p. 99.
17. Pascal, *Pensees,* Number 131.

Chapter Eight
1. Edmund P. Leach, "When Scientists Play the Role of God," *London Times,* November 16, 1978. Quoted in Francis Schaeffer, *Whatever Happened to the Human Race?* (Old Tappan, New Jersey: Fleming H. Revell Co., 1979), p. 122.
2. Michael Novak, *Belief and Unbelief* (New York: The MacMillan Company, 1965), pp. 35,37.
3. Ibid., p. 57.
4. Quoted in Francis Schaeffer, *Back to Freedom and Dignity* (Downers Grove, Illinois: InterVaristy Press, 1972), p. 14.
5. Timothy Leary, *The Politics of Ecstasy* (New York: G. P. Putnam's Sons, 1968), p. 361.
6. Aldous Huxley, *Ends and Means* (London: Harper, 1937), pp. 312, 316.
7. Francis Schaeffer, *How Should We Then Live?* (Old Tappan, New Jersey: Fleming H. Revell Company, 1976), p. 205.
8. Daniel Yankelovich, *New Rules* (New York: Random House, 1981), p. 1.

9. Ibid., p. 176.
10. Woody Allen, "Woody Allen Wipes the Smile Off His Face," *Esquire* (May 1977), p. 72.
11. Bertrand Russell, "A Free Man's Worship," quoted in H. J. Blackham, *Objections to Humanism* (Riverside, Connecticut: Greenwood Press, 1967), p. 106.
12. Ibid., p. 119.
13. Wayne McDill, *Evangelism in a Tangled Worlds* (Nashville: Broadmen Press, 1976), p. 54.
14. C. S. Lewis, *The Discarded Image* (London: Cambridge University Press, 1964), pp. 74-75.
15. James M. Childs, *Christian Anthropology and Ethics* (Philadelphia: Fortress Press, 1978), p. 5.
16. Leslie Flynn, *Man: Ruined and Restored* (Wheaton, Illinois: Victor Books, 1978), p. 81.
17. Arnold Toynbee, "Perspectives From Time, Space and Nature," *Man's Concern with Death* (New York: McGraw-Hill Book Company, 1968), p. 84.
18. Reinhold Heibuhr, *The Nature and Destiny of Man* (New York: Charles Scribners Sons, 1948), p. 166.
19. Ibid., p. 266.
20. Blaise Pascal, *Pensees,* Number 409.
21. Bertrand Russell, *Has Man a Future?* (Hamondsworth: Penguin Books, 1961), p. 110.
22. Fran Schumer, "A Return To Religion," *New York Times Magazine* (April 15, 1984), pp. 93,90.

Chapter Nine
1. For more information on the theology of nonbiblical religious systems, see *Handbook of Today's Religions* by Josh McDowell and Don Stewart (Here's Life Publishers, 1983), *The Kingdom of the Cults* by Walter R. Martin (Bethany House, 1968), *Confronting the Cults* by Gordon Lewis (Baker Books, n.d.), and *The Theology of the Major Sects* by John Gerstner (Baker Books, 1960).
2. Wayne McDill, *Evangelism in a Tangled World* (Nashville: Broadman Press, 1976), pp. 29-39.
3. C. S. Lewis, *The Last Battle* (New York: MacMillan Publishing Co., 1956), p. 102.

4. C. S. Lewis, *The Screwtape Letters* (London: Geoffrey Oles, LTD, 1942), pp. 64-65.
5. Jonathan Edwards, "Man's Natural Blindness in the Things of Religion," *The Works of President Edwards*, 4 vols., (New York: Robert Carter and Brothers, 1864), 4:26.
6. Blaise Pascal, *Pensees*, Number 430.

Chapter Ten
1. The Lausanne Committee for World Evangelization noted: "Great numbers of Roman Catholics are considered to be outside the grace of God by the church itself. Our studies reveal that 500-600 million of the 742 million are living as non-participating Catholics"; "Christian Witness to Nominal Christians Among Roman Catholics," No. 10 Thailand Report (Wheaton, Illinois: Lausanne Committee for World Evangelization, 1980), p. 13.
2. "Christian Witness to Nominal Christians Among Protestants," No. 23 Thailand Report (Wheaton, Illinois: Lausanne Committee for World Evangelization, 1980), p. 5.
3. Blaise Pascal, *Pensees*, Number 100.
4. Campbell N. Moody, *The Purpose of Jesus in The First Three Gospels* (London: George Allen and Unwin, 1929), p. 141.
5. C. S. Lewis, *Mere Christianity* (New York: The MacMillan Co., 1960), p. 111.
6. Pascal, *Pensees*, Number 534.
7. "The Religious Personality of the Populace," *Christianity Today* (December 21, 1979), p. 15.
8. George Gallup, Jr., *Religion in America, 1979-1980* (Princeton, New Jersey: The Princeton Research Center, 1980), p. 23.
9. George Gallup, Jr., *The Search For America's Faith* (Nashville: Abingdon, 1980), p. 134.
10. Gallup, *Religion*, p. 16.
11. Ibid., pp. 90,106.
12. "The Christianity Today Gallup Poll: An Overview," *Christianity Today* (December 21, 1979), p. 14.
13. Ibid.
14. "Heaven Has Room for Those Born Once," *Minneapolis Tribune* (Sunday, December 11, 1983).
15. George Gallup, Jr., "The Latest Trends in American Religion," *Christian Herald* (November, 1982), p. 24.

16. Gallup, *Religion,* p. 6.
17. Gallup, "Latest Trends," p. 24.

Chapter Twelve
 1. *Letters of Flannery O'Conner, The Habit of Being,* ed. Sally
    Fitzgerald (New York: Farrar, Straus, Giroux, 1979), p. 229.
 2. Murray J. Harris, "II Corinthians," *The Expositor's Bible Com-
    mentary,* ed. Frank E. Gaebelein (Grand Rapids: Zondervan,
    Vol. 10, 1976), p. 350.
 3. Michael Green, *Evangelism in the Early Church* (Grand Rapids:
    Eerdmans, 1970), p. 249.
 4. George Jackson, *The Fact of Conversion* (New York: Eaton &
    Mains, 1908), p. 234.
 5. "Less Pressure, More Loving," an interview with Jerry Cook
    in *Leadership* (Spring, Vol. V., Number 2, 1984), p. 16.
 6. John Stott, *The Lausanne Covenant* (Minneapolis: World Wide
    Publications, 1975), p. 18.
 7. The Thailand Statement came out of the Consultation on
    World Evangelism held in Pattaya, Thailand, June 16-27, 1980.
 8. C. S. Lewis, *The Weight of Glory* (New York: MacMillan
    Company, 1949), p. 15.
 9. C. S. Lewis, *Christian Reflections* (Grand Rapids: William B.
    Eerdman's Publishing Company, 1967), p. 33.
10. Friedrich Gerhard, *Theological Dictionary of the New Testa-
    ment, Vol. 6* (Grand Rapids: William B. Eerdman's Publishing
    Company, 1969), p. 682.
11. Ibid., 8:157.
12. Jackson, *Conversion,* p. 234.
13. Samuel Shoemaker, *How to Become a Christian* (New York:
    Harper Brothers, Publishers, 1953), p. 74.

Chapter Fourteen
 1. David Wells, *Search for Salvation* (Downers Grove, Illinois:
    InterVarsity Press, 1978), p. 45.
 2. Joe Aldrich, *Lifestyle Evangelism* (Portland: Multnomah Press,
    1981), p. 79.
 3. Art McPhee, *Friendship Evangelism* (Grand Rapids: Zonder-
    man, 1978), p. 45.
 4. James Jauncey, *Psychology For Successful Evangelism*
    (Chicago: Moody Press, 1972), p. 123.

5. Aldrich, *Lifestyle Evangelism,* p. 84.
6. McPhee, *Friendship Evangelism,* p. 45.
7. See *rhetoric* and *rhetorical* in the *Oxford English Dictionary,* p. 2535.
8. Becky Pippert, *Out of the Salt Shaker* (Downers Grove, Illinois: InterVarsity Press, 1979), p. 65.
9. C. E. Autrey, *Basic Evangelism* (Grand Rapids: Zondervan, 1959), p. 91.
10. Aldrich, *Lifestyle Evangelism,* p. 84.
11. Earl Palmer, "Evangelism Takes Time," *Leadership* (Spring 1984), vol. 5, no. 2, p. 21.
12. George MacLeod, *Only One Way Left* (Glasgow: Iona Press, 1958), p. 38.
13. Aldrich, *Lifestyle Evangelism,* p. 20.
14. "Less Pressure, More Loving," an interview with Jerry Cook in *Leadership* (Spring 1984), vol. v, no.2, p. 13.
15. Aldrich, *Lifestyle Evangelism,* p. 29.
16. Ibid., pp. 36-37.
17. C. S. Lovett, *Witnessing Made Easy* (Baldwin Park, California: Personal Christianity, 1979), p. 76.
18. Aldrich, *Lifestyle Evangelism,* p. 19.
19. Colin Brown, ed., *The New International Dictionary of New Testament Theology,* 3:1043-44.
20. Allison A. Trites, *The New Testament Witness in Today's World* (Valley Forge, Pa: Judson Press, 1983), p. 12.
21. Brown, *New Testament Theology,* 3:1044.
22. J. H. Bavinck, "Introduction to the Science of Mission," quoted in Trites, *New Testament Witness,* p. 8.
23. See chapters 2 ("The Gospel" A Precise Message") and 4 ("A Look at New Testament Evangelism").
24. Alan Walker, *The New Evangelism* (Nashville: Abingdon Press, 1975), p. 71.
25. Leighton Ford, *The Christian Persuader* (New York: Harper & Row, Publishers, 1966), p. 78.
26. Will Metzger, *Tell the Truth* (Downers Grove, Illinois: InterVarsity Press, 1981), p. 109.
27. Carl F. H. Henry, "High Time for a Bold Sharing," *World Vision* (May 1982), p. 8.

Chapter Fifteen
1. Walter Bauer, *A Greek-English Lexicon of the New Testament and Other Early Christian Literature,* trans. William P. Arndt (Chicago: The University of Chicago Press, 1979), pp. 630-31.
2. Robert L. Thomas, "I, II Thessalonians," *The Expositor's Bible Commentary, Vol. 1,* ed. Frank Gaebelein (Grand Rapids: Zondervan, 1978), p. 250.
3. Jim Elliot, *The Journals of Jim Elliot* (Old Tappan, New Jersey: Fleming H. Revell Company, 1978), p. 186.

Chapter Sixteen
1. Walter Leifeld, "Luke," *The Expositor's Bible Commentary, Vol. 8,* ed. Frank E. Gaebelein, (Grand Rapids: Zondervan, 1978), pp. 918, 937.
2. Tom Hanks, "Would Jesus Stoop to Canned Evangelism?" *Eternity* (September 1973), p. 24.
3. Ibid.
4. George W. Peters, "Contemporary Practices of Evangelism," *Let the Earth Hear His Voice,* ed. J. D. Douglas (Minneapolis: World Wide Publications, 1974), p. 182.
5. Eric Black, "When the Pressure's Really On, They're at Their Best" *Minneapolis Star and Tribune* (May 20, 1982), pp. 1B, 8B.

Chapter Seventeen
1. Hendrik Kraemer, *The Communication of the Christian Faith* (London: Lutterworth Press, 1957), p. 30.
2. David Hesselgrave, *Communicating Christ Cross-Culturally* (Grand Rapids: Zondervan Press, 1980), p. 31.
3. Encoding can also include the use of nonverbal, nonliterate codes. Pictures, signs, physical gestures and voice tone can also be vehicles that carry messages.
4. John R. Wenburg, *The Personal Communication Process* (New York: John Wiley & Sons, Inc., 1973), p. 91.
5. Kraemer, *Communication,* p. 28.
6. William R. Bright, *How to Witness in the Spirit* (San Bernardino, California: Campus Crusade for Christ, 1971), p. 33.

Chapter Eighteen
1. David Hesselgrave, *Communicating Christ Cross-Culturally* (Grand Rapids: Zondervan Press, 1980), p. 45.
2. Ibid., pp. 20-21.

3. Norman Geisler, "Some Philosophical Perspectives on Missionary Dialogue," *Theology and Missions,* ed. David J. Hesselgrave (Grand Rapids: Baker, 1978), p. 241 (quoted in Hesselgrave, *Communicating Christ,* p. 235).
4. John R. W. Stott, "The Bible in World Evangelization," *Perspectives on the World Christian Movement,* ed. Ralph Winter (Pasadena: William Carey Library, 1981), p. 6.
5. John R. W. Stott, *Christian Mission in the Modern World* (Downers Grove, Illinois: InterVarsity Press, 1975), p. 121.

Chapter Nineteen
1. Blaise Pascal, *Pensees,* Number 16.
2. Lyman Steil, "Secrets of Being a Better Listener, *U.S. News and World Report* (May 26, 1980), pp. 65-66.
3. The Lausanne Committee, "An Exposition and Commentary," John Stott (Minneapolis: World Wide Publications, 1975), p. 14.
4. John Drakeford, *The Awesome Power of the Listening Ear* (Waco, Texas: Word Books, 1967), p. 72.

Chapter Twenty
1. John R. W. Stott, "World Evangelization: Signs of Convergence and Divergence in Christian Understanding," quoted in Alfred C. Krass, *Evangelizing Neopagan North American* (Scottsdale, Pennsylvania: Herald Press, 1982), p. 239.
2. Ibid.
3. C. Peter Wagner, *Your Church Can Grow* (Glendale, California: Regal Books, 1976), p. 82.
4. George W. Peters, "Contemporary Practice of Evangelism," *Let the Earth Hear His Voice,* ed. J. D. Douglas (Minneapolis: World Wide Publications, 1974), p. 195.
5. Aristotle, *The Ethics of Aristotle* (London: Walter Scott LTD, n.d.), p. 45.
6. Leon Morris, *The Gospel According to John* (Grand Rapids: William B. Eerdman's Publishing Co., 1971), p. 692.
7. See Joe Aldrich, *Lifestyle Evangelism* (Portland: Multnomah Press, 1981), pp. 211-14 for a helpful discussion of how those structures can be utilized for your evangelistic ministry.
8. This is suggested by C. Peter Wagner, *Your Church Can Grow* (Glendale, California: Regal-Gospel Light, 1976), p. 77.
9. Aldrich, *Lifestyle Evangelism,* pp. 79,81.

10. George W. Peters, "Contemporary Evangelistic Methods," Tape 9a, Part I from the International Congress on World Evangelization, Minneapolis, 1974.
11. Joe Aldrich offers an excellent section, "Evangelism and You," in his book, *Lifestyle Evangelism*. This section probably is the best material available discussing the ins and outs of establishing an evangelistic witness within your natural sphere of influence.
12. For more information write the Lay Ministry of Campus Crusade for Christ.
13. For more information on church evangelistic programs write: Evangelism Explosion, P.O. Box 23820, Fort Lauderdale, Florida, 33307, or The Lay Ministry of Campus Crusade for Christ, Arrowhead Springs, San Bernardino, California 92404.
14. For more information on neighborhood evangelistic Bible studies write, Neighborhood Bible Study, Box 222L Dobbs Ferry, New York 10522. See also Joe Aldrich's *Lifestyle Evangelism* for an excellent discussion of home evangelistic Bible studies, pp. 187-99.
15. Peter Wagner, *Your Church Can Grow* (Glendale, California: Regal Books, 1976), p. 82.
16. See Aldrich, *Lifestyle Evangelism*, pp. 219-35 for an excellent discussion on how to relate the gospel in the context of a friendship without needlessly threatening your relationship.
17. Donald McGavran, *Understanding Church Growth* (Grand Rapids: William B. Eerdman's Publishing Company, 1970), pp. 410-11.